Cam Ranh Bay

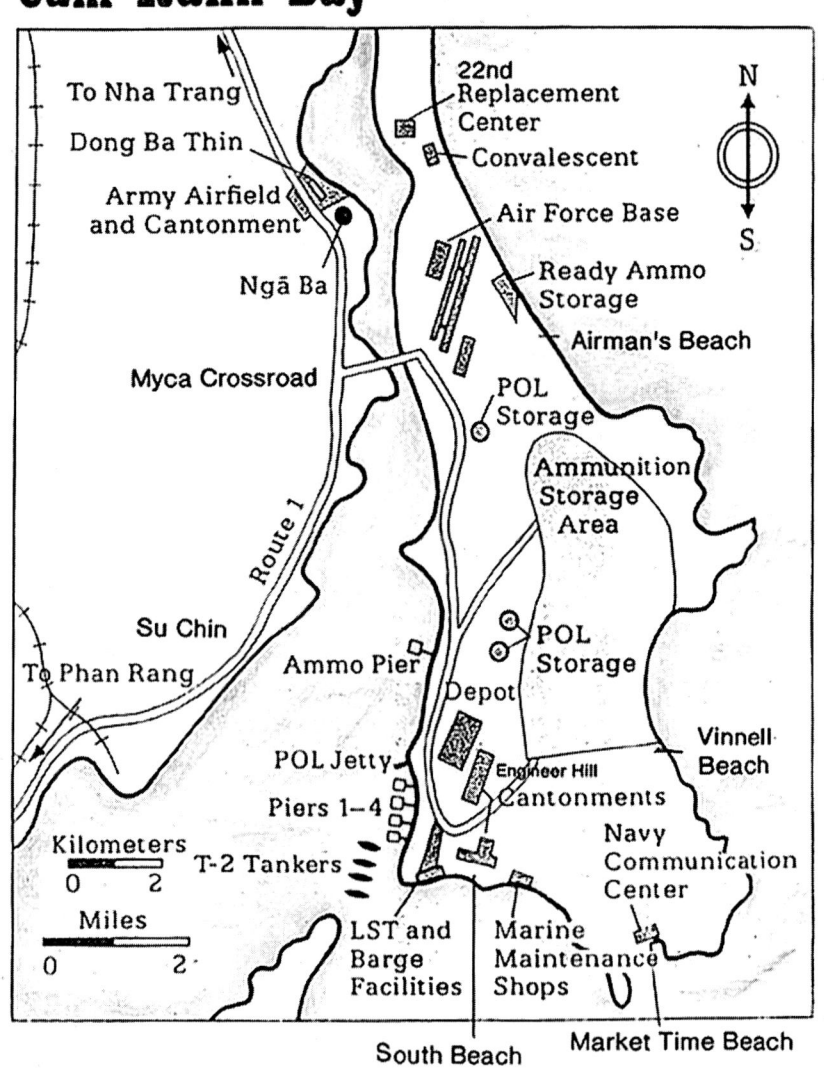

Like Boy Scouts with Guns

Memoir of a Counterculture Warrior in Vietnam

ROGER S. DURHAM

McFarland & Company, Inc., Publishers
Jefferson, North Carolina

All photographs are by the author and Ralph Dunn, Jr.

LIBRARY OF CONGRESS CATALOGUING-IN-PUBLICATION DATA

Names: Durham, Roger S., author.
Title: Like boy scouts with guns : memoir of a counterculture warrior in Vietnam / Roger S. Durham.
Other titles: Memoir of a counterculture warrior in Vietnam
Description: Jefferson, North Carolina : McFarland & Company, Inc., Publishers, 2021 | Includes bibliographical references.
Identifiers: LCCN 2021037502 |
ISBN 9781476684727 (paperback : acid free paper) ∞
ISBN 9781476642437 (ebook)
Subjects: LCSH: Durham, Roger S. | Vietnam War, 1961–1975—Personal narratives, American. | United States. Army—Biography. | Vietnam War, 1961–1975—Campaigns—Vietnam. | Soldiers—United States—Biography. | United States. Army. Engineer Brigade, 18th—Biography. | Counterculture—United States—Personal narratives. | BISAC: HISTORY / Military / Vietnam War
Classification: LCC DS559.5 .D87 2021 | DDC 959.704/34092 [B]—dc23
LC record available at https://lccn.loc.gov/2021037502

BRITISH LIBRARY CATALOGUING DATA ARE AVAILABLE

ISBN (print) 978-1-4766-8472-7
ISBN (ebook) 978-1-4766-4243-7

© 2021 Roger S. Durham. All rights reserved

No part of this book may be reproduced or transmitted in any form or by any means, electronic or mechanical, including photocopying or recording, or by any information storage and retrieval system, without permission in writing from the publisher.

Cover image: Roger Durham with 11 months in-country; stop sign 1970 (author collection)

Printed in the United States of America

*McFarland & Company, Inc., Publishers
Box 611, Jefferson, North Carolina 28640
www.mcfarlandpub.com*

Like Boy Scouts with Guns

Memoir of a Counterculture Warrior in Vietnam

ROGER S. DURHAM

McFarland & Company, Inc., Publishers
Jefferson, North Carolina

All photographs are by the author and Ralph Dunn, Jr.

Library of Congress Cataloguing-in-Publication Data

Names: Durham, Roger S., author.
Title: Like boy scouts with guns : memoir of a counterculture warrior in Vietnam / Roger S. Durham.
Other titles: Memoir of a counterculture warrior in Vietnam
Description: Jefferson, North Carolina : McFarland & Company, Inc., Publishers, 2021 | Includes bibliographical references.
Identifiers: LCCN 2021037502 | ISBN 9781476684727 (paperback : acid free paper) ∞
ISBN 9781476642437 (ebook)
Subjects: LCSH: Durham, Roger S. | Vietnam War, 1961–1975—Personal narratives, American. | United States. Army—Biography. | Vietnam War, 1961–1975—Campaigns—Vietnam. | Soldiers—United States—Biography. | United States. Army. Engineer Brigade, 18th—Biography. | Counterculture—United States—Personal narratives. | BISAC: HISTORY / Military / Vietnam War
Classification: LCC DS559.5 .D87 2021 | DDC 959.704/34092 [B]—dc23
LC record available at https://lccn.loc.gov/2021037502

British Library cataloguing data are available

ISBN (print) 978-1-4766-8472-7
ISBN (ebook) 978-1-4766-4243-7

© 2021 Roger S. Durham. All rights reserved

No part of this book may be reproduced or transmitted in any form or by any means, electronic or mechanical, including photocopying or recording, or by any information storage and retrieval system, without permission in writing from the publisher.

Cover image: Roger Durham with 11 months in-country; stop sign 1970 (author collection)

Printed in the United States of America

McFarland & Company, Inc., Publishers
Box 611, Jefferson, North Carolina 28640
www.mcfarlandpub.com

For the Phantom

The story is true.
Names have been changed to protect the guilty.
No one was innocent.

Experience is the hardest teacher.
She gives you the test first and the lesson afterwards.
—Oscar Wilde

Table of Contents

INTRODUCTION	1
1. The Lost Boys	7
2. The Tunnel at the End of the Light	15
3. Flirting with Disaster	30
4. Like Boy Scouts with Guns	49
5. The Good, the Bad and the Indifferent	77
6. Dudes, Duty and Diversions: 18th Engineer Brigade	87
7. Heavy Weather	109
8. A Temporary Reality	117
9. Duty Calls	130
10. "Who is this chick? Where the hell am I? What am I doing here?": R&R #1	143
11. Stand-Down, Let Down	167
12. Crusader Switch: 35th Engineer Group	177
13. Like There Was No Tomorrow: R&R #2	186
14. Dudes, Duty and Diversions: 35th Engineer Group	206
15. The Incorrigibles	222
16. Bourke Street Again: R&R #3	236
17. Straight On Till Morning	250

18.	Wandering and Wondering	266
19.	To the Wicky Wick Woods	279

Roger S. Durham Service History   291

Index   293

Introduction

Most Vietnam literature is focused on the combat aspects of the war but there were far more people serving in the combat zone than there were serving in combat. Soldiers in support roles were vital to the war effort, moving supplies, equipment, and personnel to where they were supposed to be. For every grunt who pulled a trigger, there were about thirty manning typewriters, phones, radios and transports to get the ammunition, food and support to that grunt and his buddies.*

While there have been a number of published memoirs about life "behind the wire," a large part of the Vietnam experience has not been fully addressed. This book is intended to fill a small part of that void, and to tell the story of another large yet underrepresented group: the men who fought the war while opposing it.

In the turbulent times of the 1960s and early 1970s, untold numbers of young men fought against the war and the draft by demonstrating, resisting, and being involved in political and social causes, only to be eventually drafted and sent to Vietnam. Their opposition to the war did not end when they were inducted. It continued with a change of location and means of resistance. Among these "counterculture warriors," opposition became a bond among those of like mind, and there were many soldiers who knew that bond. If it was not the genesis of the "FTA" attitude, the bond certainly perpetuated it. They were warriors in the sense that they were soldiers, but they were also warriors of resistance to a conflict they felt was not in our national interest, or their own.

---

*Michael Clodfelter, *Vietnam in Military Statistics: A History of the Indochina Wars 1772–1991* (Jefferson, NC: McFarland , 1995), 238–239. Clodfelter notes that the ratio of combat troops to support troops varied by the year depending on total troop strength. He indicates that in 1967 there was a total force of 473,200 soldiers in Vietnam, of which 49,500 or 10.4% were combat soldiers. Artillery and Engineers made up 12% of the total and Headquarters and Logistics was 75% of that total. In 1968 the total force increased to 542,000 soldiers of which 88% were Headquarters and Logistics. By 1969 they were trying to fight the war with eight times as many soldiers in Headquarters and Logistics as there were in combat roles which represented only 6% of the total force.

It was a divisive time in our history, a time of contrasts and irony. The country celebrated the Civil War Centennial during the first half of the 1960s, marking the one-hundredth anniversary of the event that ended slavery. Yet the struggle for civil rights was still going on as black Americans fought for the equality they'd won a century earlier, while the country became involved in another civil war, in Southeast Asia. As with our own Civil War, the nation fragmenting once again as fault lines developed along pro-war and antiwar lines, the draft, civil rights, race, religion, gender, cultural and generational divisions. People found themselves at odds with each other over any number of these issues—the United States didn't seem to be so united.

As the 1960s progressed, widespread tensions developed in American society, and the counterculture became identified with the rejection of conventional social norms of the 1950s. Counterculture youth rejected the cultural standards of their parents, especially with respect to racial segregation and initial widespread support for the Vietnam War. The Baby Boom generation came of age during this time, shunning their parents' values and filled with an excitement over what could be. They were imbued with President Kennedy's clarion call to "ask not what your country can do for you, but what you can do for your country."

However, their country was already telling them what they could do—there was an increasing need for soldiers and the draft answered for recruiting deficiencies. Freedom isn't free and there were dues to be paid, so the bill was presented to selected young men for payment. I was one of those young men.

The boomers came on the scene like they had something to prove. They were driven to make a difference and as they came of age, they sought to establish a collective identity separate from their parents. The realization that, over the years, their government has misled them made boomers distrustful of authority and contributed to a growing dissatisfaction with the status quo. It was very much an "us" against "them" mentality. This was part of the fundamental attitude that colored their perceptions of society, and the times, and influenced their judgments. This dissatisfaction was a unifying element for the nation's young people, their shared attitudes and beliefs the foundations of a mass countercultural movement across the nation. A unified antiwar ethos was fueled in part because television, for the first time in history, brought film images from distant battlefields into American households on a nightly basis, along with statistics of war dead—theirs and ours.

A separate cultural phenomenon came out of California, rising from the roots of the beat generation, with its heart in San Francisco and embraced by many Boomers. This youth movement was more social than political, but polarized by the issues facing the country, and how they impacted them. It was a grass roots movement that arose from opposition to the war. This social phenomenon included a drug subculture that popularized and spread itself as shared drug use became a basis for trust and solidarity among those in the counterculture—so much so that it became one of its identifying characteristics. Psychedelic drugs were embraced as routes to expanding one's consciousness. The attitude of the times was reflected in its music, literature and art, which were dismissed as superficial or subversive by much of mainstream society.

The counterculture integrated many ideals and indulgences of the time—peace, love, harmony, music and mysticism. The movement divided the U.S. population. To some Americans, the attributes reflected American ideals of free speech, equality, world peace, and the pursuit of happiness; to others, they reflected a hedonistic and self-indulgent, pointlessly rebellious, unpatriotic, and destructive assault on America's traditional moral order. Parents argued with their children and worried about their children's safety; their children worried about the world's future.

White, middle-class youth made up the bulk of the counterculture. They also had access to a media eager to present their concerns to a wider audience. Demonstrations for social justice created far-reaching changes affecting many aspects of society. "Hippies," "Freaks," and "Weirdoes," were epithets often hurled at these people, who took them as compliments rather than insults, adopted them as an identity and used them to bond with others who thought the same way. They became the largest countercultural group in the U.S., banded together by music, politics, Vietnam, the draft, and drugs.

Many who fought against the war and the draft were ultimately drafted and found themselves facing military service, with an all but guaranteed trip to Vietnam. Options were limited. One was not reporting for induction, a felony regarded among the counterculture as the ultimate act of defiance. But a significant number of these politically and philosophically opposed individuals did not shirk their duty when drafted. In spite of personal feelings about the draft and the war, they chose to serve a cause they did not believe in. Some rationalized that they served their country, not their government. Many served simply because they saw no alternative. Whatever their individual reasons, they went to Vietnam with a bad attitude about what they were participating in.

For many young men forced into military service who did not believe in the Southeast Asian crusade, drug use within the military was seen as a form of protest rather than a behavioral problem. Often these young men first encountered recreational drugs through friends or during college. Others began to use drugs in the military, many while in Vietnam.

The Vietnam War introduced a significant number of Americans to marijuana, which had long been used in Southeast Asian countries as medicinal treatment for pain, nausea, skin disorders, burns, constipation, premature aging, and blood poisoning, to name a few. Thus it was already "in-country" long before Americans arrived—but Americans would take it home.*

As many as three out of four American servicemen tried marijuana during their tour of duty and three out of ten were regular marijuana smokers. "Vietnamese pot became our path to sanity, our lifeline," noted a veteran helicopter pilot. "It was a simple yet very effective way of maintaining peace of mind amidst the chaos of the conflict—an escape from the horrendous reality of our daily lives." A machine-gunner recalled "Even in combat situations and on week-long patrols in the jungle, we smoked pot several times a day," His experience was not unusual. A Congressional Medal of Honor winner said he was stoned on marijuana the night he fought off two waves of Viet Cong soldiers and earned America's highest honor. Smoking marijuana was not just a political statement; for many soldiers it was a coping mechanism.†

The young men who did not partake of the accepted alternative, alcohol, found drugs to be a better choice because they did not impair the senses the way alcohol did, and did not leave the user hungover. Moreover, young men isolated on scattered bases of varying sizes and degrees of danger, with little to occupy their free time, understandably found release in drug use and the camaraderie associated with it.

The Vietnam War produced many stereotypes, one of which is the spaced-out, doped-up, hippy conscript. Just about every reference to these counterculture warriors depicts them as dazed, out of touch with their surroundings, and dangerous to their fellow soldiers. Many young men did become consumed with drug use to the detriment of themselves and their units. These are the ones many vets remember. Yet there were many non-drug users who also fell into this category, and those who used alcohol met these criteria as well. While this in no way excuses the behavior, it does illustrate how unfair the stereotype is because it does not take into account the young men who did their jobs with dedication while keeping their "heads"—a gesture of protest seen as "gettin' over" on the Army. "You have my body, but my mind belongs to me."

The rank and file were drawn from those young men most likely to be opposed to the war, and thus most likely to already be familiar with recreational drugs when they were drafted. Alienated by the military in which they served, they found acceptance and a common identity in a subculture that accumulated within the ranks—a subset of civilian opposition to

---

*Saul Rubin, *Offbeat Marijuana: The Life and Times of the World's Grooviest Plant* (Santa Monica, CA: Santa Monica Press), 75; Grinspoon, Lester. *Marijuana Reconsidered*. Harvard University Press, Cambridge, MA. 1971. p. 267.

†Novak, William. *High Culture: Marijuana in the Lives of Americans*. Cannibis Institute of America, Cambridge, MA. 1980. p.168; Brecher, Edward M. and the editors of *Consumers Union Reports*. *Licit and Illicit Drugs*. Consumers Union, Mount Vernon, NY. 1972. p. 426; Dalat, Dr. "Heart of Dankness," *High Times Magazine*. August 2005.

the war that permeated the pool of draftees. Its motto was "Peace," its universal greeting the two-fingered "V" peace sign, with recreational drug use a part of its credo. Counterculture warriors served everywhere the Army served—Germany, Korea, etc.

This book takes the reader into that society of soldiers who used drugs as a form of recreation, protest, and as an aid to coping with their circumstances. But, as their fathers before them, they did their jobs, supported the mission, and let neither their comrades nor their country down. When their tours of duty were over, most went home to become productive citizens. The young men in these pages were real. I couldn't make up these characters. My experience suggests there were thousands of other counterculture brothers who served in Vietnam, young men who toked and smoked and did their jobs to the satisfaction of those who commanded them.

The counterculture began to collapse by 1973, due primarily to the fact that most of its political goals—civil rights, civil liberties, gender equality, environmentalism, and the end of the Vietnam War, were politically stated and/or accomplished to one degree or another. Its most popular social attributes, particularly a "live and let live" attitude in personal lifestyles, were co-opted by mainstream society. The counterculture values, though, continue to influence social movements, art, music, and society in general. The post–1973 era mainstream society has been in many ways a hybrid of the 1960s establishment and counterculture. The straining of the social contract between the American people and their government that pushed the boundaries of convention and trust during the Vietnam era helped create the society and culture that has and is evolving today.

For me, the irony was that for as long as I fought going to Vietnam, in the end I did go, and then turned down a chance to go home early, extended my tour, and when it came time to go home, I was almost afraid to. Life in Vietnam was simple. Life in the World was complicated, the home front filled with unrest. I had been afraid to go to Vietnam because it was a dangerous place where people got killed. But when it was time for me to go home, I was afraid because the World was a dangerous place where people got killed.

A counterculture warrior, I fought but did not wage war. This is a perspective of the counterculture in the military, the resistance, the "underground" mentality, the struggle to maintain one's individuality amidst overwhelming conformity. It is the boredom, the drugs, the duty, the combat, the work, the friendships, the good times, the bad times, the living of life on the edge, the outrageousness, the absurdities, the insanity, and the "who gives a shit?" attitude. Even today those of us who went, and many of us who didn't, struggle to understand and interpret what happened to us in those early years of manhood, as the nation struggled to come to grips with the reality of the Vietnam War.

1

The Lost Boys

The intercom came on and the pilot's voice filled the interior of the airliner: "We are approaching the coast of the Republic of South Vietnam and will be arriving at Cam Ranh Bay Air Base within 20 minutes. If you look out the windows to your right you will see the coastline." Below, the vast blue-green expanse of the South China Sea could be seen divided by a narrow line of white beach and rocky outcroppings of the Vietnamese coast.

Here we were, a plane load of rather dejected military personnel preparing to land at Cam Ranh Air Force Base in Vietnam. The beast had stalked me the past six years—now, I was moments from setting foot in the home of the war. What'd I do to deserve this? In the silence inside the plane, my thoughts turned back to where this road began—college.

I went to college not for an education but for a deferment to keep me out of the draft. Enrolled at a branch of the University of Wisconsin, I found two things that impacted my life. One was the antiwar movement. The other was drugs. My involvement in the antiwar movement started after I attended an open forum discussion on the Vietnam War and the draft. At that time, I'd supported my government's policies on the conflict in Vietnam, but my curiosity led me to attend the discussion.

It turned out to be a more interesting evening than anticipated. I found myself agreeing with much of what they had to say. After the meeting, I talked with several attendees, and the turning point came when one of them said: "Well, if you support our government's policies in Vietnam, what are you doing here? Why aren't you over there fighting for what you believe?" I had no response: I was there to maintain a student deferment so I wouldn't have to go over there and fight. It was a contradiction I had a hard time coming to terms with. It was OK for me to support the war, as long as someone else did the fighting.

This was the beginning of my war against the war. I wanted to do all I could to bring an end to the war and the draft, so I joined the ranks of youth aroused to protest the war. I supported protests on my own campus, participated in the Dow Chemical Company demonstrations in Madison,

Wisconsin, in October 1967, where I first experienced tear gas, and went to the Democratic Convention in Chicago in August 1968. I'd watched college friends leave school to be drafted and sent to Vietnam. In my third year of college, the war got closer to me and I was resigned to the fact that it would eventually get me too, no matter how hard I tried to avoid it. I could see Vietnam looming on the tree line of my future then. Now I was on the threshold of that future.

College also brought me into contact with recreational drugs. In my small hometown, drugs were perceived as a big city problem. Princeton, Illinois, was a long way from being any kind of big city, and we were thoroughly indoctrinated against drugs. But in college I met people my age who told me what I had learned about drugs in school was not true so I began to learn about a variety of recreational drugs.

I put in three years before flunking out of school and had to go home for a semester before I could go back, while the draft waited like a wolf at my door. I reapplied, was accepted and all packed to leave for my last year of college, when the day before my departure the mailman tramped a path to my door, delivering a letter from the government that began with "Greetings." My draft notice had arrived. I was not going back to school. I struggled with whether to go in for induction or not and considered going to Canada. In the end, it came down to how I felt when it was time to go.

There were no good options. Each had good points and bad points. If I did not go, someone else was going in my place, assuming the fate that would have been mine. It might require that young man to lay down his life and his parents to grieve his loss rather than mine. Then again, if I decided to go, perhaps I would prevent another young man from having to face the reality that lay before me. In the end, I went. Flunking out of school was the start of the road that led me here, on this airplane about to land at Cam Ranh Air Base.

During basic training at Fort Bragg, North Carolina, we endured weeks of abuse by loud-mouthed drill sergeants who'd already done

One of the campus "weirdoes" 1967.

1. The Lost Boys

Basic Training. Me (front row, second from left), with my 5th Platoon comrades. I'm not happy.

tours in Vietnam, while the threat of our own deployments hung over us. We learned the intricacies of the M-14 and M-16 rifles, bivouac, first aid, KP, gas warfare, hand-to-hand combat, bayonet drill, close order marching, physical training and the grenade range, where we took our first casualty after a trainee dropped a live grenade in the pit. The detonation killed both the trainee and the instructor, who was a 'Nam vet. This happened right in front of me, since I was next in line for that pit.

After basic, it was Fort Lee, Virginia, where I trained as an Armorer and Supply Specialist, then got orders for Vietnam. We were told to go home on leave, put our affairs in order, make out a will, and say goodbye to family and friends because many of us would not be coming back.

On 15 July 1969, I reported to Fort Lewis, Washington, for overseas processing. But, when I arrived at the Seattle airport I ran into one of my Fort Lee classmates who was guiding arriving soldiers to Fort Lewis transportation. He told me there was a chance we wouldn't go to Vietnam because President Nixon was beginning his de-escalation and people headed for 'Nam were being sent to other assignments.

At the initial processing the NCO in charge called off a list of MOS (Military Occupation Specialty) designations that were on hold—those so designated were to stay after the briefing. My MOS was on the list. After the briefing we were sent to an NCO in an adjacent building, who sent us to a barracks to await another call.

When we finally got our orders, mine were for Hunter Army Airfield, Savannah Georgia. I'd thought maybe Vietnam would pass me by and I wanted to believe it.

Upon my arrival at the Hunter Field reception station, an NCO reviewed my records and asked: "Can you type?" I acknowledged I could, whereupon he asked me to sit down at his typewriter, opened a book to a random page and said: "Type this page." I proceeded to peck out the words from the selected page until he told me to stop. "I can get you a good job." he said. With that he handed me my records and told me to come back to see him on the following morning.

Typing. My father had insisted I take a typing course a few years back. As a young man, in those pre-women's-liberation days, I perceived typing to be a feminine skill meant for secretaries and clerks. But my father insisted so I learned the basics of typing that summer of 1963. But that wasn't enough. When I returned to high school that fall, he insisted I take the typing course offered there. In the years since, I had not done much typing. But in spite of all the good Army training I'd just completed, in the end my typing skills were all they were interested in.

The following morning, I was interviewed by a big, burly First Sergeant (1SGT) who looked at my records and asked: "Durham, can you type?" I responded that I could, and he told me to sit at a typewriter adjacent to him, opened a book on his desk, picked a random page and said: "Type this." Once again, I proceeded to type the page until the 1SGT said: "OK! We'll keep him." Thus I became a member of the Garrison Company,

After Ft. Lee, a studio portrait for my mother.

1. The Lost Boys

Headquarters and Headquarters Company, Number 2, and served as a clerk typist in the company orderly room. I could hear my father telling me that I needed to learn how to type. It seemed this useless skill had some value after all. Was this my guardian angel at work?

Hunter Army Airfield and Fort Stewart were a combined helicopter flight training center to train helicopter pilots for Vietnam. I settled into my job and typed duty rosters, correspondence and anything that was given to me. Our 1SGT was what I had come to know as a stereotypical "lifer," a career soldier. The other clerks were all "short," a term I was unfamiliar with—it meant they would soon be out of the Army.

I processed new people into the company, getting them on the unit roster, providing meal cards, and getting them up to speed. We had returning Vietnam veterans come into our company and I could always identify them by their dark tans and lost expressions. What I found difficult to understand was how many came back to the orderly room within weeks requesting transfers back to Vietnam. I could not understand what was happening there. Why would they want to go back?

I moved up the ranks from an E-2 to a PFC to a SP4. The short-timers left and I soon found myself the ranking clerk and primary typist for the 1SGT and company commander, Major (MAJ) Larry Wells. I was exempt from extra duty, worked an eight-hour day and could have spent my entire enlistment there typing away for the MAJ and 1SGT. As the months slipped by, I began to feel I had cheated Vietnam. Savannah was beautiful. I could have stayed there forever.

Through Jay "Antman" Barton, one of my Fort Lee classmates at Hunter, I met Everett J. Nance, or "EJ" as we knew him, who sat beside me on this plane approaching Cam Ranh Bay. He was from Portland, Oregon, and with SGT George Preston, joined our circle of comrades at Hunter. Preston was just back from Vietnam himself and was full of stories about dope and outrageous behavior he'd witnessed or participated in. His stories were unbelievable.

In the spring of 1970, members of my Fort Lee class who'd also been on my orders to Hunter were turning up on the monthly Vietnam levies. It seemed the Army had not forgotten us and was coming back to get those who'd been diverted last June. The March 1970 levy for Vietnam listed a John Durham from our company with my M.O.S. But he'd already been to Vietnam and was due to get out of the Army in May. He laughed when informed of this. I knew they were after me and gotten the wrong Durham.

The April levy confirmed my fear, as my name was on it for Vietnam. MAJ Wells became panicky since I was the only experienced clerk in the office while the rest were newbies. He'd called the Pentagon to try and get me off the levy, but it was no dice. It was a name levy. They wanted me, not someone with my M.O.S. When my buddies found out I was under orders for Vietnam they were suitably subdued, with the exception of SGT Preston who laughed and said he envied me. I felt like a condemned man.

When I got my orders, I asked for a two-week leave prior to reporting. Then, EJ Nance turned up on the same levy, so we coordinated our leaves to report at Fort Lewis together. In April we flew out of Savannah bound for Chicago, where EJ spent a week with my family before going to his home in Oregon. I returned the favor flew into Portland to visit him before we reported to Fort Lewis. We were driven there by EJ's mother and sister, followed by tearful farewells in the parking lot before we disappeared in the processing center. The procedure was the same as last year when I'd been diverted to Hunter Field. Was my guardian angel still with me?

The Fort Lewis replacement center was filled with GIs in khakis or dress greens while others wore new bright green jungle fatigues. We avoided work details and attended formations to see if we'd been manifested on a flight. That first evening after the formation we were loaded on buses, driven to the supply point and issued new OD green jungle fatigues, boxer shorts, T-shirts, OD towels and jungle boots. I felt so fresh and new in my fresh and new and green fatigues.

The day before we left for Cam Ranh Air Base, we heard our names called for the evening manifest. At the appointed time we'd cleaned our barracks, checked our bags and headed toward the assembly area. That's when we ran into a basic training buddy of EJ's who was also on his way to Vietnam with our group. Since he was a SP5, he was headed to the NCO club which, being lowly SP4s, we had steered clear of. EJ's buddy said it was "no sweat" for us to go to the club with him. After all, they were sending us to Vietnam so what else could they do to us? The biggest threat they could lay on a soldier at this time was "If you fuck up, we'll send you to Vietnam." Well, we hadn't fucked up but were being sent to Vietnam anyway.

The club was full of soldiers of various ages and rank, yelling, laughing, joking and raising a raucous din. Beer flowed to excess and this meant all over the tables, floor and various people. We sat at a table with friends of EJ's buddy. Everyone at the table was going to the Nam for their second tours. One slightly inebriated Puerto Rican buck Sergeant began telling us about his first tour and how he'd been shot by the VC in a firefight. This led to him pulling up his pant leg so we could see the rather nasty looking scar on the calf of his leg. He couldn't wait to get back to his old unit.

After getting our fill of the NCO circus we made our way to the assembly area where NCOs began calling off the manifest and issuing tickets to board the buses. EJ and I were soon on the bus. The drivers appeared, the buses rumbled to life and we headed down the street in silence through the slumbering installation bound for McChord Air Force Base, past neon signs of motels, restaurants, bars, fast food places and gas stations.

"Goodbye America" someone said.

"Ya, fuck the Army, screw Uncle Sam" another answered.

We entered McChord Air Base with dark, silent, empty looking buildings and only streetlights glaring in the night, the brightly lit terminal ahead, and looming ominously behind it a DC-10 jet bathed in floodlights. The P.A. announced, like the crack of doom, our immediate boarding and departure for Alaska, Japan, and Cam Rahn Bay. EJ and I joined the trickling mass of green, through the gate toward the tarmac.

We stepped into the cool summer night and toward the boarding ramp, the darkness held back by the glare of floodlights. The DC-10 stood like a queen bee, being serviced by a score of tiny drones. The lettering on the side: "Flying Tiger Airlines." We chuckled to ourselves when we realized it. "FTA." "Fuck the Army."

Crossing the Pacific Ocean, a feeling of excitement began to fill my mind. The dark mood I'd experienced in the past few days was being replaced by a new sense of adventure. EJ and I kept each other occupied with conversation, which brought to mind a quantity of speed I had tucked in my pocket. We snorted some, and as I inhaled, I heard a voice speak up.

"Hey, man, what's you doing there?"

I sat back and looked over at two black faces across the aisle, scrutinizing us. "A little speed, man." I managed to say. "You want a hit?"

A flash of grinning teeth. They turned out to be from Chicago, which was pretty close to home for me. They were Dan and LeRoy, and as the speed took effect the four of us began a very long and involved conversation and in no time we'd bonded. We talked on and on, the plane flew on and on, and so did the time. I no longer cared.

Landing at Yakota Air Base in Japan, we were guided by Air Force personnel across the tarmac toward the terminal, where we were halted while another group filed out across the tarmac to board another DC-10. They were all deeply tanned and dressed in khakis. Having finished their tours in Vietnam, they were on their way back to Fort Lewis, going home. We were green and a little scared, on our way to take their places. They looked much older than we, and as they passed, we heard them snickering and jeering at us. We lost our sense of adventure for a moment and walked dejectedly toward the terminal as the other group passed us.

After entering the terminal, the unpleasantness of the meeting was forgotten, and we shuffled off to check the attractions. As we stood at the counter of one shop, a young warrant officer stepped up to us and asked EJ "Aren't you Specialist Nance?" EJ turned around and a flash of recognition crossed his face. They greeted each other warmly. The WO had been a warrant officer candidate back at Hunter Field in the school company that EJ had been assigned to. They had become acquainted there until the warrant officer graduated and shipped out to Vietnam.

"Are you on our flight?" EJ asked him. He was, explaining that he'd been back to the States as an escort to return the body of a friend to his family. The deceased officer had also been in the same class at Hunter and EJ had known him. They'd been shot down flying a Cobra helicopter. It made me feel funny just being in the presence of this warrant officer who was on his way back to the Nam after escorting the body of his deceased friend home.

The call came to board for the last leg of our flight to Cam Ranh so we filed out and onto the DC-10 and were soon airborne, cruising south. The flight seemed all too short.

The pilot came on the intercom once more: "Please return to your seats, fasten your seat belts, and put your tray tables into the upright and locked position. We are beginning our approach for landing at Cam Ranh Air Field."

As we made our final approach, I could see glimpses of brush-covered hills and little buildings aligned neatly in rows, and jeeps and trucks inching along roadways. In the back of the plane, someone began humming a familiar tune. Others quickly picked it up then one person began singing it aloud. It was Country Joe McDonald's "Fixin' to Die Rag" and in a flash the entire plane was singing in unison as the plane bumped onto the runway. We had arrived.

2

The Tunnel at the End of the Light

There were signs of life as we passed rows of wooden barracks—crudely constructed with galvanized roofing and screens covering the windows, they looked like something out of World War II's Pacific Theater. To the north a large mountain with rough, rocky peaks. To the west another long, rocky spine of peaks.

The 22nd Replacement Battalion was housed in a cluster of ramshackle wooden buildings, painted a sickly pea green, the sun glinting off their roofs, white sand everywhere and nary a tree in sight. The entire facility was surrounded by a veritable wall of concertina and barbed wire with bunkers and guard towers at intervals. Large floodlights sat on poles aimed over the wire. It looked like a cross between a frontier fort and a prison camp.

It appeared as if the entire compound was overrun with people. We passed small groups wearing swim trunks and carrying towels walking out the gate and down the road. Others were wandering around in civilian clothes. Some were dressed in faded green fatigues and battered boonie hats, wearing beaten boots whose once-green colored canvas uppers were now red and brown. These contrasted sharply with the men in new green fatigues and boots. I couldn't imagine them walking the streets in the "World."

As we disembarked from the bus, the NCO yelled over the loudspeaker for us to fall in on the hardstand. I began to get a little paranoid about the packet of speed in my pocket.

In spite of the open screened windows, the processing building was hot and stuffy as we filed in and sat at tables placed around the room with perspiration soaking our fatigues. We were all hot, hungry and uncomfortable. A SP4 mounted an elevated wooden podium and addressed us over a loudspeaker. We filled out forms for the next of kin notification, MACV currency conversion cards, and turned in our personnel records.

As we filed out, I recognized my chance. While we assembled on a wide, covered wooden boardwalk, I ventured out of the sheltered boardwalk to find a suitable place to stash the stuff.

Every little bit of shade was occupied by hot, sweating, miserable newbies. I wandered past the orderly room and looked around. Between each building were bunkers constructed of large, corrugated metal culvert pipes set in wooden frames and thoroughly sandbagged. A plywood skin covered the sandbags, and each bunker could be entered from either end or through an opening in the center. Many bunkers were already occupied by newbies seeking shade, even though signs indicated: "For Use Only During Red Alert. Stay Out!"

At the entrance of an empty bunker I ducked in, dropped to my knees in a sandy corner, dug a hole, deposited the package of speed, covered it and carefully withdrew from the bunker, brushing away sand that stuck to my sweaty hands. I was already wringing wet from the heat, humidity and exertion, felt light-headed, exhausted, hungry and jet-lagged.

We turned in our U.S. currency, our completed forms and I.D. card, and were given MACV currency conversion cards, I.D. cards and a wad of colorful currency that looked like play money. These were Military Payment Certificates or MPC, the only currency authorized for use on U.S. installations in Vietnam.

My bags weren't hard to find since I could easily spot my guitar case and duffle bag, the fattest one there. I struggled to get the bag and guitar over to the counter where an MP impatiently waited. "Get 'em up on the counter!" he demanded. I obliged. He placed his hand on the duffle bag as I handed him my customs form. Without examining the bag, he directed a torrent of questions at me. "You got any ... narcotics, marijuana, LSD, pornography, U.S. currency, communist literature, propaganda, firearms, etcetera?" I smiled and said "No."

The stream of people coming from the customs building soon swelled the number of people with baggage seeking relief in the shade under that shelter. While it was wonderful, it was no relief from the heat and the humidity and the stupidity. I knew at that moment, in an air-conditioned office in one of the buildings around us someone was making decisions about where we would be sent. Our fates were being determined by others as we waited in the hot shade.

We found the only source of drinking water was a small green, wheeled water trailer where we waited our turn in line to drink warm water from a chewed Dixie cup that was provided. It barely satisfied our quest for a drink but it did wash away the sticky saliva.

Our search for a place to urinate was aided by the permeating smell of the "pisser." I never before had my nostrils assaulted by the stench of urine that had been cooked in the hot sun day after day for who knew how long.

2. The Tunnel at the End of the Light

The pisser consisted of a few sheets of plywood set up around four pipes buried in the sand with about two feet of pipe protruding. The stench was unbearable! I held my breath, fought my way through the flies and took my place inside, relieving myself into the crusty, smelly pipe. It wasn't at all what I'd imagined Army facilities here would be like. But, then again, I had no idea what to expect.

When we returned to the shelter, we were told we had to go to the central issue facility (C.I.F.) where we acquired an OD laundry bag filled with goodies such as a helmet, canteen, web gear, rain poncho, etc. Then we returned to our spot under the shelter feeling confident we'd touched all the processing bases, so I retrieved the speed I'd stashed earlier.

Later, as the sun settled on the western horizon, we stood in line at the mess hall to get our first real meal, then gathered for the 8:00 p.m. formation as cooling darkness descended upon us. I knew there were a lot of newbies in the replacement center but now they were literally coming out of the walls of the barracks. A whistle blew and everyone assembled on the flood-lit hardstand. Crowded, ragged ranks were established as the orientation was given by an NCO in the white hut.

He called off manifest lists for different destinations while everyone fidgeted and milled about and we listened, not expecting to hear our names since there were many others ahead of us. When names were called people made their way through the crowd to answer and after an hour of sitting and listening to manifests being called off for destinations all over Vietnam, there remained only a small group of us sitting on the hardstand.

When the NCO finished he leaned out of the window of the little white shed and called to us. "You guys come here and let me see your I.D. cards." Like fools we obeyed. He collected our I.D. cards, put them in his pocket and said, "I want you all to stay together as a group." Since we had no barracks, yet we followed another NCO to the covered walkway which was still littered with our assembled baggage from that afternoon.

"Get your bags and come inside the customs building" he said, so we extracted our baggage and followed our companions inside. The interior was brightly lit by bare bulbs dangling overhead. There were only a few bags on the luggage racks and the money conversion window was locked up tight. The NCO instructed us to gather around. There were about fifteen of us there with our bags. "We've got 800 bunks in these hooches..." he said, "and we have over 1,000 people here tonight. You'll have to sleep in here on the luggage racks." He turned and walked out slamming the door behind him as he left. We stood there momentarily looking at one another before the group began to break up and look for a comfortable spot on the empty luggage racks. "Fuckin' K.P.!" a black PFC said in disgust as he threw his bag onto a rack.

"No use trying to leave. They got our I.D. cards" someone said.

"Should never have given that lifer my card!" EJ said to me.

"Well what the fuck?" I replied as I chained and locked my guitar and duffle bag to a 2 × 4 support beam of the luggage rack. I spread my poncho over the 1 × 6 boards in the rack, climbed into the narrow space and rolled up using my blanket for a pillow. The only thing that crossed my mind in that moment was that my first day in the Nam was at an end. I realized that five years earlier on this same night I was attending my senior prom.

It seemed as though I had just closed my eyes when a loud voice began yelling at us to get up. I opened my eyes and could see the light bulbs still glaring overhead but there was no way to tell if it was day or night. "OK, fall out! Where's Anderson?" the NCO yelled. I could see he had our I.D. cards. "When you get your card, take your bags and fall-in outside." I rolled out of the luggage rack and folded up my poncho. As the NCO called out names, guys collected their I.D. cards and went outside to where another NCO waited.

"Durham!"

I retrieved my I.D. card. EJ had his card and shouldered his bag. "See you outside" he said as I struggled to collect my gear and unlock the padlock that held my guitar and bag to the 2 × 4 post. The NCO walked out and switched off the overhead light. Darkness fell about me and I saw the last two newbies rush out the door and into the bright sunlight to join the group outside. I cursed silently as I struggled to dial up the combination on the padlock while expecting the NCO to descend upon me at any second for being late. At last! The numbers fell into place and the lock clicked. I gathered my bags and rushed to the doorway.

When I walked into the bright sunlight there was no one there. The group was nowhere in sight. Where was EJ? No trace of any of them. I looked around. Maybe the NCO would come back looking for me but I had my I.D. card and thought I better get away from the customs building. EJ was caught and that was too bad but I had slipped through their net. The heat was building and I was hungry but felt the mess hall was not a place for me to be around today. I noticed there were fewer newbies due to several manifests having flown out during the night.

I wandered over to the admin building where I entered and found several GIs leaning against a counter. There was some baggage stuffed behind the counter and against the wall so I inquired as to whether I could leave my bag and guitar there. One unconcerned SP4 nodded so I stuffed my bag under the counter and padlocked the guitar to a support. With my stuff secured I went outside to settle back in the shade under the eave of a barracks behind the admin building.

2. The Tunnel at the End of the Light

About noon I wandered down the street to an S-4 office that advertised sodas for sale and waited in line to purchase two lukewarm cans of orange soda. I drank one as I walked, then cautiously crept to the mess hall, walked in the exit and found EJ wiping off tables and grumbling to himself. I hurried over to him. "Here man, check out this soda!"

"Can use it. Thanks!" he replied as he sat down and opened the can. "Fuckin' DRO (Dining Room Orderly)" he mumbled between drinks from the can. "What happened to you?"

"They missed me. I'm just keeping clear."

"I won't be out of here until about 7:30 tonight. Muthafuck!"

"I'll catch up with you at evening formation" I replied as I edged toward the exit.

I returned to my spot in the sand, relaxed in the shade under the eave of the barracks and dozed in the heat. When I awoke, I noticed a paperback book lying in the sand near me. I reached over, picked it up and began reading it. After I read a few chapters I placed fifteen chocolate-flavored cigarette rolling papers that I had in my pocket, in the book as a bookmark. I wished I'd had some smoke to roll in them, but I had not come across any of that famous Vietnamese pot.

About 7:00 p.m. I wandered back to the mess hall where I met EJ as he came out. We walked to the hardstand for evening formation and found a crowd already forming there. We went behind the processing building where we ran into our two traveling companions, Dan and LeRoy, the two soul brothers we'd been with on the flight over. They were walking around with eight other soul brothers but we recognized each other at the same instant.

"Hey! What's happening' Dudes?" LeRoy said.

"Not much. What are you guys up to?" I replied.

"Shit! We scored some smoke from Mamasan...." LeRoy said as he dug around in his pocket, retrieved an L&M cigarette package and handed it to me "...but we got no pipe or papers to smoke it in!" He shrugged his shoulders in a gesture of disgust.

I looked into the package stuffed with that green, aromatic vegetation. "Hey LeRoy...." I said as I handed the package back to him "...I got a few rolling papers I'm using as a bookmark."

His eyes lit up. "You wanna get your head?"

"I'll trade you some of my papers for a buzz" I said.

"Can you roll joints?" Dan said.

"You betcha!" I replied. "Let's go somewhere where I can work."

"My man, my man" LeRoy said patting me on the back. "This dude's always prepared."

There was a general mumble of approval from the assembled soul brothers, whose mood brightened with this development.

We walked around the processing building and sat along the white picket fence near the far corner of the hardstand. The floodlights in the area gave off enough light so I pulled out my book and LeRoy handed me the L&M package. Everyone's eyes were on me as I proceeded to construct one well-packed, chocolate-papered joint and held up the finished product. A grunt of approval ran through the group. I handed it to LeRoy and he fired it up while I rolled another one and another one. About the time the first joint made its round, another was lit, and the loudspeaker called the formation to order. We sat in the darkness beyond the formation area and I continued rolling several joints, saved papers to mark my place in the book and returned the remaining weed to LeRoy.

By this time the NCO in charge of the formation was calling off manifests. LeRoy and Dan were called for the Bien Hoa manifest so they went up to get their records and orders. When they returned they were even happier to know where they were going but they had to leave since they had to go with the others on their manifest as they would ship out together.

Suddenly we heard EJ's name called over the loudspeaker. He ran to the little white shed to get his records and orders and returned with a smile on his face. "Going to Nha Trang!" he said. "That's just north of here. Fifth Special Forces. I gotta go with the others on the manifest. We gotta stay together 'cause we all go out together."

"OK" I replied. He disappeared in the dark as the loudspeaker continued to call out names.

"The following people are staying in the Cam Ranh Bay area. SP4 Rhodes, SP4 Garrett, SP4 Bender, SP4 Reed, SP4 Durham, SP4...."

Wait! That was my name!

I ran to the handstand and made my way through the group gathering in front of the white shed where the NCO waited. "I'm Durham!" I said as I made my way to the front of the group. The NCO handed me my orders and records.

"You're going to the 18th Engineers. You'll be paged when your transportation arrives."

I turned and walked back toward the white picket fence to find EJ waiting for me. "Hey, I'm staying in Cam Ranh!" I told him.

"We'll be pretty close then" EJ said. "I had to get a bunk with the group in one of the barracks. We won't leave until tomorrow." We walked through the sand while my mind rushed with visions of what staying in Cam Ranh for my tour might be like although I wasn't quite sure what "The Engineers" meant. I wondered what I'd be doing with them. Typing, I supposed. The evening formation broke up and people wandered off in small groups as quiet descended upon us.

As the evening wore on, I began to feel the rub and stickiness of the

2. The Tunnel at the End of the Light

dirt, sand and perspiration on my body. "Bet the shower rooms wouldn't be too crowded now." I said to EJ With only two shower facilities for the number of GIs in the area it was almost impossible for everyone to use them as EJ and I found out earlier. As a result we just hadn't bothered.

"Sure could use a shave" EJ said as he rubbed his chin.

"I'll meet you at the shower" I replied. We hurried off to collect our things. I retrieved my soap, shaving gear, clean T-shirt, a towel from my bag still secured in the administration building and walked to a shower room located near the U.S.O.

The night was clear and calm and the sound of the showers could be heard before we got there. They were small, single-story buildings with showers in one end and a row of sinks and mirrors down the center of the building. We found a line of people waiting. Water stood about an inch deep over the floor so I waded in and claimed a sink. As I washed myself, EJ came in and we washed and shaved in silence. It felt good to get rid of three days of grit and sweat.

We made our way to the barracks along the metal walkway that ran over the sand by the back-bay where about a mile to the west, across the bay, we could see the glimmering lights of that military installation I'd noticed earlier. As we walked along, we heard the siren first and then we

The installation across the back bay as seen from where EJ and I watched it being attacked our second night in-country. This was Dong Ba Thin.

heard the thumping coming from across the water. When we looked across the bay, we could see the installation coming to life and heard the distant sound of a siren. There were flashes of light followed by the delayed sounds of explosions while searchlights from guard towers swept over the compound and parachute flares blossomed in the night sky over the area, floating slowly across the sky with their glaring light illuminating the darkness.

We stopped to watch. On this quiet evening, there was the war. They were under attack and we watched the flares and flashes and listened to the muffled explosions. There were green tracers arcing through the darkness and drifting into the compound followed by red tracers from the compound arcing back into the darkness. Then there were helicopter gunships in the air working over the area outside the compound with rockets and mini-guns sending tracers flying everywhere.

We stood transfixed. There was the war! We weren't even out of the replacement center and there was the war. We watched the fireworks and listened to the noise until it subsided and then walked on somewhat dumbfounded by it all.

"I'm gonna put my stuff away." I told EJ.

"OK. I'm in the third barracks, upstairs. There is a bunk next to mine."

It began to rain as I stashed my things in the admin building, grabbed my guitar and ran to barracks #3, where I stumbled up the stairs at the end of the building. The light over the door at the top of the stairs glared brightly as I entered the darkened interior. A row of iron-framed army bunk beds spread out on either side of me and as I walked down the darkened aisle, snoring GIs lay in all the sagging bunks. Duffle bags lay by the bunks and comic books, magazines and assorted trash lay strewn about the floor. As I approached several vacant bunks near the end of the aisle, I heard a voice whisper my name. It was EJ lying on a lower bunk. I could see why none of the beds around him had been claimed. There were only bare bed springs, but I was beyond caring at that point. I locked my guitar to the bed frame, climbed to the top bunk with springs protesting loudly, and lay down. No pillow. It didn't matter. I listened to the rain on the corrugated tin roof.

I slept fitfully during the night. At one point an NCO came through the darkened barracks yelling for everyone on the Bien Hoa manifest to get up and fall out. I dozed again. He returned, yelling and banging about the Bien Hoa manifest. I dozed again. I awoke later and found half the barracks empty and it was still dark outside. I dozed again.

Wooden floor. I sat up to greet my third day in the Nam then jumped down from the top bunk and woke EJ. After a bit of yawning and getting our act together we walked out into the new day We skipped morning formation since we had our orders. No sense wasting time there so we wasted it at

2. The Tunnel at the End of the Light

the Red Cross building where we read, played cards, and ate greasy toasted ham and cheese sandwiches with cups of diluted lemonade.

About noon we ventured back to the formation area. The loudspeaker called out: "Attention in the company area. All those on the Nha Trang manifest fall in on the hardstand with bag and baggage. I repeat. All those...."

"Hey!" EJ said. "Gotta get my shit!"

"I'll catch you at formation." I yelled as he sprinted off towards his barracks. There was already a large group of newbies milling about with their baggage, smoking and talking when I got to the assembly area where three OD buses were lined up at the bus stop. I stood along the white picket fence near the trash point until I saw EJ with his duffle bag join the group collecting on the hardstand. The formation was brought to order and the manifest read off. As each name was called that individual boarded a bus. EJ's name was called and I walked to the bus to meet him.

"Well, I'm on my way" he said. "You got my address?"

"Fifth Special Forces. You bet!" I replied. "Be sure and write me."

"Take care of your head, Buddy!" EJ boarded the bus and disappeared.

As the 1:00 p.m. formation was called, the buses drove off down the road and out the gate. Now I was alone. After all we had been through together, it was hard to see EJ leave. In later years he acknowledged that leaving me at that moment, after all we'd been through together, was one of the scariest moments of his life. I felt much the same way.

I returned to my spot in back of the admin building in the shade under the eave. The place seemed deserted. I read my book and dozed yet no word for me passed over the loudspeaker until 3:30 p.m. when the loudspeaker crackled to life. "Attention in the company area. All those going to the 18th Engineer Brigade report to the processing building with bag and baggage immediately. You are shipping. I repeat...." I'd heard this phrase so often in the past few days that I almost ignored it until it hit me that I was going to the 18th Engineer Brigade! I shoved the book in my pocket and headed for the processing building.

I walked into the office where I saw a couple of soldiers lounging about. "What do you want?" a SP5 asked me rather ominously.

"You called me. I'm supposed to go to the 18th Engineers." I replied as I looked at the other soldier sitting in a chair. He was wearing wire-rim glasses and had a bushy moustache not at all conforming to Army regulations. It was plain to see that he was a "freak" and I could tell he'd smoked his share of pot before.

"Throw your bags on the truck outside" the little freak said. I hurried around the counter where my bags and guitar were stashed and dragged them outside to a deuce-and-a-half parked along the picket fence where we'd smoked the night before. Two newbies were already in the back of the truck and a third was throwing his bag on board when I approached. He grabbed my duffle bag and threw it up to the newbie waiting in the back. I climbed up and sat down. There was no canopy over the truck bed, so we sat in the open making small talk. Soon, the little freak climbed into the cab, and the truck rumbled to life. We headed out the gate, past guard towers and fields of sand, barbed wire, and bunkers. We drove past sand hills, rows of barracks, and on past the airport. We could see the bay to the west and a bridge ahead that spanned the water. By the presence of more bunkers, searchlights, concertina wire, and guards I realized this was the entrance to the Cam Ranh Bay installation.

Beyond the bridge was a checkpoint and beyond that lay those expansive mountains on the distant western horizon. We approached a junction in the road and the truck slowed to a halt. From here the road to the left went on down the coastline; a right turn would carry us across the bridge and out of Cam Ranh.

The truck began moving and gradually turned ... right!

Wait a minute! We're going over the bridge! What are we leaving Cam Ranh for? I'm supposed to stay in the Cam Ranh area! I can't do that if I leave it. The truck picked up speed and we approached the bridge. I thought maybe I'd gotten on the wrong truck, but I remembered that the others with me had all said they were going to the 18th Engineers just as I was. Where were we going?

We drove over the bridge and approached a checkpoint with a large single-story building in the center and traffic routed around both sides of it. Everything was surrounded by chain-link fencing, more concertina wire and bunkers and guard towers on the perimeter. The truck halted at the checkpoint where an MP talked to the little freak while another MP eyed the five of us in the back. "Where you headed for?" the MP asked our driver.

"Dong Ba Thin" he replied.

This was the first time I'd heard the name of Dong Ba Thin. It wasn't Cam Ranh but it was the Cam Ranh area. We drove out of the checkpoint and left all U.S. Army protection behind. A row of shabby ramshackle shacks appeared along the roadside with little stands where sodas, C-rations and other goods were being sold. Vietnamese soldiers stood eyeing us suspiciously as we passed. Beyond the checkpoint, the road junctioned with another road and at the corner sat a number of three-wheeled motor cars or lambrettas that the Vietnamese used as a taxi service. We turned right and headed north on highway QL-1. It was the main north-south road that ran the length of the eastern coastline of Vietnam. The countryside was unimpressive, scrub brush, small trees, and occasional Vietnamese farms where small children herded skinny cows in the brush. In the distance I could see

2. The Tunnel at the End of the Light 25

a military installation that I realized was the place EJ and I watched being attacked the night before!

We passed a small compound that even I could see was some kind of ARVN (Army of the Republic of Vietnam) installation but the American installation was located next to it. When I saw the gate to the western compound approaching, I strained to feel any change in the truck's momentum indicating we were slowing down to turn in but we continued past the gate. Ahead we approached the gate to the eastern compound and again I held my breath, hoping the truck would slow down. There were no more military compounds beyond that gate.

The truck gears whined loudly, and I was relieved when he turned in at the gate and into the compound. The first thing that caught my eye was the wreckage of a UH-1 "Huey" helicopter in a field off to the side of the road. Opposite were the runway and flight line facilities for helicopter and fixed wing aircraft. The road was filled potholes and we passed equipment yards, motor pools filled with large trucks, cranes and vehicles, while on the other side of the road we passed long, single-story "hooches" built with the same ventilated walls, screen windows and corrugated tin roofing. Every building was surrounded by a four-foot-high revetment made of sand-filled fifty-five gallon barrels with layers of sand bags piled on top. A sign identified the area as the "553rd Float Bridge Company."

We rounded a curve and proceeded down a road running parallel to the beach passing a radio station, the enlisted and NCO clubs, then a section of run-down, unused hooches identified by a faded sign as the "Dong Ba Thin In-Country R&R Center." Bunkers dotted the edge of the road and more wire and spotlights filled the beach area. Across the bay I could see the 22nd Replacement we'd left a half hour ago. We passed a chapel and more hooches, then the truck slowed, made several right turns and we were on a back street behind all the hooches we'd just passed. On a small concrete basketball court a group of soldiers were sweating through a game of basketball. The truck backed up to the door of a small building adjacent to the basketball court and the engine went silent. The little freak climbed out of the cab. "Put your stuff in the hooch and report to the orderly room with your records and orders." With that he walked off.

I pulled my bags and guitar off the truck and faced the building we had been directed to. A sign over the door read "18th Engineer Brigade Transient Barracks." It looked more like a small garage. I opened the screen door and entered to find metal frame bunk beds, sagging mattresses and bare bed springs. Comic books, magazines and empty soda cans lay strewn about the floor. A newbie sat writing at a table while another lay on his bunk reading. Several of the newbies I arrived with started a conversation with the two already inhabiting our quarters as I dragged my stuff in and settled on a lower bunk. There was sand all over the mattress, but I sat down and dug my records out of my bag. One of the newbies already occupying the building oriented us to where the PX was, and where to get drinks.

I took my records and orders and joined the procession out the door. We entered a small office filled with desks and file cabinets where we found the same little freak who'd driven us from Cam Ranh sitting at one desk. He reviewed our files and orders and instructed us to go to the personnel office in the building behind the orderly room.

So we trooped around to the personnel office, which was packed with desks and file cabinets and one large aisle that ran up the center of the room. An NCO greeted us as we entered, then asked us to sit and wait while he interviewed us individually. While waiting, I leafed through my personnel records and was surprised to find a letter of recommendation from MAJ Wells calling attention to my typing skills and attesting to my hard work at HHC #2, Hunter Field, Georgia. It was an unexpected gesture on his part. I knew he'd tried hard to get me out of the levy, but in the end this letter of recommendation was all he could do, and I was unaware of it until that moment.

Viewing down the street toward 18th Brigade HQ area with the HQ at the end of the street and Tower 17.

As each person finished, they left. Then I was called so I sat down at the desk as the NCO looked over my records. "You type?" he asked.

"Yes, sir" I answered, a sense of déjà vu swept over me.

"Here, type this" he said as he handed me a paper and gestured toward a vacant typewriter.

I proceeded to type away until with a nod of approval, he stopped me and said he believed I could type. He continued looking through my records. "Hmmmm.76 Yankee. Supply. Hmmmm" he muttered to himself then looked at me, handed my records to me and said "Take this to the office next door and see Master Sergeant (MSG) Florence."

I collected my records, went next door and found myself facing an NCO sitting at a desk with a sign reading "MSG FLORENCE." The NCO at the desk was a staff sergeant. "I'm supposed to see Sergeant Florence" I said.

"He won't be in today" the NCO replied as he sat back and turned the page of a girlie magazine he was reading. I turned around and went back to the personnel office to see the NCO.

"No Master Sergeant Florence" I said.

The NCO looked at me. "Give me your records and you go back to that office tomorrow morning at 7:30 a.m. He'll be there then. Tell him I sent you." This sounded good enough to me so I returned to the transient hooch.

When I entered the other members of my group were there chattering about their assignments. "Where you goin' Roger?" one of them asked. "We're going to Phu Bai. The 45th Engineer Group" he said as he motioned to the guy sitting next to him on the bunk.

"Fuckin' Phu Bai!" one of the newbies already inhabiting the hooch said disgustedly. He walked up the aisle taking on the stance of a lecturing college professor. "That place is way north of here, up by the DMZ and Da Nang. Too close to trouble for me."

"Where are you headed?" another newbie asked him.

"Qhin Nhon. 937th Group" he replied.

"I'm staying here." I said as I walked past the newbie standing in the aisle and sat on my bunk. "I gotta see someone here tomorrow."

By this time everyone was ready to go check out the EM club so they stumbled out the back door. I was alone. It was quiet. I walked out the back door and leaned against the sand-filled barrels of the revetment surrounding the building. Everything seemed primitive, drab and without color. My eyes fell on the sign over the door of the building directly behind the transient hooch. It said "Shower." Another sign on the wall of the building warned "Non-Potable Water. Do Not Drink." I walked over to the screen door and stepped into the darkened interior. No mirrors, no sinks, just a bench, some nails driven into the wall and eight water pipes without shower heads scattered around the wall. A shower, no matter how primitive, would be most acceptable so I returned to the hooch, dug out clean underwear, a towel, a bar of soap and went back to face the shower.

I waded barefooted through the warm, stagnant water covering the uneven concrete floor. The shower head spewed forth a single stream of water like a garden hose. The hot water tap was warm, and the cold water tap was warm—it all came from the same water tank mounted on a wooden platform high above the building, heated by the sun. The water heater had apparently ceased to function. It didn't matter. It was a shower. The sweat and grime washed off as in any other and in no time I was refreshed and in clean clothes. All I needed now were clean sheets, but none were forthcoming from the locked supply room.

I sat on my sandy bunk and wrote a few letters to keep the folks at home posted on where I was. When finished I sealed them in envelopes and wrote "Free" in the upper right-hand corner exercising my new right to free postage by virtue of being in Vietnam. As the sun slipped into the western sky, I walked to the mail drop at the orderly room and deposited my letters.

Suddenly I was hungry and walked to the mess hall. After explaining

The 18th Engineer Brigade HQ area. Officers hooches to the right, NCO hooches to the left behind the two raised water tanks, enlisted hooches beyond. Admin buildings out of sight to the left.

my status to the headcount man, I was allowed to obtain a tray of food and sat down in the dining room where groups of GIs sat at little tables. I ate alone.

I left the mess hall and walked across the street where I noticed a building with a large sign reading "Re-Up Army." "Fat chance" I thought as I walked past the re-enlistment building.

Dong Ba Thin sat on the sandy, coastal plain surrounded by large, rocky mountain ranges to the north and west and I wondered who was up in those mountains looking down on us. When my newbie comrades returned, I went in the hooch and relaxed on my bunk to read. I became aware of the movie running so walked outside into the darkness where I could see the flickering ray of light from the projector with cigarette smoke drifting through it. I found the whole area filled with people in the bleachers and those in their lawn chairs or laying on ponchos or blankets on the ground. I found a seat in the bleachers and proceeded to watch the movie "Gaily, Gaily" with scenes filmed in Galena, Illinois, near where I'd attended college. Thus I was familiar with Galena having been there many times during those college years. I felt homesick as I watched the movie.

It proceeded with minor delays due to changing reels on the single projector but it was like no other movie theater I'd ever been to, particularly the audience participation. When the villain appeared or seemed to be gaining the upper hand the screen would be instantly pelted with a barrage of soda cans, beer cans, cigarette butts and anything that could be flung at the screen. Good scenes, such as explicit love scenes or an attractive female in scanty attire were run and rerun several times for the gratification of the audience before proceeding with the movie.

When it was over everyone wandered off in little groups talking, laughing, grumbling, leaving the theater area littered with a carpet of beverage cans and assorted debris. I wandered away somewhat amazed and returned to the transient hooch where I laid on my bunk. The other transients sat talking but I settled back and slept my first good night's sleep since arriving in-country despite the intermittent sounds of grenades exploding out on the compound's perimeter.

3

Flirting with Disaster

An NCO came through the hooch yelling at us to get up and sweep the place out, then was gone slamming the screen door behind him. My watch read 7:15 a.m. so I dressed, got my things and walked out of the hooch. GIs carrying steel helmets, flak jackets, web gear and M-16s wandered up the street as I walked past the supply room, personnel office and continued to the next building. I entered the office I'd been sent to the day before and found myself facing a small man with a severe flat-top hair cut and a mousey looking face sitting behind the desk. His fatigues were so starched and pressed they appeared to be cardboard. His nametape read FLORENCE in bold, black embroidered letters. "You our new man?" he asked before I could say anything. "Come on in" he said as he rose from his desk. "The Major isn't here right now. You sit down here and let me look at your records." He stood barely over five feet tall and looked more like a little kid than a forty-seven-year-old man with twenty-eight years in the Army. He'd seen service in World War II, Korea, and had been in Vietnam longer than I'd been in the Army.

The office was long and narrow with desks, file cabinets and bookcases down either side of the building with an aisle down the center. To the west end near where I sat was a plywood partition behind which sat the O.I.C. (Officer in Charge) and his assistant. There were several clerks sitting at one desk conversing quietly and casually glancing my way. I noticed steel helmets, flak jackets and M-16s hung on nails driven into the exposed 2 × 4 wall studs. An SFC sitting at his desk next to the partition rose, walked over to me and handed me an oversized paperback book. "You might want to look at this" he said. It was a PACEX catalog filled with stereos, cameras, and other merchandise. I was told that since I was in the Southeast Asian Theater I was authorized to purchase from this catalog and its prices were quite reasonable when compared to the same items back in the "World." He introduced himself as SFC Hagberg. While I perused the catalog Hagberg walked over to confer with SFC Florence.

The screen door slammed and I heard new voices. Two clerks

3. Flirting with Disaster

appeared around the row of file cabinets that framed the entryway. One of them, loaded down with flak jacket, rifle and gear, walked over to his desk. The other was a tall, well-built SP5 with a well-trimmed, regulation moustache and a big smile on his face. His dark tan and faded fatigues gave clear evidence that he had been in-country for a long time. "Hey Sarge, we got a new man?" he asked MSG Florence as he walked over to me to introduce himself. "I'm Jim Walters. Where you from in the World?"

We shook hands and I responded "I'm Roger Durham and I live near Chicago."

"Chicago, eh? I'm from Milwaukee. Hope you're staying with us."

"So do I" I mumbled softly.

"You're probably gonna take Jimmy Ferrill's place. He's only got thirty-two days left. I got sixty-eight days and I'm going on R&R in two weeks."

SFC Hagberg walked over. "Walters, why don't you leave him alone now?"

"OK, OK. I gotta go to the hooch, Sarge" he said to MSG Florence. "Nice meeting you. I'll see you later" he replied as he left, slamming the screen door behind him.

"Do you type, Durham?" SFC Hagberg asked.

"Sure do" I replied with that déjà vu feeling coming over me again.

"Then sit down over here at this typewriter and type this" he said indicating a typewriter and handed me an open tech manual. I sat at the typewriter and typed the designated page. "OK, pretty good" was his response. I couldn't help but reflect on how my typing abilities got me placed when I processed in at Hunter Field and how they now played a role in my assignment here at 18th Engineer Brigade HQ. I returned to the empty desk.

There was conversation and laughter at the far end of the office. "Good morning Sergeant Florence" I heard a voice say just as I saw a man in starched fatigues with gold, embroidered oak leaves on his collar, polished boots, and an OD baseball cap, walk swiftly past my desk followed by the little Master Sergeant. I knew this was the man who had the final word on my assignment.

MSG Florence turned and motioned to me. "Go in and report to the Major."

I stood, stuffed my baseball cap in my pocket and entered the office. I came to attention in front of the Major's desk and saluted. "Sir! Specialist Durham reporting."

Major Marks waved a quick return salute. "Sit down, Durham" he said as he indicated a small couch beside his desk. He was probably in his mid-forties with a face like chiseled stone and a close-cropped haircut that resembled sandpaper more than hair. He looked at me with steely, blue eyes. "Where you from in the States?"

"Near Chicago, sir" I replied.

"Well, I'm from Florida." We talked casually about my previous duty assignment at Hunter Field, my M.O.S., whether or not I could type (again), my civilian schooling and so on. At last he looked at me and said: "So you think you wanna work for us, Specialist Durham?"

"I'd sure give it my best shot, sir."

"OK. Captain White!" he called to the captain who was writing at a desk just outside the Major's office. "Meet Specialist Durham." I stood as the captain looked up from his desk. He was young, in his late twenties, with a heavy build. He smiled.

"Glad to meet you, Specialist" he said as I shook his hand. "Welcome to the S-4 shop."

Major Marks stood up and looked over the partition. "Sergeant Florence, tell personnel we'll keep him" he yelled. I heard a voice in the office respond and then Major Marks turned to me and said, "Sergeant Florence will take care of you."

With that I saluted, turned, walked out of his office and found MSG Florence waiting for me. "You'll be taking Specialist Ferrill's place. You'll be driving and some typing as well."

It sounded good to me. The screen door slammed again, and I heard the shuffling and clumping of boots on the rough concrete floor. Two more people whom I'd not yet met came in. The nametape on one identified him as the Specialist Ferrill I was to replace.

MSG Florence spoke up: "Ferrill, this is Specialist Durham. He'll be replacing you." I stood and shook hands with a thin, pleasant looking fellow with a well-trimmed moustache and the hint of a southern accent. We talked momentarily about the usual topics. He was from South Carolina.

I was then introduced to SP4 Ronald Hardwick who was MSG Florence's clerk. Hardwick was tall and lanky with fair skin, dark hair and a rather unconcerned expression. He spoke quietly and smiled as we shook hands. Hardwick was from Pittsburgh and had been "in-country" about four months. It was inevitable that with a name like "Hardwick" his nickname quickly became "Hard Dick." It seemed as though everyone had a nickname, usually bestowed upon them by their comrades whether they wanted it or not. Like probably all the Rogers who served in Vietnam, it was not long before I was dubbed "Ramjet" after "Roger Ramjet" a cartoon character we'd all watched on TV as kids back in the World, and as with most nicknames, it stuck.

The three of us talked momentarily before the screen door slammed again and I saw SP5 Walters whom I'd met earlier. MSG Florence said

"Walters, take Durham down and get him squared away in the hooch." He turned to me. "Tomorrow morning take your finance records and catch the duty driver to take you over to process at Finance. Don't come in here tomorrow morning. You'll have to get up around 0630 to catch him 'cause he goes off duty at 0700." I nodded and collected my records. "Don't worry about the rest of the day" he said as I followed Walters out the screen door, slamming it behind us as we walked out into the morning sunlight.

We walked in silence for a few minutes before Walters spoke up. "What do you think of Sergeant Florence? He's a rotten little fucker. Sure glad I'm getting out of here in 62 days." We walked and talked of "The World," previous duty assignments and the S-4 office. "You got stuff in the transient hooch?" he asked. I nodded so we went to the transient hooch which was deserted except for my things. Walters shouldered my duffle bag and I grabbed my guitar, bags, and followed him out the back door, across the street, past a heavily sandbagged bunker and into a courtyard between two hooches. A small, Vietnamese girl sat near the bunker amid a row of jungle boots she was polishing. "How you doing, Mai?" he said as we walked past her. She smiled and yelled something back that I couldn't even begin to understand. "Ya, a new man!" he yelled back to her as we walked into the shade under the eave, opened a screen door and entered the hooch.

It was a large room with exposed 2 × 4 beams overhead, rough concrete floor, louvered plank walls, screen covered windows and seven bunks, one unoccupied. Each corner was occupied by a bunk, wall lockers, foot lockers and conveniences such as cassette players, fans, lamps, a refrigerator, etc. The degree of comfort depended on how long one had been "in-country."

Walters let my bag drop by the empty bunk. I noticed a small Illinois state flag on the wall over the bunk next to mine and a Vietnamese guitar stuffed behind the wall locker. "Who's from Illinois?" I asked.

"Oh, that's Willy Anderson. He's the Major's driver. You'll meet him later."

"Plays guitar, too?"

"Ya, sorta Country stuff" Walters said as he walked to his bunk in the corner. His bed was made up with a camouflaged poncho liner and there were bamboo mats covering the floor. He rummaged through his wall lockers and came out with a new bright, green, boonie hat like everyone in the company wore. "Here…" he said as he tossed me the hat "you don't wanna wear that screwy baseball cap. This is more comfortable. They're hard to get 'cause everyone wants one and they're phasing them out. Engineers are one of the only units authorized to wear them now and they are supposed to be issued to us but our supply room hardly ever has any." He walked over where I stood examining the hat which was brand new. "Got that the other night from a drunk newbie lieutenant. Fell down in the street and left his hat in the ditch. I picked it up. Got two already. Don't need it and there is no sense in you not getting one for a while."

We sat down on a couple of foot lockers while I tried on my new hat. Walters smiled his approval. It already made me feel like an old-timer even if I wasn't one. "Everybody here works at the S-4 office?" I asked as I surveyed the empty bunks in the room.

"Well, almost. Bob Gregson's here…" he indicated a bare bunk and locker behind me. "…he's a newbie. Just got here last week. Works in the dispensary. Everybody here and in there…" he indicated the adjacent room beyond his bunk "…works in S-4 or the Maintenance Office at the other end of the office building. In this room we got Jimmy Ferrill, Ronnie Hard Dick, Willy Anderson, Andy Witner, Bob Gregson and me. In the next room is Chris Beshak, Bob Boone, Tom Franklin and Stu Berdman." I nodded my understanding. "You want a soda?" he asked.

"Sure."

He went into the next room with me trailing behind. Inside the doorway was a large refrigerator with a chain and lock on it. Walters pulled a key off one of the 2 × 4 wall stud, opened the refrigerator and turned to me. "You want Pepsi, Coke or R.C.?" he asked quite seriously.

Quite a choice I thought to myself. "Pepsi, I guess."

He pulled out two cans, opened them and deposited some of the colorful play money in a box inside the refrigerator then handed me a can and we sat down on footlockers.

"What about this duty driver thing tomorrow?" I asked him. "Where do I find him?"

"Oh, take your finance records, go to the headquarters building and tell them to have the duty driver take you to finance. MSG Florence will pick you up when you're ready."

It sounded simple enough but I knew that nothing was ever simple in the Army. Could the Nam be any different? "Say…." I knew what he was going to say before he said it merely by the tone in his voice. "…you smoke grass?" I couldn't tell if he approved or not.

"Well, I've been known to" I admitted.

He sat back. "I thought you might. Don't let Sergeant Florence or Sergeant Hagberg find out. They don't look too kindly on pot heads." I still didn't know where he stood on the issue. "You'll meet Robards and Sanger. They live next door and work in the P.I.O. (Public Information Office)."

"You smoke?" I asked.

"I have but I don't do it too much anymore."

The screen door slammed and the smiling little Vietnamese girl shuffled in on flip-flops carrying several pairs of polished boots that she placed under certain bunks.

"Hey Mai! You get on the stick and defrost the refrigerator. It's a mess! I told you yesterday and I want it done today!"

"OK, OK! I be beau coup busy! I do!" she replied in a voice thick with a Vietnamese accent before walking out of the hooch, slamming the door behind her.

"Little bitch!" Walters said.

"How do I go about getting a house girl?" I inquired.

"They cost $5 a month. You sign up at the supply room and pay for 'em on pay day. They make your bed, polish your boots, clean the hooch and so forth." He finished his soda and threw the can in a waste basket. "I gotta get back. If you need something come to the office. I'll have Mai get you some sheets. The supply room never has any. Fuckin' gooks hide 'em."

Mai, our hooch girl.

He walked out and I heard him talking to the house girl. They walked off together. I was alone in the hooch so began to unpack when Mai came in with sheets and a blanket. She laid them on the bed and smiled at me. "You be newbie boy, eh?" I nodded. "You want me work for you? You pay me?"

"Ya, I'll pay the right people." I responded. She smiled and turned around to leave.

"See you fuckin' G.I." she said as she walked out.

I settled back to unpack and was not aware of the passage of time until noon when the clerks from the S-4 office returned. Walters introduced me to Willy Anderson, the Major's driver, from Centralia, Illinois, who bunked next to me. He was a quiet fellow with a wide smile. Then came the others, each one introducing themselves to me. There was Stuart Berdman, a studious fellow with glasses and a thin, sandy moustache who was known as "Groucho." He was followed by Chris Beshak, known as B-Chuck, another old-timer, Tom Franklin from Tennessee, a thin, friendly fellow with dark frame glasses, and Andy Witner who was tall, blonde, well-built and Nordic in appearance. He was from Vermont and spoke with a pronounced New England accent. Then there was the medic, Robert Gregson, known to everyone as "Red" due no doubt to his red hair. He was tall, stocky and had a very pleasant personality. He bunked across the aisle from me, was from New Jersey and I learned we shared the same birthday although he was born earlier on that day so he was older by a few hours, and never let me forget it.

Several of the group left for lunch when a new person entered the room. He was a short, stocky, barrel-chested fellow with a round head, a bulldog face, a wide mouth, no neck, a beer gut, an arrogant attitude and an obnoxious laugh. He ignored me completely and launched upon a laughing conversation with Walters and Willy about his exploits in the local ville the night before. He was SP5 Bob Boone and I immediately sensed that we had very little in common. He was the King Grit of the office and obviously of the hooch as well. Suddenly their banter was interrupted by the sounds of the musical group the Byrds, singing "Jesus is Just Alright with Me" being played at full volume and coming through the plywood wall from the room next door.

"Sounds like Robards and Sanger are home." Walters said to me.

"Goddamned fuckin' Hippies! Wish they'd cut that shit out!" Boone said as he turned and stalked into the adjacent room. The song ended and quiet returned.

"Come on" Walters said. I followed as we walked out of the hooch and entered the next room. I was shocked by its appearance in comparison to our room. This room had a plywood ceiling painted white, and plywood panels serving as walls painted alternating red, white and black. Day-glow posters were on the walls and a black light hung from the ceiling. A wall locker, bookshelf with a tape deck, speakers, turntable and amplifier stood against the rear wall with a desk and television on it. Two fellows were sitting in low-slung lawn chairs on the floor.

"How you doin' John, Mike?" Walters said as we entered. "We got a new man in today."

I was introduced to John Robards, a tall, thin fellow with a friendly smile and a face that reminded me of Howdy Doody; and Mike Sanger, who was about my size and wore horn-rimmed glasses. They both seemed genuinely happy to meet me and we clicked right away. We were already Brothers and we talked about home, what was going on back in the "World," the latest music and such. They each had about four months of their tours left so they were old-timers. Walters said he had to eat so he left us. After his departure Mike walked over to where I sat on a bunk and knelt down on the floor in front of me. "You smoke pot?" he asked.

"I've been known to," I replied.

They smiled at one another. "We thought so. Stop by tonight. We'll get together."

"I'll be there." I responded. "Right now, I think I'll go get something to eat."

"OK, we'll see ya later. Nice meeting ya" they said as I left and headed for the mess hall.

When I returned to my hooch it was empty as everyone had returned to the office. I continued unpacking and when finished pulled on my new boonie hat, and took a walk down the road to find the PX I'd been told was down there. I walked until I saw a complex of buildings that contained the post office, craft shop, tailor shop and PX.

The small PX was air-conditioned which was nice but it was only a small room with shelves of canned foods, souvenir curios, toiletry items and similar necessities. Two Vietnamese girls sat unconcerned in one corner by the entrance where the cash register was. I bought a can of Ritz crackers and a mirror for shaving since the shower room had neither sinks nor mirrors. The crackers were of no concern but the can they came in would hold water for shaving and would serve admirably as my sink for many months to come. It seemed that everything came in cans, particularly candy and hard candy at that. No chocolate would last long in this heat and M&Ms were the only chocolate there was.

I returned to the hooch. As the afternoon wore on, the S-4 boys drifted in as things closed down. They were talking and laughing, carrying their web gear, flak jackets and weapons and piling them in their wall lockers. Everyone was friendly and spoke to me with the exception of Boone who ignored me.

"Hey, Hard Dick, we're going to eat. You coming?" Walters yelled to the fellow who was MSG Florence's clerk. He said he would be along, then walked to where I sat on my bunk.

"How're you doing?" he asked. "Going to eat?"

"Naw, I'm not really hungry."

"You met Robards and Sanger yet?"

"Ya, this afternoon. They want me to come over after supper."

"I can imagine why," He responded with a knowing smile.

When the sun disappeared behind the mountains the hooch came to life. Stereos and cassette players turned out Ike and Tina Turner and Led Zeppelin, in competition with Lorretta Lynn and Merle Haggard all playing in unison from opposite corners of the hooch. When Boone, Willy and Walters headed out for the EM club, Hard Dick and I went to Robard's and Sanger's hooch.

Their room was bathed in black light when we entered. Others were already there as I found the "gang" was gathering. I was introduced to Dan Rosberg, another "short-timer" who had barely thirty days left before going home. I could hardly imagine being in that position since I still had at least an entire year ahead of me. He soon left and others came in. I was introduced to Bob Wilks, a tall, lanky, easy-going fellow with a "Tommy Chong" stoner personality and a sense of being perpetually stoned. Bob was a character. He wore sunglasses all the time because his regular prescription glasses were usually broken. Why were they broken? Well, Bob had trouble coordinating his feet. He fell in the theater bleachers at least once a week and once, when bending over to retrieve the hat he'd dropped on the ground next to a bunker, he banged his forehead on the edge of a 55-gallon drum in the bunker wall, necessitating stitches.

One Sunday afternoon, he passed out at the beach and cut his head on the rocks when he fell. Another time he fell through a wall in a hooch and finally, he fell asleep while driving his truck and rolled it on a wet curve on the way to Nha Trang. He was banged up but not seriously injured. He was always limping or had a bandage somewhere. He was a very likeable fellow and everyone kept an eye out for him because he was always injuring himself. It was as if a little cloud of disaster always hung over Bob.

Considering his ability to court disaster, it seemed ironic that Bob worked in the communications section at the C.T.O.C. (Combat Tactical Operations Center). This was located in a heavily sandbagged bombproof bunker behind the S-4 office. It was surrounded by high fences of concertina wire and considered key to the compound's security since the radios and company communications network was located there. It was *the* headquarters when the compound was attacked and the commanding general directed operations from the C.T.O.C.

Bob's companion was Glenn Fields, a stocky, well-built individual with a Peach fuzz moustache, who was just passing the mid-point of his tour and ready to celebrate. When it was time to move out for the evening's operations the group left the hooch and wandered out of the company area, walking down the darkened road toward the PX on the route I'd walked that afternoon. I felt as though we were being very obvious as we stumbled in potholes in the road and shuffled noisily through the sand. I followed the crowd since I had no idea where we were going. At one corner of a yard filled with collapsible pontoon bridges, the wire fence was trampled into the sand. I followed the group, jumped the ditch and entered the yard. I could clearly see from the well-worn path that a considerable amount of foot traffic had crossed this trampled wire.

We entered the yard, climbed up into the stacks of pontoon bridge frames and settled into a spot at the top of one stack. The litter of beer and soda cans gave testimony to the popularity of the place. Sanger lit up a fat

3. Flirting with Disaster

joint he'd pulled out of a little plastic bag filled with them, and then passed it to me. I noticed that Fields and Wilks were loading pipes from a plastic bag of loose pot. I drew on the joint and the rich, sweet tasting smoke tasted good. Suddenly I was aware of Hard Dick nudging me and I turned to find a pipe awaiting my attentions. I took it although unaware of where it had come from since Wilks and Fields were just lighting theirs. We sat in silence as the three pipes went around, followed closely by several joints. Frequently I found myself with a pipe in my mouth and one in my hand and a joint waiting for my hands to be freed.

Things certainly were different back in the "World" where every grain of the precious herb was carefully rationed, and nothing wasted. Back there each joint or pipe was judiciously passed around and smoked down to the very last bit of dust. Up to this point in time I had never seen so many pipes and joints all burning at the same time, particularly considering the number of people in our group. When the joints were smoked down to the "butt" or "roach," I was shattered to see them being carelessly tossed aside like cigarette butts.

The pipes soon burned out and the roaches dropped to the ground. I was *blasted*. I had no idea where I was or how to get back to the company and much to my chagrin, they loaded up the pipes again! Why smoke anymore? I hung on determined to show I was as "Hardcore" as they were. My previous concepts of "excess" paled by comparison to the level of abuse and excess practiced by this bunch.

I realized just how zapped I was, so I pushed the thoughts out of my mind. The pipes continued to pass around, and my throat began to burn. "Someone's coming!" I heard a voice say. Everyone froze. Three figures entered the bridge yard through the downed fence and approached our hiding place. My heart almost stopped as they walked straight over to us and began climbing up onto the piled bridge frames. "It's Rosberg, Taske and Little Gomez."

The three climbed up to where we sat. "Thought you guys would be out here" one of them said as they joined us. I recognized Rosberg, having met him earlier at John and Mike's. The newcomers pulled out their own pipes and bags and in no time we had five pipes making the rounds. By this time I toked on each one as it came by. The technique of "shot-gunning" was very popular with this crew. This was done by placing one's mouth over the pipe bowl and blowing into it which caused the smoke to stream out the stem with great force. I had seen this in the "World" but these fellows were regular disciples. They each took a shotgun blast, coughed, hacked and turned red in the face which was evident even in the dark, yet after recovering, were back in line for another hit from whoever was administering the punishment.

During a break to reload pipes, I was introduced to the newcomers. Little Gomez was a small, Puerto Rican fellow who was very friendly and I liked him immediately. There was also another Gomez in the company and he was a very large fellow known as "Big" Gomez. In this way people would know just which Gomez you were talking about. The other fellow was Frank Taske, pale and thin with very blond hair, steel blue eyes from Madison, Wisconsin. Since I'd gone to school near there, had many friends there and had spent much time in Madison myself, we struck up a conversation. Frank worked with Bob Wilks in the C.T.O.C. and ran the radios during the late-night hours. When the compound was hit, Frank ran the radios and coordinated operations in the compound with the helicopter gunships that provided overhead cover. He was stoned all the time, and everyone marveled at his ability to function under pressure. It appeared that we were in good capable hands with Bob Wilks and Frank Taske in the C.T.O.C.

Since I was the new guy, I was meeting these fellows for the first time, so the usual questions ensued about where I was from back in the World and how long I'd been in the Army. One of them asked me: "So what do you think about this place so far?"

"I hardly know what to think." I responded.

Another voice chimed in: "It's not so bad. You'll get used to it. It's kinda like Boy Scouts with guns." Everyone burst out laughing and then someone added "…with free ammunition and no adult supervision…" which brought more laughter before the conversation moved off in a different direction. I was amused at the comparison, but having been a Boy Scout, I understood. Many young men of the Vietnam era had been Boy Scouts. It was their first real exposure to the military environment with its system of rank, authority, and standards of organization and conformity. In the Boy Scouts they learned survival skills, first aid, teamwork, map reading, marching and they went to the field and camped out and conducted field problems. All of which they would also find in the Army. Basic Training was just a refresher course for many. The Army merely added firepower to the mix and placed these young men in an environment where everyone, good guys and bad guys, had guns. It was the element of being in a combat zone that made the difference. It was like Boy Scouts with guns.

By the time the pipes were going again, my rear end protested the hardness of the bridge frames and awkward positions necessary to stay perched atop the pile. One by one the pipes flickered and died and at last, put away. We then wound our way out of the bridge frames and made our way through the hole in the fence although I no longer had any idea what lay beyond. I was lost with no sense of direction. Rather than betray my ignorance I kept quiet and followed Hard Dick who, out of the group, did

3. Flirting with Disaster

sleep in my hooch and since I knew he must have some idea of where he was going, I followed him. We walked along the main street past illuminated hooches with sounds issuing forth and entered the company area just past the theater where a movie flickered on the screen, and finally to the hooches. There, everyone collected in Mike and John's hooch which glowed with black light. Luke-cold sodas appeared and were passed around. Some people left and others came in. I was right next door to my hooch, so I was no longer worried about being lost. However, it wasn't long before I was ready to find my bunk, so I excused myself and went next door. My hooch was an entirely different world. Hard Dick, who I had not even noticed leaving John and Mike's room, lay on his bunk. The stark realities of my room compared to the black light, day glow and music next door seemed unreal.

I sat on my bunk. Hard Dick came over and we talked until interrupted by the rest of our hooch mates returning from the movie. Boone was laughing and being obnoxious and horseplay ensued between him and Walters. Hard Dick returned to his bunk, and I grabbed my book. Failing to comprehend what I was reading, went to bed and struggled to find sleep amid the noise of a card game my considerate comrades had developed on a card table at the foot of my bed.

Sunlight was filling the hooch when I awoke. The card table with cards, beer and soda cans scattered over it, still sat at the foot of my bed and each bunk held an inanimate lump under the covers. I looked at my watch and sat up. It was 6:20 a.m.! I had ten minutes to catch the duty driver. I dressed, grabbed my finance records and hurried outside. It was quiet as I rushed to the HQ building at the end of the street. All the doors were secured except for one so I entered and stood facing a 1st Lieutenant. "I'm supposed to have the duty driver take me to finance." I said.

"He's at the mess hall. Should be here any minute" the lieutenant responded before walking to a back room. It was not long before a SP5 entered. He was tall with dark hair and complexion and a neatly trimmed moustache.

"You the duty driver?" I asked.

"Ya, and you gotta go to finance, I suppose" he replied, looking at my new fatigues and the records under my arm. "Come on."

We climbed in the truck and roared off down the street but didn't get far as the truck broke down before we reached the gate, so I had to hitch a ride back to the S-4. As I approached the office, I could see MSG Florence looking out the screened window and when I walked into the office he said angrily "What are you doing here? You're supposed to go to finance!" I began to dislike him right there. He thought I'd totally forgotten to go to finance and assumed I couldn't follow simple instructions. I explained the circumstances and in no time, we were headed to Cam Ranh with SP Ferrill at the wheel of a three-quarter-ton truck.

We flew down highway QL-1, past scattered Vietnamese farms and shacks in the scrub brush until we reached the road leading to the Myca ("Me-ca") checkpoint. We cleared through there, continued over the bridge and approached the junction where the road turned off north toward the airport and the 22nd Replacement center. Here we turned south down the road into a new area for me. The road wound along the bottom of brush and tree covered slopes and bluffs. The blue/green waters of the bay lay on the west side obscured at times by brush covered sand dunes. Guard towers and bunkers stood starkly on the bluffs and along the tops of the sand dunes. It was a tropical paradise spoiled only by the miles of rusting concertina and barbed wire along the beach and out into the shallows. We passed other Army vehicles on the road and traffic picked up as we continued past storage yards carved out of the sand hills, then entered an area with two-story barracks and long, low single story office buildings. A large, rocky peak towered over the area from behind the buildings making an impressive backdrop. We turned off the hard surfaced road, onto a packed sand road and then into a sandy parking lot filled with jeeps and trucks sitting in front of a large, single story building constructed of rough-cut, weathered siding looking like something out of an old-time western movie set in Arizona. This was the finance office. Our truck plowed into the loose sand until halted at the front door. I climbed out. MSG Florence motioned to the door of the building. "You go inside and we'll pick you up this afternoon." With that they were gone.

There were newbies sitting in the sand alongside the building as I entered. The interior was dark and as my eyes adjusted, I noticed bleachers against the back wall. The entire place was already filled with hot, sweating newbies holding their records. There were probably thirty newbies seated in the bleachers and in front of that was a wooden railing, behind which was a vast array of desks, filing cabinets, lights, fans, typewriters, calculators and clerks wandering around in T-shirts and fatigue pants. I noticed a sign that read: "Incoming Personnel Report Here" so I walked to that desk. The clerk there told me to sign in, leave my records, and take a number. I would be called when my voucher was ready. I took a number. It was number 18. I was not reassured by all the newbies waiting and filling up the bleachers. If I was number 18, where did those fellows fit into the picture?

I spent the day there, afraid to go anywhere lest I miss my call, and yet suffering from hunger and thirst. As I sat outside in whatever shade I could find, I noticed a jeep pull up bearing HHC 18th Engineer Brigade bumper markings. A black newbie got out and went inside as the jeep departed. I knew what he would meet in there so I waited. In no time he was back

3. Flirting with Disaster

outside and eased himself down next to me. "Fuckin' Army!" he muttered half to himself and half to me.

"I'm hip to that!" I replied. "You 18th Brigade, too?" He turned to look at me with his dark, brown eyes. He was about my height, rather stocky with a round face.

"Ya, you too?"

I nodded. We sat in silence. Somehow, introductions were unnecessary. The nametape on his jacket read "McGregor" and mine said "Durham" just as plainly. He didn't offer conversation and we sat there quietly. Then he spoke up. "You see that big PX over the hill when you came in?"

"No, I didn't."

"I'm going to wander over there. You want anything?" I declined and he trudged off through the ankle-deep sand. Shortly after, there was a call for a briefing that I sat through with the other newbies, but it didn't tell me much beyond the fact that I had to wait for my name to be called and if we missed our call, we would go to the end of the list. This tended to make sure we didn't wander too far off.

Surprisingly, my number was called pretty quickly, and I sat with a clerk while we went over my records. I was then informed I would be called when my pay voucher was ready, and once I had that I could take it to the pay window and get some money. Then I would be finished. I retreated outside where I found out the shade was disappearing as the sun reached the sky overhead. No sign of McGregor. I wandered around the building and found a snack bar annex down the road where I was able to get something for my thirst. As I sat on the revetment my attention was drawn to the wooden ammo boxes comprising the blast wall revetment. "Ammo. 155mm" the faded lettering read. The entire corner where I sat was covered with names, slogans, drawings, unit designations and other criticisms and witticisms written, carved, and scratched into the wood. It seemed like everyone who had been here had left his mark in some way. I realized that this was something of a registry so I grabbed my pen and scratched "SP4 Durham 70–71 F.T.A." in the cleanest spot I could find. Now I had registered.

The day wore on with agonizing slowness. McGregor returned and we talked to pass the time. He was from Detroit and had just arrived in-country same as me. By late afternoon I was fighting the panic of thinking I'd been forgotten. I had no idea how to contact my office at Dong Ba Thin or how I would go about getting back over there. McGregor shared the same fate.

By 4:00 p.m. we were sitting inside on the bleachers waiting for our vouchers to be called when I noticed that the little NCO standing at the end of the bleachers looked familiar. It was MSG Florence and SP5 Ferrill. I approached them, thankful for having not been forgotten.

"You all finished?" Florence asked.

"No, I haven't been paid yet. They're just now handing out pay vouchers."

"Well, we can't wait. We'll bring you back tomorrow and you can get it."

"But ... but...."

"Come on!"

"But, I got another guy from our company here. Can he get a ride with us?"

"OK. Come on! We gotta hurry" Florence said as he turned to leave. I motioned to McGregor and we climbed into the back of our office truck, old #22, and sped out of the parking lot heading for Dong Ba Thin, leaving finance behind.

When we pulled up to our hooch at Dong Ba Thin, MSG Florence said "You be in the office in the morning." We climbed out and as the truck sped away McGregor thanked me for the ride before heading toward the orderly room. I went to the hooch. It was quiet. I sat on my bunk momentarily lost in thought until I heard the screen door slam next door. I walked over to the next hooch and found Mike Sanger there. "Come on in" he said as he offered a big, welcoming smile. "I got to get some shit. You wanna listen to some tunes? Go ahead." That sounded good to me so I picked out some albums and placed one on the turntable. Mike gathered his things and headed for the door. "I gotta go for a bit. You can stay as long as you want."

"No sweat!"

The first music sounded from the huge speakers and I heard the screen door slam as Mike departed. I settled back in a lawn chair and relaxed but in a short time heard the screen door slam again. I turned to see the little red-haired freak who had driven me over from the 22nd Replacement a few days before. He was short, bare to the waist wearing only fatigue pants and flip flops. His face was round, and his skin deeply tanned and freckled by the sun. The look on his face told me he was surprised to see me as he expected Mike or John to be there. "I heard the stereo, thought Mike or John was here. I wanted to listen to a couple of new albums my sister sent me."

"Oh, it's OK. Mike said I could listen to some albums. Shouldn't think it would matter if they were his or yours."

He smiled and hurried into the room. "Got the new Crosby, Stills, Nash and Young" he said as he began working with the turntable. "You assigned to the company?"

"Ya, at the S-4 office."

"My name's Bill Casick" he said. "You're Durham, right?" I nodded. "Figured you for a freak when I picked you up."

"That was a mutual assumption" I replied and we both laughed.

He was from California, worked in the orderly room for the company commander, 1LT Burns, which seemed out of character for Bill. He was obviously a Head and the word was that Burns hated the Heads. However, Bill was the resident Head of Headquarters Company and had been in the Nam for 18 months already. In the course of our conversation, I learned that he had been living in the village of Tanh Tonh, up the road, with some Vietnamese girl for the last three months, which was not exactly approved quarters, but had been forced to return to the compound.

We listened to albums until about 5:30 p.m. when he departed. The offices were closing for the day and people were returning to their hooches prior to supper. I returned to my room to find Hard Dick, Walters, Ferrill and Beshak already there. After a trip to the mess hall, we returned to the hooch and it was not long before I heard the strains of the Byrds singing "Jesus is Just Alright with Me" at full volume which signaled that John or Mike were in their hooch.

I went next door to visit until the others showed up. Mike came after supper and Bob Wilks and Frank Taske from the Commo Section. Since Glenn Fields and Dan Rosberg had guard duty on Tower 19, the group decided to go out and see them. This sounded rather foolhardy to me but I bowed to the experience of those who suggested it. Nine of us walked through the company area, turned out the road past the 608th Tech Supply warehouse, and toward the perimeter. Tower 19 was out there somewhere behind that huge warehouse. It was a clear evening, and I was nervous about how we would explain ourselves to anyone who might chance to question our purpose.

The rutted, sand road wound around the brigade LZ, past a line of bunkers, and the wooden guard tower that was Tower 19. It was constructed over a sandbagged bunker and had a tiny, sand-bagged, roofed-over platform about fifteen feet off the ground. We could see two figures sitting on the sandbags as we approached. They waved and I knew they were not smoking cigarettes.

We climbed up the wooden ladder until there were eleven of us perched up in the little tower along with a chair, several M-16s, a spotlight, an M-60 machinegun, an M-79 grenade launcher, flares and a multitude of ammo cans and boxes. We clustered together as a handful of joints were lit and made their way around the group in anticipation of the pipes that were being filled. Everyone talked jovially yet I couldn't help the paranoia growing in me. Here we sat in a guard tower, eleven of us, practically in broad daylight, blowing weed. I traded toke for toke with the others but as the pipes and joints made their rounds I wondered what we would do if the OD (Officer of the Day) came around as they were supposed to do.

However, I took heart in the fact that the others were not concerned in the least. I looked out across the compound perimeter stretching in front of the tower. Barbed wire and concertina plastered across the open, sandy plain. To the right, the perimeter curved outward, around to another tower standing almost in front of Tower 19. That was Tower 20 which was a more modern steel tower about thirty feet high and manned by soldiers from another company since it was not part of our unit's responsibility. To the left of Tower 19 was a tall, sixty-foot steel tower that stood at the corner of the compound with the bay to one side, the swampy plain to the front and the compound behind. "Which tower is that?" I asked.

"That's Tower 17" Bob Wilks replied.

"If this is Tower 19, where's Tower 18?"

"Tower 18 stood over by the chopper pad" Rosberg said. "Sappers blew it one night and it was never rebuilt."

"Hey, Roger! Did you hear about Tower 15?" Mike said. I shook my head. "It fell over about two weeks ago!" Everyone began to laugh.

Old Tower 15 shortly before it fell over one night with the guards in it.

3. Flirting with Disaster   47

"Ya, Little Gomez, Smith and I were on guard there." Bob Wilks spoke up.

"What happened?" I inquired.

"Who knows?" Mike said. "It used to stand between the chapel and the 'O' Club (Officer's Club). It was an old wooden tower like this one."

"Ya!" Bob Wilks laughed. "We was stoned to the max, man, and she starts leaning over. Then, WHAM! Everything is scattered all over the ground, dope and shit everywhere! Too fuckin'much!"

"Oh, ya! Little Gomez laid there and laughed for half an hour!" Mike said. "They had to call the OD (Officer of the Day) and tell him their tower had fallen over!"

Everyone broke out laughing as they recalled the incident. I wondered just how sturdy this old, wooden Tower 19 was with eleven of us up in it. By this time, I was completely blasted. I looked out from the rear of the tower across the hooches and hangers and buildings and could see a wall of clouds approaching from the west. It was still light out and I was still paranoid about being up in that guard tower with all these unauthorized people. I didn't feel it would be to my advantage to get busted just after being assigned to the company. The approaching wall of rain presented an escape

The beach along the bay with the chapel and old Tower 15 and Tower 16 beyond.

and I pointed out the storm to everyone in the tower. No doubt it was heading our way as we could see it slowly obscuring the far end of the compound over by the flight line.

With eleven people under the tiny roof of the tower, there was no way we were going to remain dry so I decided to take my leave before the rain hit. This was understandable to everyone and Frank Taske followed me. The two of us climbed down the wooden ladder and hurried back to the company area.

It was surprisingly quiet in my hooch when I returned because most of the crew were out somewhere. Jimmy Ferrill sat reading in his corner. I laid on my bunk and he came over to talk about the S-4 office and personalities to be aware of. He was glad to be leaving it all behind.

The rain came but it failed to impede the progress of the movie that had just started outside our hooch. Jim got his lawn chair and poncho and left to watch the movie. I settled back with my book. Tomorrow I would start work in earnest.

4

Like Boy Scouts with Guns

I was awakened in the morning by the sounds of activity in the room. There was no alarm clock, bugle call, nor anyone knocking on our door. Everyone was up except Ronnie Hard Dick who remained a motionless lump beneath his blanket. I dressed and followed everyone from our hooch up to the morning formation in front of the orderly room. The formation was no more than a roll call for the benefit of the 1SGT who stood in front of everyone. 1SGT Sergeant Harris was tall and stocky with a furrowed face and a booming voice.

After the formation concluded, the four platoons were marched off in different directions to perform that time-honored Army activity known as "police call" for picking up the litter. Our platoon shuffled along in a relaxed walk while the platoon sergeant called off cadence like we were in basic training. Everyone spread out talking and joking as we picked up cigarette butts, beer cans and litter left by the officers the night before. Once finished we stashed the collected trash in the nearest trash barrel or behind a revetment and wandered off to our hooches.

I grabbed my Ritz cracker can and headed for the shower to get some water to shave. The growing pressure in my loins forced me to take my place in line at the piss tube. The pisser behind the shower was a heavy duty one compared to the ones we'd used at the 22nd Replacement. This one was a fifty-five-gallon drum buried in the sand, filled with rocks, and had two sections of curved metal culvert surrounding it for privacy. As always, the stench was extreme. I had to take a breath, rush in, hold it for as long as I could and take care of my business while slowly exhaling.

For those who had to take a crap, we had an 8-hole "shitter" that was a frame structure like every other building with screened windows and a corrugated metal roof. Beneath each "hole" was a half of a 55-gallon drum where people did their business. Once these filled up they were pulled out through doors at the back, mixed with diesel fuel, and burned. Vietnamese were hired as "shit-burners." Their job was to stir the burning mixture until

The "Pisser."

it was consumed. The smell and the black smoke rising into the sky was a ritual played out all over Vietnam every day.

When I finished, I made my way to the fresh air by the shower room. I retrieved my water can and returned to the hooch to shave. There was something pleasant about standing in the bright, morning sun, brushing my teeth, shaving with cold water and using a small, round mirror propped up on the sand bags of the revetment. It was the same at every hooch where the guys lined up along the revetments busily performing that morning ritual of shaving.

A slow procession of people burdened under the weight of helmets, flak jackets, web gear and rifles, began to troop past me, heading for the offices. When I finished, I stashed my gear and headed to the office with the others for my first day at work. MSG Florence gave me a hard look when I walked in. "Where's your alert gear?" he demanded.

"I haven't got any" I responded.

"Ferrill, take him over and get him his alert gear!"

Jimmy Ferrill grabbed his hat. "Come on" he said as we headed out the door. "Fuckin' Florence really chaps my ass" he said. "Sure glad I'm leavin' this place." We walked to the supply room where a tall, thin, black

4. Like Boy Scouts with Guns

Burning the shit. The Brigade motor pool across the road.

G.I. listened to Ferrill, then issued me a flak jacket, two ammo pouches, four M-16 magazines of ammo and my very own M-16. I signed the required forms and promised not to kill anybody without permission and left.

When we returned to the office, I added my gear to the rest hanging on the wall and then assigned a bunker to go to during alerts so I wouldn't be running around with no idea of where to go when that time came. I spent the morning with Jimmy Ferrill as he explained the intricacies of his job as the Stock Control Specialist and office duty driver, doing the driving for anyone and everyone in the office. Added to this was the responsibility of keeping track of various supplies and hand-carrying requisitions through supply channels at Cam Ranh.

At 11:45 a.m. the clerks started filing out of the office to beat the lunch rush on the mess hall. I followed the group to the mess hall where we sat on the sidewalk in the shade of the eave until the hall opened. The line grew steadily as each office let out for lunch. The mess hall door opened and we filed through. It was the same uninspired food. I ate and headed back to the hooch. I noted in a letter to my brother: "To give you an idea of the heat, yesterday at noon it was 101 in my hooch. About 115 outside…."

That afternoon MSG Florence got SP Ferrill, grabbed me and said: "Let's go for a ride. You haven't gotten your money from finance, right?" I grabbed my hat, we headed for the truck, I climbed in back and we were off for Cam Ranh. We soon pulled into the same sandy parking lot at finance and parked in front of the same weathered building. Nothing had changed since the day before with scattered newbies sitting around outside. The scene inside the building had not changed either with newbies sitting bored and disgusted on the bleachers. I approached a counter near the pay window and snared the clerk behind it. He was sweating and a little flustered. "What do you need?"

"I need my pay voucher. I processed here yesterday but couldn't stay to get my pay voucher." He grumbled, took my name and disappeared. In a moment he was back with my file in his hands. "Here" he said as he handed the voucher. I stepped to the pay window where I received a wad of M.P.C. for my back pay, travel pay, and so on. With a smile on my face and cash, such as it was, in my pocket, I left the newbies to their fates and we drove back to Dong Ba Thin.

Mail was important. There were two mail calls each day, one in the morning and one in afternoon. I couldn't stand to see mail call go by without something for me so I needed to get letters out to family and friends and get a flow of mail coming in. Home was my anchor, and I was already feeling a little adrift in this sea of insanity.

When the office closed at the end of the day, I retrieved my alert gear and followed everyone back to the hooch. I was hot and sticky and could hardly stand to feel the grittiness of my own skin, so I headed for the showers. Practically everyone converged on the shower room so I waited my turn for those few refreshing moments under that stream of lukewarm water. Feeling clean, I shuffled back to the hooch, put on my blue jeans and a T-shirt. Soon the mess hall migration began and as evening settled around us we heard the Byrds singing "Jesus is Just Alright with Me" so we knew Mike and John were in. I walked to their hooch to get another evening under way.

We trooped out to the bridge yard to smoke pot like a bonfire. After abusing our lungs we wandered back down the rutted, dusty road to the company. A few last joints were passed around and as we approached the company the "roaches" were flicked into the ditch along the road as we continued toward the movie. It was at this moment that the realization finally sunk in that I actually *was* in Vietnam! *This was Vietnam!* The reality I had dreaded all those years. Here in three days, I'd seen and smoked more pot than I'd seen in one place at one time! Pipes were haphazardly filled, spilling dope all over!

4. Like Boy Scouts with Guns

And then there were those pre-rolled joints that were so evident everywhere. I'd never seen anything other than hand-rolled joints and now to see them looking like manufactured cigarettes was amazing. Why roll joints when you could buy them already made up? They generally came in little plastic bags of twenty pre-rolled joints although I later saw them in sealed commercial cigarette packages. They called them "decks" and I was told you could buy one for about $2. The pot was so abundant and cheap that there was no worry about saving every precious scrap as we had back in the World.

A "deck" of 20 pre-rolled joints.

Thursday, I woke and followed everyone to morning formation which was just as informative as the day before. Police call followed, then to our hooches before joining the office migration for another day When I arrived, the office was getting into gear on the day's work. By mid-morning the office was a maelstrom of clattering typewriters, doors slamming, phones ringing and people yelling. The phones completely mystified me. They were dial phones, but the dials were never used. Down in the Maintenance Section at one end of the building, an NCO stood with a phone to one ear, his hand over the other and yelling "I can't hear you! Can't you speak any louder?"

I witnessed SFC Hagberg pick up a phone and ask "Could I have Crusader Switch, please?" and talk as if he was calling a store downtown. I was afraid to be close to a phone for fear I'd have to answer it. I could hardly be expected to know who the call was for even if the caller told me since I only knew the names of a few of the people who worked in the office. But I struggled on and about 10:00 a.m. the phone rang, and MSG Florence answered it. When he hung up, he looked at me. "Durham, the C.O. wants to see you." My heart leapt into my throat! Sheeeeiiiiiiit! I'm busted for sure! With my heart pounding I grabbed my hat and ran to the orderly room expecting the worst and wondering what I'd done that would warrant the C.O's attention.

The orderly room consisted of a few small rooms stuffed with desks, file cabinets and typewriters. I walked in. A clerk behind a desk looked up and said "Oh, Durham, have a seat." As I sat he said the 1SGT wanted to see me when he came in. I wondered what this was about.

A few moments later the screen door slammed and there was 1SGT Harris. He saw me and said "Oh, Durham, come on in here." I followed him to his office where he motioned to me to sit down next to his desk. I could see the C.O.'s office was empty, so I knew he was not in yet. Strangely enough, the 1SGT smiled at me. "Well, Durham, how do you like it here?"

"It's all right, so far."

"Well, I'll tell you what this is all about. I am required to brief every new man who comes in and the C.O. is required to do the same. He'll be in shortly." I felt a wave of relief as I realized this visit was merely procedure and not due to anything I'd done. "Now in this company, you'll be required to pull guard duty. It comes up every five or six days. Before you can pull guard you'll have to go to the transition fire range. This is required and we go every Saturday morning. You report here at 9:00 a.m. with your rifle and alert gear."

He explained what happened when the compound was attacked and the various "alerts" I needed to pay attention to. Yellow alert meant enemy activity was expected and bunker guards were put out on the perimeter, but the one that mattered most was "red" alert. There was no way to ignore a red alert because it was generally preceded by incoming rocket and mortar rounds followed by the siren going off. At that signal we were to grab our weapons and man the perimeter to defend the compound. My alert station would be assigned to me by my duty section NCOIC (NCO in charge). He talked about company work details, other duties that could come my way, then closed the session with words of advice about how I should do my duty, keep my nose clean, my head down and I'd go home all right. About this time, I heard the door slam and the 1SGT looked up. "Good morning, Sir." I turned to see a tall, well-built young man with close cropped curly blond hair and rough masculine facial features. I took him to be a college frat boy. A silver bar on his hat told me that this must be the company commander, 1LT Burns.

"I got Durham here, Sir. You want to see him now?"

"Send him in when I call, First Sergeant" the C.O. said as he went into his office, came back out again and reappeared with a cup of coffee. He disappeared back into his office and it became quiet. "First Sergeant, send Durham in"

"OK, report to the C.O."

I stood up, took a deep breath and walked into the C.O.'s office. He sat expectantly behind his desk looking at me with authority and purpose blazing in his cold blue eyes as I stood before his desk. "Sir, Specialist Durham reporting." He returned my salute.

"Sit down, Durham." I pulled up a chair and sat. "Where you from back in the World?"

4. Like Boy Scouts with Guns

"Near Chicago, Sir."

He nodded. "Where you working now?"

"I've been assigned to the S-4 office, Sir."

Again he nodded. "Has the First Shirt filled you in on guard duty, transition fire and alert procedures?"

"Yes, Sir."

He briefed me on company policies, procedures and rules I was expected to adhere to. When he was finished, he leaned forward, rested his elbows on the desk, looked me squarely in the eye with his blue eyes boring into mine, and said, "Durham ... you ever smoke pot?"

The question hit me like a ton of bricks. I was unprepared and my mind rattled. How can I answer that? I could say "No" but my face, my eyes, my moustache that tested the limits of Army approval, my wire rim glasses, my attitude, all said "Yes." Maybe honesty would be the best policy. Maybe they'd already seen me associating with known "Heads" in the company. My whole army career, indeed my entire life, might be riding upon my answer to this question. I realized that my silence was almost as damning as any answer I might give. Yes, be honest, but to a degree. You can lie, a little. "Uh, yes Sir, I've been known to, but that was back in the States when I was in school. S'been a long time, though."

He smiled and leaned back in his chair. I held my breath. "The stuff they got over here is 100 times as potent as anything you ever smoked in the States. (He was telling me?) If you know what's good for you, you'll steer clear of it while you're here. If we catch you messing with pot while you're in this company, you'll be shipped out so fast it will make your head swim!" He told me we were the "cream of the crop," hand-picked from all the incoming newbies and as such we had been chosen to work at brigade headquarters. It was a privilege not to be taken for granted, nor abused. He leaned forward with a stern resolve forming in his eyes. "Do I make myself clear?"

"Well, Sir, I didn't plan on becoming some kind of dope fiend while I'm here. I know what it can do and I know this place requires you to have your wits about you at all times. I'm not stupid, Sir." (Crazy, perhaps but not stupid.)

He smiled and leaned back in his chair. He was not much older than me, if at all, but I didn't like his arrogance. "Durham, you're pretty lucky to be here. The 18th Brigade is in charge of all construction projects in the first two military regions in Nam. We have an A.O. (Area of Operations) that covers almost 70 percent of Vietnam. Your record got you an assignment here at Brigade headquarters. This is the top. You fuck up here and you can only go one direction. Do we understand each other?" He gazed at me as if he expected me to fall on my knees and kiss his feet in grateful humiliation at being allowed to work in their little club.

"Yes, Sir...." I answered. "...we understand each other."

"Check with the First Shirt and see if he's got anything for you. That's all." I stood, saluted, checked with 1SGT Harris, then headed back to the S-4 office.

At the close of the day trash from all over the office was dumped into a large garbage can and two clerks duly detailed by MSG Florence, hauled it to a trash point, out past the LZ near the perimeter, where it was burned. The can, filled with paper trash, weighed a ton and it was no cake walk to haul that thing out to the burn point which was one reason people avoided the detail if they could. The burn point was just a few rusting barrels where everyone in the headquarters offices burned their trash. It was a dirty job and no one wanted to do it. Thus there were never any volunteers but MSG Florence made certain everyone had a chance to perform this duty.

At 5:30 p.m. the day was over, we trooped back to our hooches and the run on the showers began. I joined in since the day's accumulated grime and sweat and grit was usually more than I could bear. A big 5,000-gallon water tanker was pulled up beside the shower room pumping water into the water tanks above the building.

After supper, the sounds of the Byrds singing "Jesus Is Just Alright"

My little corner of the hooch.

came blasting through the wall at full volume so I walked next door where the group was gathering to get another evening under way.

Friday the routine continued. I awoke to another day, followed the bleary-eyed people to morning formation, shuffled through police call, then back to the hooch to face that stinking pisser again and shave. If nothing else woke me up, the stench of that pisser in the morning always did. I prefer coffee, though. The office routine was also falling into place. I could even answer the phone without trouble, since it was never for me I merely had to locate who the call was for. I was also becoming better acquainted with the clerks. For the most part they were friendly and eager to help with the exception of Boone who remained aloof from me.

I didn't dislike Boone. He'd been in the Army for eight years and was happy in his role as a Clerk Specialist. He didn't want to advance, had twice refused promotion to E-6 and detested long-haired Hippies, rock and roll music, anti-anything protests and anything he didn't understand which encompassed a considerable range. The only things that interested him were women, booze and country music. I didn't attempt to get acquainted with him as he made it apparent he had no use for me or what I represented to him. It was useless to try especially when there were so many others who were friendly. I merely kept up a polite acceptance of him and our conversations were generally brief and to the point.

Part of the S-4 crew outside our hooch. Left to right: Bob Boone, Willie Anderson, Gary Arecon, myself, and Chris Beshak.

Friday evening, we collected at John and Mike's room again. My routines were still based on a five-day work week and I felt like I did on any Friday night. Tomorrow was Saturday. However, there would be no time for cartoons on TV or sleeping in. Saturday was another workday in Vietnam. There was a war on and it was a seven day work week. The office would run as usual on Saturday and I would go to transition fire to complete my in-processing.

We wandered out in scattered groups past the theater area, the security guard's hooches, the shitter and out the rutted road. We walked out past the Rock Pile, but this time we went on to the "Pond" which was nothing more than a huge mud puddle. A grassy field flanked it to one side where there was another of the 553rd's bridge yards where they stored inflatable bridge pontoons, so it was often littered with large, black rubber bundles.

We went single file along the pond bank and made our way to a clump of brush. I could tell by the way the tall grass had been beaten down and the number of discarded soda cans and "roaches" littering the bank that this was another well-utilized smoking spot. We sat in a cluster shielded from view by the bushes. The pipes were filled, a bag of joints passed around, and

The Pond with the flight line beyond.

a radio turned to AFVN. I sat watching the sun setting behind the mountains, casting long, shinning rays across the land and reflecting brightly off the muddy excuse for Pond. The warm air, the bright sun setting and reflecting on the calm water could look so nice yet we were still in Vietnam sitting around a big mud puddle listening to the hum of helicopter engines on the flight line.

"Hey, somebody's coming!" Every head turned toward the road where a shadowy figure was seen heading our way weaving among the rubber pontoons. Glenn turned down the radio and we sat in silence.

"It's Little Gomez," Bob Wilks said. A wave of relief swept the paranoia away and the radio came back on.

Steve Gomez walked in among the group. "What's happenin' guys?" he asked as he found a spot in the midst of the group. Everyone mumbled a greeting in response and then he pulled out a plastic bag and said "Try some of mine."

"Wow, man!" Wilks exclaimed. "Fuckin' O-Jays!" His exclamation brought a prompt mumble of approval from everyone. O-Jays were regular pre-rolled joints except they were dipped in liquid opium. They looked like little brown cigars and were sticky to the touch and sweet to the taste. He passed them out and we each had our own. They were a big hit with everyone and a new highlight for me. I was pretty blasted before I'd smoked half of mine, but I persevered and produced a fairly good roach that I tossed into the Pond with everyone else's.

The sunlight faded behind the hills and as I sat lost in thought, listening to the radio, I was struck by just how much Vietnam was like life itself. I looked at my new-found friends clustered around me. They had been in there for months and I listened as they talked about friends who had gone home. It was as if they were talking about people who had died. Going back to the "World" was almost the same as going to Heaven. Vietnam was their life now. It was home to them. One day they would be gone, and I would speak of them to newbies in the same manner. I realized Vietnam would become my home as time went on. It was a rather revolting thought at that moment, but it was true. As my routine became more established, my past life in the "World" would seem like it never happened. My friends clustered around me would go home and I'd probably never see them again just as if they had died. I would meet new friends and someday I'd return to the "World" and it would be as new and strange to me as Vietnam was at that moment.

I hated to think of calling Dong Ba Thin my home but I knew there was no fighting it. I had yet to face my first alert but had listened to them talk about the last one I'd witnessed from across the bay. It was as if they were discussing a football game. It worried me and I'd been unsettled because I knew facing the reality of an attack was a certainty over the next year.

The stress and anxiety could eat me up if I'd let it. How did they do it? I remembered briefings before coming to this place, and statistics we'd been fed about our chances of survival. I realized that the way to deal with concern over the unknown was to accept it, accept my mortality and the fact that I was already dead but just didn't know it yet. When you have no tomorrow, you live like there's no tomorrow. As Jim Morrison of the Doors said: "The future's uncertain and the end is always near." The secret was in making the most out of each moment, each hour, each day and not worrying about tomorrow or yesterday. Right now was the moment that mattered. I stopped worrying and began focusing on this one moment known as "the present" because it was all I had. When I let go of the anxiety it was liberating and I found that mind-set I had seen in my comrades, that "who cares?" live-for-the-moment mentality.

"Let's go cop some sodas and check out the flick" someone offered. Amidst mumbles of agreement, we rose and stumbled along the pond's bank to carry on.

Saturday morning and time for Transition Fire. We sleepily fell in for morning formation, police call, held my breath and face that stinking pisser, shave, and head for the office. About 8:30 a.m., I collected my gear and trudged over to the orderly room where I met other newbies in their alert gear, and carrying weapons. They were obviously going to transition fire so I waited as others joined our group. I saw another soldier coming slowly in our direction. He was a soul brother and as he approached, I recognized McGregor, the Brother I'd processed through finance with. He grinned when he saw me. "What? Durham, you too, eh?"

"Better than spending Saturday in the office." I replied. 1SGT Harris told us to board the deuce-and-a-half parked at the end of the building. We found it loaded with ammunition boxes, M-60 machine guns and M-79 grenade launchers. As we climbed aboard, the unit armorer and the supply sergeant came out of the supply room climbed in the cab and we took off down the road.

The truck proceeded south on QL-1 toward the Myca crossroads. The highway was filled with military vehicles going in the opposite direction and Vietnamese Lambrettas weaving sickly with their burden of luggage, boxes and baskets lashed to the top and overcrowded with people inside and hanging precariously from the back steps.

We passed the road at Myca that led to Cam Ranh and continued south.

"We're going to Su Chin" McGregor said to me. I'd heard that name in the course of conversation between Boone and Waller and others in our hooch. Su Chin was the "ville" about five miles south of Dong Ba Thin. At Su Chin we made a right turn into a narrow alley and followed until the lane opened into a broad, rolling area, heavily vegetated with brush. Ahead of us a huge, rocky hill rose abruptly, its face jagged, rocky and bare. I stood in the back of the truck as it jerked along and wondered who might be up in those rocks peering down at us. We drove to a small ridge and halted at what was intended to be a firing range. It extended over rolling ground to the base of the rocky mountain where an old French tank, a battered jeep and a truck sat as targets.

We were instructed on the M-16, the M-79 grenade launcher, M-60 machinegun, and the M-2 .50 caliber machinegun and parachute flares and fired each weapon. I liked the M-79 grenade launcher, known as a "bloop" gun from the sound it made when fired. It took a cartridge about five inches long and two inches in diameter and was particularly fun to shoot. I fired two rounds downrange on high, arching trajectories. One exploded directly on top of the tank turret and with a minor adjustment I put the second round down the open hatch of the tank turret. That impressed everyone. I didn't know until then just how dangerous I was with an M-79.

We finished, picked up empty brass casings, loaded the truck and retraced our way back to Dong Ba Thin. At the orderly room everyone climbed out and drifted off in anticipation of lunch. McGregor and I were fingered to clean the weapons after lunch. Since this involved a couple of machine guns, and several M-79 launchers, I knew I could handle it alone, relying on my armorer training which was probably why I was fingered for the duty. I told McGregor he didn't have to come in since I was willing to do it alone.

After lunch I went to clean the weapons and as I stood in the stifling heat of the supply room, McGregor walked in. This surprised me but he felt he should do his part since we'd both been tasked for the job so he pitched in and the work passed quickly. Once we'd cleaned the weapons to the supply sergeant's satisfaction, we returned to our jobs.

Saturday night descended on us but it was no different than the night before or the night before that. The only difference was that tomorrow was Sunday and that was usually a half-day off. About dusk everyone collected at the theater to catch the movie. I continued going to Mike and John's hooch where the gang gathered. I found John plunking noisily on an old, battered Vietnamese guitar like those I'd seen in the PX gift shops. He didn't know how to play it but he enjoyed fooling around with it, so I sat down, tuned the guitar, and played some tunes. I showed John some basic fingering chords so at least when he beat on the thing, it might sound like more than just noise. The group soon gathered and wandered off to the bridge yard.

When we got back I went to the hooch and played my guitar for a while before Hard Dick came over to me and smiled. "I think you're going to get a new job" he said. I looked at him, trying to figure out if he was being serious or if this was leading to a joke. "You're going to take my job and I'm going to take Ferrill's."

"When did this come about?" I asked.

"Today. Sergeant Florence was talking about it. He doesn't like me. You'll be filing and typing mostly."

"How come?"

"When I came here the other clerk had already left so I had to learn this job alone. It's been a bitch! The files are all messed up and I can hardly make heads nor tails of them. Besides, I've had very little experience as a clerk and don't type very well" Hard Dick confided. "I came over here as an 11 Bravo (Infantry M.O.S)." I looked at him incredulously. "Ask Walters or Ferrill if you don't believe me."

"It's true!" Walters interjected from his corner of the hooch.

Hard Dick continued. "Sergeant Florence found out you have more clerical experience so you'll be his clerk and I'll be taking over as office duty driver. I'd rather do that anyway." He smiled and returned to his corner of the hooch. I went to bed to think over this new development.

For my first Sunday in the company there was no morning formation, so I slept in a little longer than usual. The Sunday office schedule consisted of a reduced work force. Generally, after lunch only a designated NCO and clerk remained, allowing everyone else the afternoon. This was "Sunday Duty" and everyone pulled it on a rotating schedule that meant it came around about once a month. On my first Sunday I had yet to be put on the Sunday Duty roster, so I had the day off. When I awoke the whole hooch was still in bed. I climbed out of bed and as I rummaged under my bunk for my flip-flops, I heard bed springs squeaking across the room. I sat on the edge of my bunk and looked over at Hard Dick who was looking back at me through wrinkled eyes still groggy with sleep. I grinned at him and he waved. I pulled my fatigue pants on while he struggled out of bed and sat there. Others in the hooch were now starting to stir as well.

Hard Dick walked over to me and stood by my bed. "You working today?" he asked.

"Nope."

He yawned. "You wanna go to the beach?"

"Sure. I'd like to get outta here for a while."

"Ferrill will probably get a truck. He usually does."

"What time does he leave?"

"After lunch" Hard Dick said as he walked back to his corner.

I walked out into the sunshine and sat on the bunker outside the door of the hooch where I mulled over the news that Hard Dick had laid on me

4. Like Boy Scouts with Guns

the night before. In a way, I was happy about it and then again I was disappointed. The whole thing seemed like a rather large challenge.

Jimmy Ferrill came from the showers and approached the bunker where I sat. "You wanna go to the beach today?" he asked as he leaned against the bunker next to me.

"Ya. Hard Dick said you would probably be going. What time should I be where?"

"Just have your shit together and be in the hooch about 12:30" he said.

It seemed as if everyone headed for the beach on Sundays. After lunch a group from S-4 was on its way to the beach with Willy, Hard Dick, Walters and me situated in the open back of old #22 as the truck sped down the highway. The traffic on QL-1 appeared to be like any day except I noticed an increased number of Army vehicles heading into Cam Ranh carrying soldiers in their bathing suits. It seemed everyone was bound for the beach.

We followed the now familiar route to Myca Checkpoint, across Myca Bridge, down the Cam Ranh peninsula to the Army installation. Once there we followed a gravel road across the mountain, past storage yards and ammunition dumps, and were soon rewarded with a magnificent view of the South China Sea. It lay before us all bright blue and clear and stretching to the horizon. We passed other beach areas amongst high, rocky outcroppings and soon arrived at a place that a sign noted was "Vinnell Beach."

We pulled into a parking area among other Army vehicles where we lurched to a stop and everyone piled out. I was amazed at the beauty of the place. The high, rocky mountains and outcroppings behind and around us, the white, sandy beaches, the pure blue of the water before us. People were scattered all over the beach and, in the water, little groups gathered everywhere, even up into the nooks and crannies of the rock outcroppings. At first glance it looked like a typical day at almost any beach but when I looked closer, I noticed there was one thing missing. There were no women! All these people enjoying the beach were men. It was the Army.

We unloaded and found a spot on the beach and the balance of the day was spent relaxing in the sun, taking a swim in the cool water and letting time pass pleasantly by. After we'd had our fill of the sun, sand and sea we headed back to Dong Ba Thin.

Monday morning when I reported for work I found Ronnie Hard Dick and I were indeed switching jobs. He'd been serving as MSG Florence's clerk but had trouble doing the job due to personality conflicts with Florence and the fact that the files he inherited were in terrible shape. Ronnie had little prior clerical experience and once it became known I had more experience it was determined we should switch jobs.

Hard Dick and Florence were pleased with the change. MSG Florence, a feisty little guy with a bad attitude and a huge chip on his shoulder, loved

Inside the S-4 Office. Left to right: SP4 Gary Arecon and SFC Sparks.

his position of authority and became extremely upset if challenged. He was also deluded, believing he was always right even if proven wrong. His way was always best. Ronnie hated him.

So, I became the Correspondence Clerk/Typist. MSG Florence thought the job was difficult when in reality Hard Dick could have done it with proper instruction, but it was the files being so screwed up that made it difficult. My job was to keep track of paperwork and correspondence that came in or went out of the S-4 office and its eventual disposition. All incoming correspondence and paperwork came to me, was logged into a ledger, assigned a number, recorded by date and time of arrival, who it went to in the office and where it was filed when completed. Likewise, all outgoing correspondence and paperwork leaving our office was logged out by me and sent to the proper destinations. The job was necessary since a bureaucracy such as the Army runs on paperwork and this was the pre-computer age.

When I took over the files they were in a terrible state of disarray. It wasn't Ronnie's fault since he'd inherited them in that condition and had been trying to sort them out without success. Half the job of the Correspondence

Clerk was being able to retrieve specific documents from the files when called upon to do so. Like Ronnie, I found this to be impossible. Paperwork was rarely in the file where the log indicated it should be. This was the biggest headache we both suffered through due to the ineptitude of our predecessors. MAJ Marks would want to see a specific document, but all our searching could not locate it. This would result in verbal abuse being heaped upon us as if it were our fault, so we had to bear the blame since it was our job. Ronnie was happy to move to another less stressful job and I made up my mind that I was going to do this job and fix the files.

Across the aisle from my desk was Ronnie "Hard Dick" Hardwick.

In a letter I wrote my brother I noted:

> Things over here are generally a pain in the ass.... I work as a file clerk. Got to dig out shit from the file, keep a log of all the shit coming in and going out. They ask me to find a message [from] way back in December. I look for it, can't find it so they bitch at me. It ain't my fault. I was in Georgia when that message was filed wrong. Then they bitch cause I'm behind on my filing and logging. So, when I work on that to catch up, they bitch because I ain't looking for that message that was filed last December. Can't win, can't quit.... Its' all a pisser.

So I became a member of the 18th Engineer Brigade S-4 Office. We handled brigade supply and maintenance for various units in the brigade. A variety of projects were constantly going on, ranging from bridge construction, or replacement or repair, airfield construction, installation upgrades, well-drilling, port construction, and highway paving. We had asphalt and cement plants, rock quarries and crushers to keep track of to manufacture enough of everything to meet the demands and requirements of each project. Then there was the matter of getting all the necessary materials transported to the proper job site, not to mention the continual maintenance involved with keeping up equipment such as bulldozers, paving machines, road graders, rock crushers, dump trucks, tractors, trucks and even helicopters. It was a vast job and each person in the office had a certain duty to perform.

I became acclimated to the chaos of the office. Work was a fairly loose-run thing and we never had to account for our whereabouts as long as our work was done, and they knew where we were. There were opportunities to make a trip to the PX over in the Dong Ba Thin west compound or an occasional PX run to Cam Ranh where there were several larger PX facilities.

Although we were in an exotic, far-off land, we were not on vacation. We were there to support an on-going conflict and our function was to do our jobs. Work became the focal point of our existence. We worked every day of the week, but usually we had Sunday to provide a Milestone to mark the passing of another week.

While work occupied most of each day, we did have the evenings to relax and there were some duties that provided additional time off. Guard duty gave you some down time the next day; other duties such as Sunday Office Duty, C.Q. (Charge of Quarters), and Duty Driver all brought compensatory time off. While it was nice having free time, it brought boredom too since most of your friends were at work and there was little to do around the compound and nowhere to go.

Although I was making the transition to life in the headquarters company of the 18th Engineer Brigade, I had other responsibilities. Wednesday of my second week I was still groping my way through my new job. It was the end of another day and when I walked into the hooch Ronnie Hard Dick came in behind me and said: "Hey, you're supposed to be on guard tonight aren't you?" This was news to me. I had just taken transition fire and assumed my name would be on the roster but not so soon. "Your name's on the roster" he continued.

I ran to the orderly room to check the bulletin board and there were already several guards waiting for Guard Mount. *Damn!* Sure enough, my name was on the roster. I hurried to the hooch, gathered my gear and got into some fresh fatigues. Once again, Hard Dick came to my rescue. "Is your rifle clean? They'll inspect it." *Shit!* Of course it wasn't clean! I'd only had it long enough to look at it, shoot it at transition fire but not to give it a thorough cleaning. "Here, you can take mine. It's clean but be sure to memorize the serial number. They'll ask you that."

I accepted the weapon and attempted to memorize the serial number as I collected my gear and scrambled over to the orderly room. The Sergeant

4. Like Boy Scouts with Guns

of the Guard (SOG) was forming the group as I slid into line. When roll call was taken, we were one man short. At that moment, the missing man shuffled across the street. It was none other than my newbie partner, McGregor, with whom I'd struggled through finance processing and transition fire. "Shit! I just now found out I was on guard!" he said as he slipped into line behind me.

"Same with me" I whispered over my shoulder. We were assigned the only two open shifts left which were the shifts nobody wanted on Tower 17. We marched up the street to Brigade headquarters where two flag poles stood, one flying the U.S. flag, the other the Vietnamese flag and drawn up in two ranks facing the flags. The sergeant spoke up and four troopers came from the ranks and took their places by the two flag poles. After a few minutes we were called to attention as the Officer of the Day (OD) appeared. He was a young lieutenant dressed in crisp fatigues with a pistol strapped to his hip. He ordered us "to arms" as the flags were brought down. The color guard folded the flags, lined up and marched off.

With this formality over we were brought to parade rest and the OD inspected us. I realized the color guard didn't stand this inspection and I understood why everyone volunteered to take the flags down when we formed up. When the OD inspected me, he made comments about my fatigues and that I didn't know the serial number of my weapon.

Once the inspection was finished, the soldier the O.D. deemed to be the best and had his act together the most, was designated the "Supernumerary." That person wouldn't stand guard and would merely be on call in the event that someone needed to be taken off the tower for some reason. At the conclusion we marched to the orderly room.

Since McGregor and I had the first two shifts on Tower 17 we went on duty right away. In the evening light Tower 17 looked like something out of a movie as we approached it. A shadowy figure peered down at us from sixty feet above. A rope pulley swung lazily beside the tower. We attached our weapons, gear, etc., to be pulled up. The ladder, enclosed by a circular cage to keep one from falling off, looked like a formidable climb. We climbed the ladder, swung into the little enclosure, then pulled our gear up on the pulley. The man we relieved gathered his gear and left.

The tower was about twelve-feet square with walls and floors protected by two layers of quarter-inch steel plates. There were two cots, a footlocker filled with ammunition on one end and an M-60 machine gun on a pintle. Under an azimuth were wire terminals to detonate Claymore mines scattered in front of the tower. There was a hand-held spotlight, a telephone, an M-79 grenade launcher hung on a hook and tube flares lay stacked in one corner next to a chair with leg extensions to make it sit higher off the ground.

McGregor doing guard duty on Tower 17.

Located high over the compound we were rewarded with a breathtaking panorama of Dong Ba Thin stretching out before us and the distant mountains where the fading sun was fast sinking. To the east lay the expanse of the bay, the Cam Ranh peninsula and the 22nd Replacement Battalion directly across the water.

The evening was beautiful, and the hum of generators and helicopter engines were the only sounds disturbing the night. We popped parachute flares during the night, listened to grenades detonating around the perimeter, and played with the Starlight Scope, a new toy for us. The ability to look into the dark see things as if it were daylight was a wondrous piece of technology. I did my turn on duty and slept on the cot, using my flak jacket as a pillow. It was like camping out, like the Boy Scouts.

With the dawning of another day, the three of us on Tower 17 went our own ways except for our four-hour shifts. Being first shift I pulled the hours from 6:00–10:00 a.m. I watched from my perch as the sun rose and Dong Ba Thin awoke, had formation, police call and began another day. I watched helicopter traffic and peered through binoculars at planes landing and taking off at the Cam Ranh airfield across the bay.

At 10:00 a.m., McGregor relieved me so I lowered my gear on the rope and negotiated the ladder down. I had been looking forward to the free afternoon that awaited me but when I got to the hooch, I found out what that free afternoon meant—more boredom. The hooches were abandoned

4. Like Boy Scouts with Guns

since everyone was at work. There was no place to go except to walk around the compound or go to the dinky PX or the library. The EM Club wasn't open during the day. One could sleep or lay in the sun or read or write letters. I passed the day walking the roads we walked at night, visiting the PX, reading in the hooch and writing letters. The only thing to look forward to was the return of everyone from work and another evening with the crew.

Office routines and duties were one thing, but there were also work details that required the company to provide manpower. At morning formation, the next day, 1SGT Harris informed us of a work detail being formed and each platoon would provide its share of labor. I didn't think much about this until I went to the office and found out as a newbie, I was our platoon's contribution. No one knew what kind of work our detail was to perform.

When everyone headed back to the office after lunch, I wandered down the street toward the EM club where I'd been told to go. As I approached there was a group of soldiers milling about to one side. This was my work detail. I joined the group and recognized only one smiling face, McGregor, my shadow. We laughed as once again he was stuck, just like me. No one in the group seemed to be in charge and no one knew what to do so we waited. Soon a deuce-and-a-half pulled up with our friends from transition fire, the supply sergeant and the armorer. They informed us we would be stretching concertina wire in the back bay starting at the EM club and reaching to Tower 17 behind headquarters. We looked at each other in disbelief. The back bay was full of water since the tide was in and the area they were talking about was already filled with wire obstructions.

In the back of the truck, we found coils of shiny, new concertina wire. We were divided into working parties, to distribute the wire, drive stakes in the sand, stretch it between stakes and given bulky, canvas gloves with woven steel palms so we could handle the razor wire without injuring ourselves. The only problem was there weren't enough gloves to go around and those of us who got them found they were badly worn with holes and tears between the steel weave. The gloves I got were as good as nothing at all.

The armorer got into the truck and drove onto the beach and out into the back bay. As he proceeded, soldiers in the back threw concertina coils into the water while another working party followed. There was plenty of grumbling and complaining but to no avail. I took off my shirt as did many others and waded into the water with Mac beside me. One group installed the anchor stakes at various intervals and our group did the actual wire stretching. We worked in water from knee deep up to our chests depending on where we were. The afternoon was warm and clear and the water was comfortable at first, so we were not inconvenienced. However, as we progressed, the miserable gloves I used fell apart even more. There was no way of handling the large, bulky coils of concertina wire without cutting your hands up, even with these gloves.

Added to this was the salt water we were working in, which stung and irritated the cuts on my fingers and palms. The gloves were quickly soaked in salt water and blood. We managed to stretch the entire truck load of wire before the day was over, but there remained a good bit of the beach yet to cover. That would be left for other unfortunates to contend with. We had done our duty and the lacerated fingers and palms among our group attested to that fact.

When I got back to the hooch, my hands were lacerated with numerous cuts and I noticed my back and shoulders radiated heat like hot coals. I slept well that night as the afternoon labors left me close to exhaustion. However, its effects stayed with me longer than I expected. Since I wasn't used to the Southeast Asian sun, I had not taken precautions and found that my lacerated hands were not the only casualty of the afternoon's work. I also had a serious case of sunburn. My shoulders and back turned red and blistered and the blisters broke open releasing a clear fluid. I applied all manner of creams and remedies, but the damage had been done. I suffered through the pain and peeling skin for many days. Eventually I healed but I learned a valuable lesson about sunburn and the need for suntan lotion, from that session of stretching wire in the back bay.

After going out for nightly walks with the guys I began to feel like I should be contributing to the pot we were consuming. Everyone had their own stash, and I was always smoking someone else's but I wanted some of my own rather than being dependent on others. I had no idea how it was bought and sold much less where to get it.

After about two weeks in the company, my chance came to purchase a stash of my own. It was a Friday after work, about 5:30 p.m., and we had been released from duty. I was heading to the hooch when I ran into Mike Sanger who told me he had a truck, was going to the ville to get some pot, and asked if I wanted to put some money in on the score. Of course I did. Mike had $10 and I threw in $15 toward my part of the deal so he had $25. Back in the World that amount of money would buy two ounces of smoke, and I was gauging things by Stateside standards.

Ronnie Hard Dick joined us and Mike drove us to the EM club where we waited while Mike went to the ville. We remained about an hour enjoying the activity in the club since it was Friday night. When Mike returned, we hurried out and climbed in the cab of the deuce-and-a-half. As he pulled out of the parking lot he reached under the seat. I expected a bag about the size of half a sandwich bag but much to my surprise out came a plastic bag the size of a small pillow! It was over a foot square, firmly packed with leaves, no seeds or stems. I asked Mike "How much of this is mine?" and he responded that it was all mine!

When we got back to the hooch I hardly knew where to put it since I'd never in my life had that much pot before. Where could I put it that would be safe from unwanted discovery? I kept a small amount for my use and stashed the remainder in empty aluminum flare tubes and buried them in the bunker outside the hooch. Even with that much pot I couldn't give it away and when we went out to smoke everyone had their own stash so this score lasted for a long time.

July brought the 4th of July company party at Airman's Beach and there would be food and cold drinks. On the day of the party, we rode trucks over and piled out to enjoy the day but high winds blew sand everywhere. It got in your face, your eyes, your hair, your drinks and most annoying of all, in your food. The high winds made lighting a joint almost impossible and there were not many places at the party where you could get together and smoke without attracting attention. Eventually most of the Heads wandered down the beach to a rock jetty where they were able to find some nooks to hunker down out of the wind. It was a miserable affair due to high winds and blowing sand and we were all ready to leave and were well coated with sand resulting in a run on the showers when we returned.

That evening we made the nightly walk ending up at a large pile of concrete chunks located in the middle of an open field, known as the Rockpile, where we relaxed passing pipes and joints. Suddenly all Hell broke loose on the perimeter as all the guard towers opened up with parachute flares, grenades, machine gun and small arms fire. It just exploded around us sending red tracers flying through the night sky. This was happening at every guard tower in our line of sight and at first we feared the compound was under attack. It was after all, 4 of July and would be like the VC to attack us on this date. But then again, it was 4 of July and back in the World folks enjoyed fireworks displays and that was when we realized this was OUR fireworks display. Tonight being the 4th of July this was our observance.

Every few weeks Dong Ba Thin was hit by the local Viet Cong just to let us know they were out there. This generally involved a rocket or mortar attack, sometimes both, and on occasion, a sapper attack. When this happened, we went on Red Alert. The two compounds at Dong Ba Thin sat on a coastal plain almost totally surrounded by rocky, towering mountains situated to the north and west of us. Usually, we were hit from these hills by rockets and by mortars from the coastal plain. The severity of the attack could be measured by how prolonged it was, how many rounds we took, and how close those rounds fell to our particular piece of reality. Sometimes incoming rounds were clear across the compound, other times they were too close for comfort. The two compounds comprised a large area and one of the biggest targets was the flight line with its helicopters and small, fixed wing aircraft, and adjacent warehouse of considerable size for helicopter repairs. This was frequently targeted and since our company area was downrange, we often found the over-shots falling in our proximity.

When I arrived at Dong Ba Thin I was aware that the installation was a target. The old-timers and short-timers still talked about the last attack that EJ and I had seen from 22nd Replacement. The first week or so I had a hard time shaking that sense of dread that it would happen at any moment, but I learned from the veterans that Dong Ba Thin was usually hit in the first and last weeks of the month and rarely ever in daylight.

My first experience occurred in the early morning darkness. I was sound asleep when the sound of a blaring siren penetrated my dreams. At first, I was only aware that the siren was in my dream until I gradually realized it was real and not part of a dream. I awakened. The room was dark and someone muttered "Shit!" I could hear footsteps from people running past my window, the sand crunching beneath their boots. The siren kept blaring as flickering light from parachute flares illuminated the hooch. I heard the clanging of wall lockers being opened and the creak of bed springs as my hooch mates got dressed. Then I became aware of the explosions, distant at first then closer.

Suddenly I realized what was happening. The siren was still blaring away when I sat up in bed but the hooch was still dark despite all the noise and activity. No one turned on a light. The screen door slammed as someone rushed out. I groped in the darkness for my pants and boots, managed to get dressed and collect my alert gear. I had been told to stick with Jimmy Ferrill when we went on alert and the two of us were the last people out. When we stepped outside it was as though I'd walked into a war movie. Parachute flares floated across the night sky casting their harsh glare over us and shadows darted back and forth as figures ran from one place to another. The siren wailed and one of our mortars in the motor pool began sending up more flares.

I followed Ferrill down the street and on out towards the perimeter. Dark figures dressed in helmets, carrying M-16s, moved slowly or at a run, funneling like sand through an hourglass toward the perimeter. We hurried down the road to the bunkers along the flood-lit perimeter. When I arrived at the bunker where S-4 personnel were gathered, MSG Florence instructed me to move to the next bunker down the line. In the darkness I could dimly see the black shape of the next bunker, so I stumbled along a shallow trench that led to it. As I approached, I became aware of shadows moving around the end of the bunker. It was Hard Dick, Witner and Willy. They were milling about, complaining about the inconvenience of it all, especially the sleep they were losing.

4. Like Boy Scouts with Guns

The bunker line on the perimeter as seen from Tower 17. My bunker top right.

I sat in the darkness watching shadowy figures milling around adjacent bunkers and was taken aback by the apparent lack of interest being paid to what was happening. People talked and walked about outside their bunkers and the glow of cigarettes and joints could be seen. I had pictured a line of grim soldiers peering down the barrels of their M-16s across the top of a trench or bunker embrasure but that picture was just not there. I walked around to the front of the bunker and leaned against it, peering through the illuminated perimeter wire barriers toward the darkness beyond and imagined all sorts of enemy out there and half expected to be fired on or an assault to come surging out of that darkness, but for all I knew and what everyone seemed to indicate, there was no one out there.

The distant detonations tapered off and the siren finally ceased its incessant wailing. Only the dim whining of a generator somewhere serenaded us. I could see figures moving about near Tower 17 and an occasional flare was fired up to drift its way into the darkness beyond the wire. Helicopter gunships were in the sky now, hosing down the area outside the perimeter wire with streams of red tracers, like a garden hose shooting red water, before moving off to shoot up the darkness somewhere else.

It was not long before the alert became of secondary importance and the unending wait became the primary focus. I felt as if hours had passed and my bunk beckoned as the remaining hours of my rest dwindled. I started to feel we'd been forgotten, and the "all-clear" signal had not reached us. This was reinforced by the grumbling of my fellow bunker-mates and the loud griping of those in other bunkers around us. At last, we could see people quitting the bunker line and a mass retreat began toward the company area. MSG Florence called us together and designated B-Chuck and Willie to stand bunker guard until relieved. I learned that whenever we went on alert the bunker line was manned by guards for the balance of the night. Of course B-Chuck and Willie complained and I felt certain I would get detailed for the duty since I was still a newbie but no one remembered and that possibility passed.

I wandered through the darkness toward the brightly lit company streets. By now, the flood tide of people had receded to a trickling flow. They walked individually or in small groups, talking and laughing, then dispersing toward the darkened hooches. I walked to my hooch, stowed my gear and crawled back into bed to salvage some part of the night's rest. I had survived my first alert. We learned later that the falling rounds hit the west compound and we had none anywhere near our area. I almost felt like a veteran.

The next alert a couple of weeks later was more eventful. In a 12 July '70 letter I wrote to my brother, I noted:

> We got hit again last Thursday morning, about 1:00 a.m. I heard the rockets go over our hooch and hit Cam Ranh. They woke me up, then the siren went off. I went out to the perimeter. Big things at the bridge leading to Cam Ranh. There were red flares up, indicating enemy contact. Lots of tracers and M-60's and M79's banging away. Then a couple of red flares went up across the road from me, and a couple helicopters came over and pounded some VC sappers outside the perimeter. They hit em with rockets and mini-guns, and I was maybe 50 yards from it all. WOW! Glad them gunships is on our side! I finally got stuck on bunker guard after it was over, and between the ensuing rain and mosquitos, didn't get much sleep. Found out the next day that our compound, DBT East took one rocket. The compound across the road, DBT West took several. 1 man was killed and two wounded. The Korean compound near the bridge really got hit. They lost 4 guys killed and quite a few wounded....

Sometimes the stark reality of an alert came uncomfortably close when rounds exploded nearby and you realized how close to death or injury you could be, both your own or someone else's. Even though we were required to man the perimeter at the first siren, it was not always smart if rounds were falling in your area. You were at a disadvantage running around outside the hooch while this was happening. With most old-timers, common sense prevailed and they either ducked under their beds or hit the closest bunker until safer to move around.

I learned this lesson during my third alert when I had a "near death experience." I was asleep when the first rounds came in. They were falling near our area of the compound. BLAM, BLAM! The siren blew. This was the first time that I'd experienced incoming so close. Several people ran outside and I assumed they were heading for the perimeter but later learned they were in the bunker outside the hooch. I grabbed my weapon and gear and headed out the door.

Flares were popping in the sky above and illuminating the area. BLAM! BLAM! Two more rockets hit some distance away. BLAM! Another one closer than the previous two. I was trotting down the street with a few other people who were hurrying toward the perimeter. BLAM! BLAM!—BLAM! Three more rockets and the last one hit in the intersection of a road within sight of me. The noise was deafening, and shrapnel clattered through the pisser that stood on the corner. I heard more rockets incoming and hurried down the street when the sounds became louder. I rounded the corner and headed for an intersection as a loud WHOOSH passed over my head. In a split second there was a blinding flash of light and a deafening detonation that knocked me down. I felt like I'd run into a brick wall.

The next thing I knew I was flat on the ground, hugging the dirt like it was my best friend, with a loud ringing in my ears and the feeling there was cotton stuffed in them. I was temporarily blinded by the flash and groped about trying to find my M-16 while my eyes readjusted to the darkness. I didn't see my weapon but when my hand closed on that familiar shape, I knew it was mine.

As my feet hit the ground, I headed for the perimeter bunkers. Even though my ears were ringing I could still hear the whistling of another incoming rocket. The noise grew louder, and I could see the bunker line approaching as I stampeded down the road. The noise increased and in that instant, I dove head first into the darkness of a ditch that ran alongside the road. I heard it pass overhead an instant before I hit the bottom of the ditch. No sooner had I landed in the ditch when I felt the heavy weight of another person land on top of me. The rocket exploded outside the perimeter and I started yelling at the imbecile who was pinning my face into the bottom of the ditch, but in an instant the weight was lifted as he fled into the darkness. In a flash I was in the bunker on the perimeter. Others from the S-4 office joined me but there was little conversation.

The ringing in my ears would diminish but never go away. It was later diagnosed as tinnitus. The next day I examined the shrapnel holes in the corrugated metal sheets enclosing the pisser near where a rocket hit the night before. I walked the route down the road to where the rocket struck. There was only a scorched star pattern in the surface to mark its detonation. I momentarily pondered the possibilities of what might have happened if I had arrived at that intersection a few seconds sooner. In a 28 August 1970 letter to my brother detailing this event, I noted how tragic the possibilities could have been: "I realized the next day that this happened in the early morning hours of August 26th which was Dad's birthday. If I'd have been a few seconds sooner into that intersection that rocket would have nailed me for sure. Wouldn't have been a very nice birthday present for Dad…." I began to consider that maybe I did have a guardian angel, if there were such things. It seemed that someone was looking out for me.

5

The Good, the Bad and the Indifferent

The Army in Vietnam was every bit as fragmented as the country it represented, but with additional lines of contention. There were the same racial issues, generational conflict, anti and pro-war divisions, but there were also the draftees and the regular army crowd. Enlisted personnel were divided into two distinct groups—the heads and the juicers. Although this distinction also touched officers and NCOs, it was primarily the younger ones as opposed to the career soldiers. The juicers spent their evenings drinking beer and liquor, listening to Country music, and playing cards all night. For the heads, it was pot, assorted drugs, and rock music. There was little recreational interaction between heads and the juicers during off-duty hours partially due to a belligerent attitude many juicers had towards the heads.

In my hooch we had several Juicers but the biggest juicer of them all was SP5 Boone. He seemed jovial enough, but beneath that burr-headed anvil of a head was a brain filled with prejudice, bigotry and ignorance. He was a Mom, apple pie, America, fuck Communism, and shoot all the long-hair hippie sort of juicer. He drank to the point of excess and when he drank he got belligerent. Many nights I went to sleep to the haggling and yelling of the more intelligent in our hooch as they tried to broaden Boone's horizons. Although he generally left me alone I was definitely of the same caliber as the other hippy, weirdo punks in the company he hated so much, so I gave him a wide berth. I tried to warm up to him, to reach him in some way, find common ground, but without success.

Boone's dislike of the company heads was well-known and the fact that he was surrounded by them only made for potential disaster. My neighbors, John Robards and Mike Sanger, were some of my friends at the time and since they worked in the PIO they did a certain amount of photographic work as part of their jobs. They had shown me a number of photographs depicting outrageous pot parties they had attended in the past year. Some were at the beach, some were in hooches, some alongside the road and some were up in the guard towers.

One evening, as the sun was setting, a group of us went for our usual walk toward the E.M. club. By this time new Tower 15 had been erected to replace the old wooden tower that had fallen over. The new tower was steel, about sixty feet tall and similar to Tower 17 in construction but with a larger platform on top. There were several heads on guard duty up in Tower 15 and Sanger suggested we climb up for a visit and since he had his camera with him, take a few photos. A number of the group seemed to think this was a good idea, but I didn't. I had yet to accustom myself to the idea of having parties on guard towers and I couldn't see trying to explain to the OD my presence there with other unauthorized people. So rather than face that possibility I declined as did Hard Dick. The others climbed the tower ladder while a few of us went to the bridge yard. Later when we walked past Tower 15 on our way back to the company, we could see the flashes as photos were taken. The party up there was in full swing and Mike was busy photo-documenting it. If I ever had a guardian angel, she was with me on this night.

Several days later, during lunch, Mike asked me to stop by his hooch to see a photo album he had put together about his Vietnam experiences. He'd mentioned it to me several times before, but it wasn't until I saw it that I understood what an incredibly fine job he had done. The photo album itself had a sketch map of Vietnam on the front cover and was entitled "Viet Nam Memories." Inside, Mike had various cartoons from magazines that related to drug themes and photographs from Nam parties. Words can never do justice to the hilarity of that album. Other people who saw it were equally amused. It was a masterpiece and brought laughs to everyone who saw it.

Not long after Mike showed me this album, he showed it to Boone. I guess Mike over-estimated the degree of friendship he shared with him but for some reason he showed him this photo album that many were talking about and Boone had gotten wind of. The episode on Tower 15 and Mike's photo album happened and were forgotten. Some time passed until one evening the heads gathered as usual and retired to a spot behind the motor pool. I got blasted to the point where I had to pull myself away and go to bed.

When I entered the hooch my ears were assaulted by the overpowering sounds of Loretta Lynn. Boone had appropriated Hard Dick's cassette player and he and Willie were having a party while the rest of those in the hooch tried to ignore it. Boone had been drinking and I no sooner walked into the room when he came over to me. He was full of beer and wanted me to step outside with him so he could beat my ass. He was serious and became very aggressive. I was entirely too wasted to deal with him so I merely sat on my bunk refusing to accommodate him. What did I have to gain by fighting that big ox? If I beat him he would only want to get even. I stood to gain nothing by fighting him. He wanted to kill someone and at this moment that someone was me.

Finally, he gave up in disgust and turned away. Then he made it clear to all who cared to listen that Mike Sanger was no longer welcome in our hooch and he would beat the little "four-eyed fucker" if he showed his face there. With that he left me alone.

Immensely relieved that this crisis had passed, and I could settle down to sleep, I did so, but no sooner had I gotten into bed when in walks Mike Sanger. Boone's threat against Mike had barely been spoken and it was as if that had been Mike's cue to enter the room. Mike said something to me as he came in the door and walked over to my bunk. I searched frantically for a way to tell him to get the hell out of the hooch but it was too late. Boone had not missed his entrance and immediately made tracks for the spot where Mike stood by my bed.

Boone started the same "step outside, I wanna beat your ass" routine. Mike didn't want to accommodate him and politely refused to oblige due obviously to his size which was easily half as much as Boone's immense bulk. Boone was frustrated because no one would indulge him in a little ass-kicking. Mike refused to participate and tried to be diplomatic but Boone ended up removing Mike's glasses and connecting with a rolled, knuckle sandwich squarely to Mike's mouth. Mike was on his ass on the concrete floor before he knew what hit him. Boone walked away and Mike collected his glasses and left without a word. Boone's party went on but no one dared say anything to him except Walters, who had the physical ability to beat Boone if he needed to and was the only one who could really stand up to him. Walters tried to talk to him, to make him understand the seriousness of what he had done but Boone wasn't interested.

Mike had no sooner left when he returned with the OD. He'd reported the incident and intended to press assault charges. The OD was firm with Boone and demanded to know what had been the reason for the incident. Boone hemmed and hawed as if to say "Hell, you wouldn't understand if I told you." The OD asked if anyone in the hooch had seen what had happened. Mike had no grounds to press charges without a witness. Everyone in the hooch had seen what happened but to a man they proclaimed their non-involvement by denying they'd seen anything. While they did assert it may have happened, no one would admit to having witnessed it.

Now I was mad. They had all seen it. I'm sure they had their reasons for not backing Mike but I also knew Boone would be hell to live with if he was allowed to walk away from this incident. I spoke up and said I had seen it since it happened at the foot of my bed. The OD said we could all expect to talk to 1LT Burns in the morning. With that he and Mike left and an uneasy silence descended on the room even though the music continued.

The following morning it was almost as if the incident had not happened. I reported to morning formation, police call, and went to work like always. Later the phone rang and MSG Florence told me to go see the CO right away. I knew what it was about and hurried over to the orderly room to report. 1LT Burns was upset at this incident since he didn't like people "making waves." He'd already interviewed Mike and now he wanted my version of the event. I related it to him as it happened. He seemed to think Mike and I were conspiring against Boone but the best evidence was the healthy bruise on Mike's face. I told Burns that it occurred as I related it and felt that Boone's assault was totally unprovoked. There was no reason for Boone to have hit Mike. The instigation came solely from Boone and if Mike hadn't been his victim it would have been me. 1LT Burns' last words to me were that Boone would have the chance to tell his side of the story. When I returned to work Boone got the call to report to the CO.

Within a few hours we were keenly aware that the worm had turned but not as we anticipated. Lunch time brought sickening news. When Boone went to the CO and related the reasons why he had punched Mike, he found a comrade in 1LT Burns. In a matter of minutes Boone revealed all he knew and all he suspected, imagined, or fantasized concerning the dopers in the company. The best evidence he had was his knowledge of Mike's photo album whose existence he made known to 1LT Burns. Boone was dismissed and 1LT Burns made tracks for Mike's duty station where he demanded to see the photo album in question. There wasn't much he could do except put his fate in the hands of whoever decides such things and in this instance that person appeared to be 1LT Burns.

Mike took the CO to his hooch and showed him the album. Burns silently leafed through it before making a thorough search of the room. All Mike could do was hold his breath and pray that their stash above the ceiling would escape detection. It did. Once Burns completed his search he told Mike that he was obligated to confiscate the photo album and he departed with it tucked under his arm. The anti-dopers could not have wished for a better piece of luck than to get their hands on that damning evidence. It was as good as a signed confession for many. The identity of almost every head in the company, past and present, was revealed in that album.

A shudder of fear swept through the heads when the news spread that the photo album was in 1LT Burns' hands. The brigade commander, BG Henry Schrader, was informed of developments and old General Schrader was death on dope. The "axe" hung heavily over the company that afternoon. Events moved so quickly that I could hardly believe what was happening. The rumor spread that it was "ship out" time for all the company heads. This

5. The Good, the Bad and the Indifferent

meant being sent down to a group or a battalion or a company on the line. Later that afternoon I got another summons to report to 1LT Burns.

My heart was in my throat as I walked into his office. I held one ace and I intended to milk all the advantage I could from it. My ace was that I was not in any of those photos in the album. I had also been in-country not quite two months and was still considered a newbie.

Burns opened up on me with both barrels. Apparently, he disliked the turbulence that Mike and I had stirred up regarding Boone and he intended some sort of vengeance now that he had specific goods on the heads. I was told that some unnamed person had informed him that I had been seen smoking pot. I knew that none of the heads would implicate me and I stuck to my guns stating that I knew such talk to be bullshit. But I understood that the most guilt he could pin on me was guilt by association which I knew could be enough for him to take any action he wanted to. However, I had also been known to associate with people who were not heads and as such it would be hard to make a case against me based on who I associated with. He finally let me go but told me to keep my bags packed as I could be shipping out sooner than expected.

As the day drew to a close, we gathered in Mike and John's hooch to hash out what was happening. Everyone who had been identified in those photographs had been interrogated by 1LT Burns. We found that the worst pictures in the album had been those taken on the guard tower that night. Our superiors had been shaken by those photographs of our dedicated guards getting blasted on guard duty with many other unauthorized people in the tower. However, the pictures would have been no evidence in a court of law because people were smoking pre-rolled joints that merely looked like a regular cigarette. There was no way to prove there was pot or tobacco in them but having all those people in the guard tower was strictly against the rules and that was enough to take disciplinary action. Through it all Boone was silent. The spotlight was no longer on him. No one cared that he had punched Mike in the face for no good reason.

The next day was like others except for the undercurrent of apprehension. It seemed impossible that some of my new-found friends would be facing a new duty station soon, possibly myself among them. I clung to the hope of my newbieness and the lack of any real evidence against me. The morning passed and it wasn't until after lunch that the extent of the disaster became apparent. John Robards came to the door of the S-4 office with his beat-up Vietnamese guitar.* His face was clouded, and he handed me the guitar saying that he wanted me to have it because he was leaving, being

---

*Today the Vietnamese guitar John gave me is in the collection of the U.S. Army Heritage Museum, U.S. Army Heritage and Education Center, Carlisle Barracks, PA.

shipped out to the 299th Battalion at Phan Rang. Not only was he leaving but leaving *now*, he would be gone within the hour and not only John, but also Mike Sanger, Glenn Fields and several others. Anyone identified in the photo album was gone.

1LT Burns was as good as his word. He'd told me that if I was caught smoking pot I would be shipped out so fast it would make my head swim. He was not kidding. John Robards was not shown smoking anything in the album photos, yet he was paying the price of being Mike's hooch mate and Mike's indiscretion in showing the album to Boone. It seemed that my guardian angel had done her work in keeping me from going up in Tower 15 with Mike on that fateful night.

Only a few heads of the old brotherhood survived the purge. Myself, mainly due to the lack of evidence and the fact that I was still a newbie. I gathered they felt I would straighten up since the fear of the Lord had been sufficiently instilled. Billy Casick survived because he worked with 1LT Burns and was one of his particular pets. He was not seen in any of the incriminating photographs either. Bob Wilks survived because he was a little "loopy" anyway, wasn't identified in any of the photos and worked in the important Commo Section. Frank Taske likewise managed to survive since he wasn't seen in any photos and held a good position in the Commo Section.

Still, guilt by association was enough to attach a stigma to those of us who had been friends with those who were shipped out. Paranoia gripped all of us who survived. It was not safe to smoke pot anywhere in the company area and it was even felt unsafe to congregate anywhere near the company when we went out for our evening walks. The shadow of the Bust would hang over us, and 1LT Burns would wage a ceaseless battle to nail the remaining pot smokers in the company. It wouldn't be until after 1LT Burns left the company many months later that the specter of this witch hunt would finally be laid to rest.

Boone received an Article 15 and $50 fine for his assault on Mike. This was justice but Boone walked a thin line as there was much animosity toward him and even wild talk of bodily injury in retaliation. However, in the end it was decided that he was not worth the effort and was left alone by nearly everyone. I was glad when the time came for him to leave.

Those who had been reassigned and shipped off made out surprisingly well. We learned the lower echelon headquarters would hungrily snap up anyone who had worked at the brigade level. That old adage of 1LT Burns' that we were the "cream of the crop" worked both ways. Few of those who were shipped out went below the battalion level and in most cases went to companies where pot smoking was both prevalent and accepted. Everyone who'd been transferred loved their new duty assignments and it seemed that we who'd stayed in the brigade headquarters company had really been

5. The Good, the Bad and the Indifferent

the losers. 1LT Burns continued his crusade to rid the company of heads and the Bust was a cloud that hung over us for many months to come.

After the episode with the photo album, I had nothing further to do with Boone and went so far as to move out of the S-4 hooch entirely and move in with Billy Casick. I refused to reside in the same hooch with Boone and, surprisingly, he left me alone. After my arrival as a newbie, Bill became a friend through our ties with the evening crowd and since he lived alone in a large room with a spare bunk, he offered refuge and I moved in. Bill's room was paneled with painted plywood on the walls and ceiling and a large built-in desk, bookshelf and counter along one side. We got along well, and Bill's room was a nice change from the barren group accommodations I'd shared in the S-4 hooch. Bill worked in the orderly room and I continued going to work at S-4 so no one was the wiser.

There were several duties of my new job as correspondence clerk but most important was keeping the correspondence log and files. No one envied me my job because I had to work for MSG Florence. He was abrasive, over-bearing and obnoxious at times. It was often an effort to maintain a civil conversation with him and the situation was aggravated because he seemed to think my job was difficult and I was ignorant. Eventually I had

Convoy security gun trucks were frequent visitors to Dong Ba Thin. This is the "Shadow of Death," a converted 5-ton dump truck belonging to the 937th Engineer Group, 299th Engineer Battalion.

to stand up to him which infuriated him but once he realized I had valid points he backed off. When he realized I wasn't intimidated and was actually competent he began to respect me a little more and by the same regard as I got to know him better that respect was reciprocated.

After the Bust our group's numbers were greatly reduced, and those of us who remained had to lay low. I continued living with Billy and our smoking was discrete. In the evenings the gang was smaller and our walks no longer the mass migration through the company and down the darkened streets they had once been. Bill continued to bring newbies over from the 22nd Replacement and one of our favorite past-times was initiating the enlightened brethren among them. Some would be assigned to our company but most were sent to other brigade units. While we had them, we saw that they got their heads. We would collect them from the transient hooch at night and take them on an evening walk. It was great fun to blow them away as we could always see a little of ourselves in these fresh newbies. In this way we met a lot of good people passing through the unit. Many times, these newbies were a source of hallucinogenic drugs that were almost totally unavailable in-country.

One night Billy and I were in his hooch fooling around with his tape deck. I was playing my guitar and he was amplifying it and recording it. Several guys were in the hooch with us when this newbie stuck his head in the door. None of us had seen him before. He was tall and lanky with a bushy moustache and said he'd heard the guitar and asked if he could sit in and listen. We agreed and he joined us. As the evening progressed, I learned that his name was John Valentine and he also played guitar. It became apparent he was one of us and we invited him to go for a walk so we could treat him to some of Vietnam's finest herbal refreshment. We hiked to the motor pool where we stood in the darkness smoking and talking. In the course of conversation, it came out that John was from Whitewater, Wisconsin, and we once played music at the same college music festival, he being in a band that was the product of a mutual friend! How strange that two people pass unnoticed at one point in their lives only to meet five years later under bizarre circumstances on the other side of the world.

John was now officially in the 18th BDE and while he was with us he was a member of the Dong Ba Thin Gang. After we'd gotten our heads together John divulged that he was in possession of about six hits of Purple Haze L.S.D. he'd brought with him from the States. Billy and I immediately put the deal on him for a couple of hits. We then returned to our hooch; since it was early, we decided to do up a hit that night which we did. Billy, John and I had a good visit about things in general, the war, the Nam, the World, dope, guitars, music, girls, short-timers, newbies, R&R, etc. By 11:00 p.m. the company was settling down, so we went for another walk since

5. The Good, the Bad and the Indifferent

The "Invader," converted 5-ton dump truck, 937th Group, 299th Engineer Battalion, at Dong Ba Thin, October 1970. Destroyed in an ambush, 2 February 1971.

sleep was impossible. The night was warm and quiet as we walked to the basketball court where we continued chattering.

Beyond the hooches we began to notice a lot of flare activity across the bay. Initially we didn't pay much attention to it. We heard the "pop" and "thump" of distant explosions that we shrugged off. This wasn't unusual but sudden explosions from across the bay finally got our attention and we realized that the north L.Z., firebase and PDO yard near the 22nd Replacement were under attack!

We hurried past the hooches and crossed the street to Tower 16 from where the whole panorama across the bay spread before us. Rockets were exploding and flares were dancing slowly above the whole affair providing an unreal daylight. Red tracers drifted off into the darkness like strange, dotted lines in the night sky. More rockets exploded with a silent flash of white light before we could hear and feel them from across the bay. More rockets, more flares, more tracers. Then green tracers drifted across the sky in the opposite direction. Red flares appeared in the sky denoting direct enemy contact. There was a hot little firefight developing over there and Billy and I anticipated the alert siren would go off at Dong Ba Thin. John

Smoke rising from where a VC contingent and U.S. ground forces and helicopter gunships engaged the night before.

was absolutely freaked out! He was a newbie and now he was watching his first real, live action of the war he had been sent to fight. Like EJ and I at the 22nd Replacement, he was having a hard time coping with it, particularly since he was whacked out on L.S.D. John was ready to head for a bunker, but Billy and I convinced him to sit and watch the show.

For some reason Dong Ba Thin did not go on alert and we sat under Tower 16 watching the event progress from a lot of banging and shooting to relative quiet, to more banging and shooting, until helicopter gunships arrived and tore the place up with mini-guns and rockets. At 2:00 a.m. it was still going on when we headed to bed. John was flabbergasted with it all; for us it was just another night of in-country madness. John had been suitably initiated into the circus of insanity and eventually sent to the 35th Group.

6

Dudes, Duty and Diversions: 18th Engineer Brigade

The group at Dong Ba Thin evolved as old-timers became short-timers and departed and newbies arrived to take their places. When I arrived as a newbie, I learned the ropes from the old-timers and as the old-timers I knew became short-timers and went home, I became an old-timer. New people came in and the cycle went on.

There were people who seemed to appear, and I never knew when they came into the company. One of these was Greg Kowalski. He was from Detroit and I came into contact with him through Billy Casick who worked in the orderly room where Greg was assigned. Everyone called him "Ski" and the first impression I had was him hobbling on crutches with a cast on the leg he'd broken playing basketball. His propensity for self-injury rivaled Bob Wilks' and eventually earned him the nickname "Kamikaze." He was tall with horn-rimmed glasses that were always sliding down his nose and a shock of light brown hair that never seemed to stay out of his face. He had a big, toothy grin, an expressive face and was a willing protégé of Bill's.

One night while Billy and I were out behind the motor pool having a smoke, we saw two figures approaching in the dark. One of these turned out to be Ski and the other was a newbie Ski had taken under his wing. Ski introduced John Arthur, who had been in Germany when he was levied to Vietnam. John C, as he became known, was from the Upper Peninsula of Michigan, was tall, well-built, with dark eyes and a moustache, the personification of a lumberjack.

He'd just been assigned as duty driver for the Personnel Office. After that night I had a few more contacts with John but it wasn't until we pulled guard together on Tower 17 that we truly got acquainted. We pulled first and second shifts and since I knew John was a smoker I had no qualms about offering him a joint. We came off that tower as best of friends.

Through John, I met Ralph Dexter, a tall, thin fellow from Western Springs, Illinois, who'd arrived in the company in August 1970. He was a volunteer wash-out from OCS school and glad to be back among lowly enlisted personnel. Ralph and John C. worked in the personnel office and hooched together. I first saw him as a newbie assigned to John's hooch and noticed him standing there tall and lanky, all arms and legs that went on forever, shirtless, in cut-off fatigue pants. His hooch mates teased him good naturedly and it seemed that whenever he laid down on his bunk someone would yell "Dog pile on Ralph!" and everyone in the hooch piled on, pinning him to the bed. He took it all in stride. I didn't know where his head was at but John C. clued me in. He mentioned on several occasions they'd gotten him pretty blasted so I knew Ralph was one of us, but it wasn't until we pulled guard together that our friendship was sealed.

While checking to confirm I was scheduled for guard duty on Tower 17, I noticed Ralph was listed for one of the other shifts on that tower. I mentioned this to John C. and he laughed and said we would get along great. I had no idea how right he was. It was a warm, clear evening when we climbed up the tower and I got acquainted after I offered him a joint. As we talked we both became fascinated at just how closely our interests paralleled.

He was a history major with a Masters degree, loved military history and to top this off lived a half-hour from my home back in the World! We spent that night on Tower 17 talking about history, the Army, the World, the times we lived in and comparing our reality with that of young men who had lived other realities in the past that had been far more arduous than ours. By the time we climbed down off that tower the next day, we were brothers from different mothers.

From then on Ralph and I pulled guard together almost every time, primarily because our last names placed us together alphabetically on the roster. That meant we always ended up on the same tower. Since Ralph's home back in the World was a short drive

Ralph "Hardcore" Dexter.

from my own, it wasn't long before his mother was talking to my mother. They occasionally had lunch together and talked about their "boys" as we learned.

Ralph proved himself equal to any drug consumption challenge and his ability to absorb abuse through such things as "smoke-downs" elicited appreciative comments from the boys. He soon acquired the nickname "Hardcore" and indeed he proved himself to be "the Hardcore one."

My refuge with Billy Casick did not last long after MSG Florence and SFC Hagberg found out I was not residing in the S-4 hooch. I had to move back. By this time Boone had moved into the other S-4 room and would soon go home so I moved back into the S-4 hooch. After Bill's nicely improved room, returning to the S-4 hooch was like moving back to the garage.

Work was the largest part of our day. I became more capable and eventually sorted out the file system enough that I could use it. Besides the ubiquitous typing duties, I also collected statistical data relating to things such as asphalt production, gravel production, cement production, resource consumption, project status and the number miles of road they'd paved and submitted this information directly to the commanding general's office.

The office routine was chaotic at times. Everyone focused on their job and getting it done so they could pass time and go home. At various intervals during the week a truck would come around selling ice cream sundaes just like some Good Humor truck making its rounds through the neighborhoods back home. What made this so curious was the truck always played recorded music over a loud speaker as it drove around so you could hear long before it arrived. What made this so curious was their choice of music. Generally, we heard two songs played, "I Could Have Danced All Night" and "London Bridge Is Falling Down."

On a hot afternoon you would hear this strange music drifting in from the distance. It sounded so out of place that you had to wonder if your senses were playing tricks on you. However, as it got closer, everyone in the office became agitated as orders were placed and people assigned to run out when the truck arrived. Once it hit our street, people poured out of the offices and headed to where it stopped and in no time a line formed at the truck's window. The two Vietnamese vendors inside, sometimes female, sometimes male, began dispensing cups of soft, lumpy ice cream. The menu was simple—vanilla or strawberry and sometimes, chocolate. Once all appetites had been satisfied, the music was cranked up and the truck moved off down the street to the next area and another group of soldiers who needed an ice cream break. It was one of those off-the-wall things that when I saw it, I couldn't believe it.

It wasn't long before we started seeing S-4 staff depart as their tours expired. Walters and Ferrill went home and we got replacements such as Garry Arecon who moved into the hooch. I was able to move to a corner of the small room and as an old-timer had first claim on furniture and goods left behind by departing hooch mates. This allowed me to enlarge my personal area and develop more comfortable accommodations.

By this time Ski had been reassigned from the orderly room to the Repairs and Utilities section and drove a water truck. This change meant he had to move to the room adjacent to mine. Although his room was next to mine its entrance was on the other side of the building, so I had to walk around the end of the building to get to his doorway. He shared this room with other fellows who drove water trucks and worked for the R&U section.

One was Bob McGregor, the soul brother with whom I'd processed into the company and shared all the early highlights of becoming a member of the 18th BDE. It was perhaps to be expected that we also shared similar views on dope. One of his partners was Bob Mathison, a muscular soul brother from Cleveland. Mac, Mathison, Ski and Gary Huddelman were all water truck drivers. Huddelman, known by one and all as "Hud," was an easy-going fellow from Florida who'd been brought into the circle by Ski. It seemed he was always stoned, and nothing fazed him.

Warren Schives was the last inhabitant of what was collectively known as "Ski's Room." He was not a water truck driver but worked in the R&U section so resided in their hooch. They roomed with Ski and it was that contact that brought them into my circle. Ski, Hud, Mathison and Schives all entered the company after the Bust so had no sense of how it had affected things. Ski's Room became a center of activity for the heads who remained.

With their connections to the R&U section the occupants of Ski's Room obtained plywood and materials and in no time their hooch resembled a much larger version of John and Mike's. The room was divided into four smaller rooms with black painted plywood walls decorated with fluorescent day-glow paint. Black lights added to the atmosphere, a cassette player provided music and a TV made it all complete. It was a far cry from my room.

Dong Ba Thin was not a permanent installation so there was no sewer or water systems which necessitated the use of outdoor latrines and water brought in by tanker trucks. Several large tanks set on wooden towers provided water for showers, mess hall and other points. The water truck driver's job was to keep the water tanks in the company filled so we would have water for washing, cooking, etc. To keep these tanks filled the company had a 5,000-gallon tank truck and a smaller 2-1/2 ton truck with a tank fitted on its bed. The smaller truck was kept filled from the larger tanker since the smaller truck was easier to drive to the various water tanks than the big tanker was. When the big tanker ran dry, it was time to head for a water point and refill, thus runs were made at all hours of the day or night. To

6. Dudes, Duty and Diversions: 18th Engineer Brigade 91

do this, water truck drivers had to drive about ten miles to a water point at Cam Ranh where a large well provided fresh water.

It seemed ridiculous to me that in the HQ of the 18th ENGR BDE, with well-drilling units attached, that there was no well drilled at Dong Ba Thin. The wells were in Cam Ranh and in the surrounding area. It seemed the water truck drivers were always filling the water tanks but whenever they went to take a shower there was never any water.

Sometimes the tank truck would break down and we couldn't haul water unless another could be found to help. Sometimes the roads were closed due to snipers, mines or enemy activity so the trucks couldn't make the run. On more than one occasion we were without water even to drink much less take a shower. Usually there were two drivers assigned as water truck drivers and sometimes it got to be such a pain in the butt for them that one or both would quit.

After a point in time, Mac and Mathison quit and were transferred to other duties in the R&U section. Thus, Ski and Hud became their replacements and took over their job. As water truck drivers they didn't have the same work schedule as everyone else; thus they had more free time. This was balanced by the fact they were on call at all hours.

A water truck filling the tanks for the shower facility at Dong Ba Thin.

Ski always looked for anything that could be turned to an advantage and being a water truck driver had a great potential. He was a regular customer in Tanh Tonh and there was one particular whorehouse he frequented where he got to know the girls pretty good. At Dong Ba Thin, all Vietnamese nationals had to be off the compound before dark and the gates were closed shortly after that. At one point some folks wanted to bring a Vietnamese lady in to spend the night with the 1SGT as a surprise. Ski found a way to make that happen.

The 5,000-gallon tanker had three separate compartments in it. When he filled it he would only fill two compartments, stash one of the girls in the empty third compartment and drive onto the compound. The gate guards knew Ski and his job as a water truck driver so there was nothing unusual in his coming and going in the water truck. During the day there were always Vietnamese on the compound so when the coast was clear he would take the girl out of the tank and hurry her to his hooch. In this way they were able to surprise the 1SGT with this little gift. Then, the girl stayed a few extra nights with Ski and his hooch buddies and they smuggled food from the mess hall to feed her. When the time came Ski put her back in the tanker and returned her to the ville.

Since I lived in the room next door, I was alerted by very feminine giggling heard through the wall so I investigated, became wise to the situation. Others became aware of what was going on and once word got around, there was interest in the scheme. Ski realized the potential, but he needed to find someplace other than his hooch to carry on business.

Down the street, across from the E.M. club, there was an old in-country R&R center. It was discontinued and the buildings abandoned except for a small group of GIs who lived in one room as care-takers. Ski, who could be very convincing, talked these guys into cooperating with the scheme which seemed foolproof. The R&R center was the perfect spot for Ski's plan. Basically, the same idea was used but instead of smuggling in one lady, Ski brought in several. They were deposited at the R&R center and word passed around. On the evening of the grand opening, Hard Dick and I walked down to the R&R center with others. The soldiers who lived at the R&R center provided a room for a waiting area where there were good tunes and fellowship. The adjoining rooms were where the ladies were and the rhythmic banging of the bed against the wall in the next room kept beat to the music we listened to. There was a fee, of course, but the convenience was well worth the cost. No hassle of going to the ville and getting back into the compound. Ski would leave the girls secured at the R&R center and continue business for several nights before returning them to the ville via the big water tanker.

Of course, all good things come to an end and so it was with this enterprise. The increased activity at the supposedly abandoned R&R center attracted the wrong kind of attention, the girls were discovered, recognized for what they were, and escorted off the base after being interrogated. Although nothing was ever proved, Ski and Hud were relieved of their water truck duties.

Following this he and Hud were placed in charge of the boy-sans, a group of young Vietnamese boys ranging in ages from ten to fifteen years old used as a source of labor for collecting trash, painting, clean up, filling sandbags and a variety of other odious chores. They were supervised by a soldier and the job of herding them around fell to different people depending on who was available to do it. It appeared that Ski and Hud became permanent supervisors of the boy-sans. They were quite a group since there was a language barrier to overcome and Ski and Hud were just big kids themselves, so it was hard to determine just who the adults were.

They bossed the boy-sans through all manner of duties including daily trash collection There were metal fifty-five-gallon drums scattered all over the company area. Each afternoon, Ski loaded the boy-sans into a deuce-and-a-half and drove through the area collecting the garbage. When they stopped at a trash point the boy-sans hopped out and struggled to raise the barrel over the tailgate and dump it. Team effort always worked although the trash barrel was bigger than most of them. They did all the work while Ski and Hud drove around smoking joints and reading magazines and comic books recovered from the trash. The boy-sans would sort through the accumulating pile of garbage and pass a variety of salvaged goods to Ski and Hud.

After the trash had been collected, they drove to the west compound where the dump was located.

After unloading the trash and smoking a few more joints they returned to Dong Ba Thin East.

It was quite a rolling freak show and amidst all of this attention Ski and Hud were soon dubbed "Captain Trash and Lieutenant Garbage."

Hard Dick, John C. Arthur, Ralph Dexter and I became a fairly steady foursome for the evening strolls to the bridge yard. Ski, Hud and the group living in their room provided additional members and through them we connected with other heads in our company. The most notable of these were, amazingly, the security guards.

The security guards manned the main compound gates, provided some level of local security on post, and although they weren't military police, were regarded as such. The biggest tip-off to the true nature of the security guards was when an NCO discovered one of the sandbags anchoring the roof on their hooch held several pounds of pot rather than sand. This was rather scandalous to those in authority and although it gave the security guards away, no one could be singled out as responsible for the pot being in the sandbag. Needless to say, the sandbag was confiscated and it's anyone's guess as to what became of it. We soon developed a rapport with kindred spirits amongst the security guards.

Dan Brozic was one of them. Tall, thin, with sleepy-looking eyes, and a mouth full of gaps between his teeth, he was easy-going and well-liked. He'd been in Nam for over a year and a half and planned to extend another six months. His hooch was a place we frequented during our walks and visits after dark. He would eventually leave the security guards and go to work at the NCO/EM club system on the compound.

Our leaders were important men doing important jobs but they were human, like everyone else and their personalities and capabilities ran the full gamut. The officers were like the other two groups in the Army, the enlisted and the NCOs. There were career officers who were senior in rank and position and then there were younger officers, some looking forward to careers, others looked forward to getting out. Most junior officers had more in common with the enlisted men than with the senior officers they had to socialize with. At the top of our pile was BG Henry Schrader, who took command of the 18th a month before I arrived. He was an older man with a kind face, graying hair that was almost white, and a well-built physique that spoke of a man in good physical condition for his age.

Another officer deserving mention here is a lieutenant who came to the S-4 office during the late summer of 1970 and was promoted to captain soon after. This was Captain (CPT) Calaber, a short fellow with horn-rimmed glasses and thick, black hair. He had been studying to go into the ministry when he'd entered the Army. After six years in the enlisted and NCO ranks, he reenlisted and signed up for officer's candidate school. This placed him on the other side of that line separating the lowly enlisted and NCO ranks from those of the commissioned elite.

As a result of his years as an enlisted soldier he could empathize with us and tried to be everyone's friend, going out of his way to help anyone. He invariably bought ice cream for everyone in the S-4 office when the ice cream truck came around. He was our Big Brother and at night he could be found in our hooch playing chess or cards with B-Chuck, Hard Dick or Tom Franklin. For a while that took some getting used to. You never expected to enter an enlisted hooch and find a captain relaxing among the GIs. When he first showed up on our doorstep one night, he explained his plight because as a former enlisted man he felt more at ease among the lower ranks. All he asked was to be accepted as a person. In the evenings he just wanted to be one of the guys but in the office, he tolerated no nonsense.

In return took us under his wing and didn't care about any of our bad

6. Dudes, Duty and Diversions: 18th Engineer Brigade 95

habits. The only time we objected to his attention was when he would volunteer our services for night convoys to the airport in Cam Ranh. We really didn't enjoy getting up at 2:00 a.m. to drive over to the airport because CPT Calaber was trying to score points with his superiors. But we always did it. After we got to know him, he was more accepted and was the kind of officer who seemed in short supply in the Army because he gained the respect of his soldiers.

Our company was nestled into the southeast corner of the Dong Ba Thin east compound. The perimeter was lined with guard towers at intervals and each company within the compound was responsible for manning a particular number of towers. The towers had originally been large elevated roofed over wooden platforms with

Top and above: **Hardcore Ralph on, and off guard duty in Tower 17.**

sandbagged walls built over a bunker. They could accommodate about three people comfortably but on my first visit to Tower 19 there were eleven of us crammed on that platform. The towers stood about fifteen or twenty feet high and when I arrived, these weary things were being phased out by sixty-foot-tall steel towers.

Our perimeter section was a stretch of beach on the back part of Cam Ranh Bay's west shore. Towers 15 and 16 over-looked the bay and Cam Ranh peninsula about a mile away. Tower 17 was sited at a corner of the compound with the bay to the east and fronted by land on the south and west sides. Moving south along the bluff above the beach you passed the chapel, the officer's club and then to our mess hall next to the CG's quarters. Between the CG's quarters and the mess hall was Tower 16 which faced the bay but was not as isolated as Tower 15 since it was in the midst of the company area and right in "officer country." My hooch was across the street so I was close to Tower 16 but that was its only redeeming quality. Tower 16 was as safe as Tower 15 since their locations were similar but being directly in officer's country meant it was not a popular tower to pull duty on.

The officers had to walk back and forth under the tower as they went to and from their quarters and all this officer activity, and their close proximity, tended to put a damper on the type of evening festivities generally practiced on other guard towers. The officers left us alone up there on Tower 16 but serious smoking didn't take place there until long after the officer's activities had ceased and darkness veiled our activities.

Proceeding along the bay to the south you passed the officer's hooches before you came to the brigade HQ building. It was situated in a corner of the compound with an expanse of open area behind it, and at this corner stood Tower 17 where McGregor and I stood our first guard duty.

West of Tower 17 was Tower 19, situated along the perimeter that completely faced the land side of the compound; if the VC tried to come through in our area it would be between towers 17 and 19. This area of our perimeter had the most potential for trouble and for this reason Tower 19 was not a popular tower and usually the last to have its shifts assigned. Tower 19 was situated in a remote area of the compound and wasn't close to any other company. A large warehouse and repair facility was situated to the rear of Tower 19 and this area was a choice target for rocket and mortar attacks so the tower's proximity to this target added to its lack of popularity.

To the right of Tower 19, the perimeter made an outward curve toward Tower 20 which placed it almost in front of Tower 19 but slightly to the right and some distance away. The perimeter then turned to the west so Tower 20 sat on another corner of the compound although it was manned by a company we had no direct contact with.

Certain towers became favorites such as Tower 15 situated as it was on the beach. It was not considered a risk since it was said the VC didn't like trying to get through wire barriers in the water. Tower 16 situated between the CG's quarters and the officer's club and subject to unwanted scrutiny by the officers was not so popular. Tower 17 was a favorite since those on duty there had the following day off except for their four-hour day shift on the tower. However, since Tower 17 faced some land frontage there was always the possibility of infiltration, so people were wary of duty there. Being a 24-hour post; there was always a guard on the tower and when we knew one of our comrades was on duty there during the day, we often went out for a visit. Tower 19 was the least favored tower of all because it faced the land and one never knew what was out there.

My favorite tower had to be Tower 15. It stood atop a small bluff overlooking the back-bay with a wonderful view of the water, Cam Ranh peninsula and the 22nd Replacement. The beach below the tower varied at times, depending on the tides, and barbed wire obstacles stretched along the beach and in the water, some of which I helped install. Floodlights mounted on tall poles illuminated the area at night and the water frontage and obstacles meant the VC were unlikely to come from that direction. Behind the tower was an expanse of open fields.

I generally avoided guard duty on Tower 19 because of its location, but there were times I ended up out there. One of the first times I had duty there I was with JC Arthur and Garry "Hud" Huddleman as my partners. We were on the old wooden Tower 19, it was one of those warm nights and things were very dry since we'd had so little rain. The tower faced a brushy, flat plain of land covered with tall grass and brush. JC and I had first and second shift and were manning the tower in the evening twilight. As it got dark, I fired up a parachute flare that sailed up high overhead and burst into a brightly sputtering ball of light that slowly drifted down on its little parachute. The drifting light cast slowly moving shadows.

After the flare drifted to the ground and sputtered out, JC said he thought he'd seen someone out there. We discussed this and concluded to fire another flare. BAM! I sent another flare on its way. It burst over the perimeter and began its slow descent. Sure enough, I saw two figures in the light outside the perimeter wire, walking away, heading toward the brush. John saw them too. He was right. There was someone out there!

After the flare drifted down and sputtered out we hit them with the spotlight. The two men outside the wire were Vietnamese but didn't appear to be concerned by our detection and attention. We caught them in the beam of our spotlight, but they would walk away from the perimeter. When the light was off, they would turn around and walk back toward the wire. Since they had no business being that close to our wire at that hour, regardless of who they were, I devised a plan to convince them to move off. I customized a flare for them by digging the cork plugs out of the end of the flare tube, pulling out the little parachute and cutting it off leaving only the flare and then replaced the cork plugs in the end. This was a trick that had been done before primarily for entertainment. Without the parachute the flare would sail into the air, ignite, and then fall back to earth making a large, sputtering ball of light on the ground.

By this time it was dark so JC took a regular flare and fired it. It sailed up, burst and began floating down, illuminating the area. The two Vietnamese were still there but walking away from the wire again. I readied my flare, judged the distance, aimed the tube at the two men rather than into the air, and fired. The flare sputtered, tracing a thin line of light as it raced across the perimeter and landed between the two men before bursting into brilliant, white light. They jumped and ran away while the flare ignited the tall, dry grass around it.

The Vietnamese disappeared in a hurry, probably assuming correctly that there were a couple of lunatic Yankees on that tower. However, the little grass fire the flare started continued burning but didn't seem to be any threat. Besides, it added illumination to our area outside the wire and would discourage others who may have been hiding in the brush, so we didn't report the fire. It seemed to be burning itself out when I went off my first shift. Since the tower enclosure was so small, our bunks were on top of the bunker beneath the tower platform, so I stretched out on a cot and went to sleep. Later I awakened and when I looked out across the perimeter wire, there was a huge mass of flames! The fire had grown to a magnitude I hadn't considered possible and seemed to be coming toward the wire! It was feasible it could burn right up to the tower and consume it as well! I felt some anxiety, but I knew I couldn't sleep through such a commotion and went back to sleep.

When my second shift came around, the fire was raging on a much wider scale burning off all the brush outside the perimeter wire, into the perimeter wire, and far off to our right and reaching over to Tower 17 and approaching Tower 20. I talked to Hud who was third shift and we decided to wait and see what happened. No one paid attention to it although it was a continuing topic of conversation on the phone lines connecting our towers. We eventually called in to report it to the SOG who told us to let it burn unless it became a major threat. I watched it burn while I sat for my second shift and when I went off my shift and back to the bunk to sleep it was going strong.

The sun in my eyes soon told me it was morning, and we hadn't been burned up during the night. I saw that the fire was pretty well burned out except for a few small patches that still smoldered. The landscape in front of the tower had changed dramatically to a blackened, wasteland with smoke

6. Dudes, Duty and Diversions: 18th Engineer Brigade   99

drifting in the still, morning air. The fire burned itself out but not before coming perilously close to the tower as it had burned all the brush in the perimeter wire between towers 17 and 20. When we came off the tower that morning, I fully expected there would be questions from higher authorities as to who was responsible for the fire but nothing came of it. In fact, burning the brush was beneficial since it cleared the undergrowth from a whole segment of the perimeter, and it seemed such a good idea that other companies followed suit and burned off the brush in their areas.

I preferred third shift because you could watch the movie, then go out when your shift began at 10:00 p.m. You pulled two hours, slept for four hours, then pulled your last shift from 4:00–6:00 a.m. when you could watch the sun come up, then go to breakfast. I volunteered to put the flags up at HQ in the morning because this got me off the tower a half-hour early.

While guard duty became routine, you never forgot there was a serious side to what we were doing. While on guard at night, I often heard rockets pass overhead on their way into Cam Ranh. In the early morning hours of 30 August 1970, I was on Tower 17 when I heard rockets zoom by overhead. A short time later, all hell broke loose in Cam Ranh when the

Crossing Myca Bridge on to Cam Ranh peninsula. The smoke rising in the distance is from the remains of a jet fuel storage facility that had been rocketed the night of 30 August 1970. I saw the hit from Tower 17.

Air Force compound across the bay was hit. One of the aviation fuel storage areas near Myca Bridge took a hit resulting in a huge fireball rising into the night sky and fires that raged all night. I learned later that this attack resulted in the destruction of 460,000 gallons of aviation fuel and fuel storage facilities with the combined capacity of over 2.25 million gallons.*

Sunday was our day of recreation and the beach was the most popular spot for this. Being on the coast of the South China Sea, Cam Ranh had many fine beaches, some of the most beautiful and unspoiled I'd ever seen. The Cam Ranh peninsula was shaped like a spoon with the handle running to the north and the bowl to the south. The shank of the spoon handle was mostly composed of sand dunes and stretched for miles. A road traveled north and south along the eastern portion of the peninsula and connected all of these beaches. As you traveled south you entered an area of high, rocky hills and the terrain became more mountainous and rugged. Nestled among these rocky hills was Howell Beach that had lifeguards, a snack bar and was a favorite among enlisted personnel. A short distance to the south was Vinnell Beach, another favorite probably because there were no lifeguards, and an "anything goes" attitude prevailed there. The beach was small and restricted by rocky outcroppings that extended out into the water. What made Vinnell popular was not so much the beach but the rocky hills that flanked it. These provided areas for secluded activities up in the innumerable nooks and crannies for those who took the time to climb up into them.

As the road proceeded south from Vinnell it passed through more rocky hills and mountains ending at a naval base known as Market Time. The beach at Market Time was a beautiful crescent of white sand located in a cove between two high rocky outcrops and overlooked Binh Ba Bay at the entrance to Cam Ranh Bay. The Navy had a base there so there were a number of buildings as well as a snack bar and a convenient club at the beach. Needless to say, Market Time was popular and as such could be crowded and inconvenient.

Vinnell Beach was the favored spot for most of the heads in the area. Every Sunday the area filled with military vehicles and the beach and surrounding rocky hills were alive with groups partying. We would pull in, pile out and head up into the rocks. Once we found a spot it didn't take long to settle in, break out some drinks and fire up the pipes. Some went swimming while others climbed the rocks, explored and interacted with some of the other groups scattered throughout the rocks doing the same thing as we were.

There was a great spirit of brotherhood there on those Sundays and brotherhood is definitely the term for there were hardly ever any females there. Occasionally, someone would have a few Vietnamese girls there,

---

*Fox, Roger P. *Air Base Defense in the Republic of Vietnam 1961–1973*. Office of Air Force History, Washington, DC. Appendix One, "Chronology of VC/NVA Attacks on the Ten Primary USAF Operating Bases in the Republic of Vietnam 1961–1973. p. 195 #341.

Search and destroy operations in the Rocks at Vinnell Beach. Left to right: Willie Torres, me Chris Beshak, Ralph, Ronnie "Hard Dick," and John C. Arthur.

perhaps prostitutes but it didn't matter. The sight of a female in a bikini amongst all those sex-starved men obviously drew a lot of attention. It was a very brave lady who ventured into that sea of men on those Sundays.

In September 1970 I requested an extension of my tour in Vietnam. Although my parents did not understand why I would want to spend one moment longer than I had to, my reasoning was simple. It was Army policy that if you left Vietnam with less than five months to serve, they discharged you so you got out five months early. If you had more than five months left then you served that time at some stateside duty assignment. After putting up with a year in the Nam, I knew my attitudes were such that I would have a difficult time dealing with nine more months of stateside Army BS. When I was done with Vietnam, I wanted to be done with the Army as well. In order to do this, I extended my tour by 105 days so that it would just pass that magic five month mark left in my Army enlistment. By this time, I had already put in enough time in-country to be comfortable with the existence.

There were benefits to doing this. For one, I would be authorized an additional R&R. For another, I would continue to live the simplicity of a more relaxed existence, than stateside Army duty. In Vietnam, the Army was a job and the job was what was important. In the States the Army was filled with attention to nit-picking regulations and appearances were what mattered. For me, extending my tour was a simple thing. Trying to explain it to my parents was another case entirely. Beyond the simple explanation of my motive to get out of the Army five months early, there was nothing I could say that would make their acceptance of the fact any easier. I trusted my guardian angel to keep doing her job.

When I arrived in the company, pot seemed to be readily available and all the old-timers knew where to get it. It usually came in little rubber band wrapped plastic bags with twenty machine-rolled joints inside. These cost about $2.50 a bag, or "deck" as they were called. The prizes were the pre-rolled O-Jays. These were regular joints that had been dipped in liquid opium. A deck of twenty cost about $3 to $4. They were considered the ultimate and we usually over-indulged when we managed to score these.

The car wash down the road, where you could get anything, even a car wash for your deuce-and-a-half.

6. Dudes, Duty and Diversions: 18th Engineer Brigade

Bags of loose pot could be scored in a variety of sizes. A two-pound bag would run from $10 to $15. Larger bags were generally difficult to score because the Vietnamese were wary of keeping large amounts around. The other issue with loose pot was not everyone had rolling papers. Of course, there were pipes of all kinds available in the larger PX stores and gift shops usually carried carved ivory pipes so smoking loose pot was not an issue.

For the first few months I was in-country I relied on the old-timers to score my smoke. They made runs to the ville, or to the car wash at Myca crossroads and it was no problem to lay a few dollars on them and put in my order. However, the old-timers gradually went home or to other duty assignments and when my stash ran low, I faced the lack of a source. Thus the time came to take matters into my own hands. I knew where the places were to buy the stuff but had never gone there myself. I found I was not the only one facing this issue. My buddies Ralph and Ronnie Hard Dick were in the same predicament and we decided that the time had come for decisive action.

Careful planning was called for. Ralph, Ronnie Hard Dick and I put our heads together and our money. After lunch one day we took the S-4 truck, old #22, and, headed south on QL-1 for the car wash at Myca crossroads. I had my camera and its bag and the plan was for Hard Dick to drop us off while he cruised down the road. We felt Ralph and I could score without being worried that the parked truck would attract the wrong kind of attention. While Hard Dick went down the road and doubled back, Ralph and I would conclude the transaction, stash the dope in my camera bag, and meet Hard Dick on his way back.

We approached the car wash, a cluster of several small shanties occupied by Vietnamese of all ages and sizes. Hard Dick pulled off the road while Ralph and I jumped out and walked up to a group of Vietnamese. There was a surge of boy-sans and in an instant we were surrounded by boy-sans trying to sell us something, anything, from pussy to pot. We'd come to the right place.

We hurried into the tall brush behind the car wash where we could deal without being seen from the road. There must have been fifteen or twenty boy-sans collected around us like a herd, each yelling something about what they had to sell. We were waist deep in boy-sans and it was a loud clatter of chatter that assaulted our ears until we yelled for quiet and they shut up. We confirmed that we want to buy "Ghan Sai" making smoking motions. Immediately the bidding opened. "I got good Ghan Sai, $3 a bag!" one yelled while holding up a bag of pre-rolled joints.

Another yelled "$2.50!" and still another offered "$2.00!"

It finally got to $1.50 and, when the bidding stalled, we took it and ordered thirty decks. The lucky vendor scurried off to collect the order while the others tried to convince us to buy something from them. One little fellow held up a light green thimble-sized plastic vial and said "You want buy cocaine?" The thought "cocaine?" flashed through my mind. I'd never done any before or come in contact with it. I inquired as to the price and $2.00 didn't seem to be too outrageous. I considered a purchase but then decided against it.

The boy-san returned with his arms and pockets full of decks. The exchange was made and we stuffed the little plastic bags in my camera case, then made our way to the edge of the brushy area followed by the flock of young merchants trying to make a last-minute deal. We saw Hard Dick approaching in old #22 so we strolled out to the front of the Car Wash. Hard Dick pulled off, we got in and sped off. It seemed so easy we were almost afraid to breathe. We zoomed down the road, drove through the gates and on to our hooch where the score was divided up.

As the necessity to score was a recurring one, our routine became more refined. We didn't need to go through all the motions of dropping someone off to deal with the boy-sans and now merely pulled the vehicle off the road near the car wash. The boy-sans would quickly descend upon the vehicle then all we had to do was take bids, place our order and wait for delivery. Every time we went to score some smoke, the boy-sans offered up cocaine. It seemed cheap enough and we had heard that cocaine was not addictive, so we decided to give it a try. The little plastic vials started to turn up among others in our group and word was that it was a pretty good buzz.

One night as we sat in Brozic's room at the security guards' hooch, cocaine was offered so I took a snort and sat back. I figured the "coke" couldn't be any worse than all the psychedelics I'd done. It wasn't long before I could feel the stuff drop through my nasal passages and into the back of my throat. By then I could feel a warm, mellow glow all over my body. I couldn't keep from smiling and I felt good.

When we left Brozic's room, several of us headed for the movie. I climbed up into the bleachers and the warm feeling kept coming. I felt like I was melting right into the bleachers, couldn't keep focused on the movie and lost my train of though. My eye lids were heavy, and I wanted to lie down so I climbed down from the bleachers and "floated" to my hooch.

Inside Hard Dick and Tom Franklin were enjoying a game of chess and knew at a glance that I was blasted. I laid on my bunk and relaxed. My entire body felt numb, but my mind was active. I felt good all over. Then I began to feel a little nauseous. It was an awareness that I could, if I let myself, puke it all up. I lay perfectly still and tried to fight it. After a while I went to sleep. The following morning, I was fine. I did not consider this first episode a failure or a success. I just felt that now I had some idea of what "coke" was all about.

6. Dudes, Duty and Diversions: 18th Engineer Brigade

This led me to purchase a vial of my very own on our next trip to the car wash. Being wary of getting into a habit with "coke," I tried to do it as a change of pace, usually hitting up a snort after I got off work in the evenings and before going to the mess hall. I had one occasion where the nausea in my stomach caught up with me and I puked my guts out along the revetments outside my hooch. There was an invisible line you had to find because if you went over that line you would puke it all up. If you stayed on the right side of that line, you could maintain.

Then came a reckoning. In the evening after I got off work, I was about to do up a toot.

Hard Dick came in the hooch and saw what I was doing. He came over and said: "You know, I found out there isn't any cocaine in Vietnam. I heard it from the brigade surgeon."

"Well, what the hell is this stuff then?" I asked.

"It's *heroin*!" he replied. "Plain old *smack*!"

I was only one of many who were learning the truth about the white powder we'd been ingesting. "So, this is really heroin?" The name heroin conjured up images of hypodermic needles, the ghetto, drug addicts, etc., but I realized I'd already crossed the line. I'd been fooling with it for over a month! I felt I would never come in contact with it; now I'd been consuming it, on the assumption it was something else. This information was soon verified. It was also noted that the vials sold in Vietnam were from 94 percent to 98 percent pure heroin, as opposed to the stuff sold on the streets back in the World, which was usually about 4 percent pure. This meant that if I were to continue fooling with it, I would have to be extra careful, so I didn't end up dead. A routine of use could mean a biological dependence which I didn't need.

The knowledge that coke was really smack did not affect its use at all. In fact, its use seemed to increase once people found out. When you went to score at the car wash, the first thing the boy-sans tried to sell you was the cocaine as they called it. The rise in heroin use, and availability, happened about the same time that military authorities implemented a crack-down on drugs in general but primarily on pot. We read articles in the "Stars and Stripes" about the drug crackdown and there was word about it in the "grapevine." We were only aware of a slow tightening of the local pot supply which was seen as a lack of loose pot for sale. The pre-rolled decks were always available but the one- and two-pound sacks of loose weed became scarce.

The crackdown only succeeded in making things worse. For one thing, the little plastic vials of heroin were easier for the boy-sans to carry, they could hide them easier and since the vials were so small, they could carry more of them. The vials had a greater value for a smaller amount as compared to the same value of pot which took up more space. It got to where heroin was almost all you could get. Decks of joints could be found but not always and loose pot was rarely available. Sometimes you had to order in advance.

But the military, being as efficient as they were, took measures they deemed necessary. An action brought about a reaction, and it amazed me that they could not understand the correlation between the rise in heroin use and the crackdown on pot. They were blind to the repercussions of suppressing the pot markets. If they'd left it alone, the heroin problem would never have become as intense as it did. As pot became harder to find, heroin use became more prevalent. Many who were used to smoking pot to get their head found no alternative other than heroin. The crackdown on pot actually drove many to heroin as a substitute. If the authorities had left pot alone, they would never have had the heroin problem in 1970–72.

More soldiers got involved with the white powder because it posed less risk of the user getting caught. It could be snorted almost anywhere including the office, the hooch, the mess hall, and on guard duty, and it could easily be smoked in a cigarette with no one knowing since heroin did not give off any smell. Thus it could be smoked anywhere a cigarette could be smoked.

Many soldiers were not educated about the stuff and got hooked. Then there was a painful price to pay to overcome their dependence on it. There were also cases of overdose, many fatal. Overdose cases were caused by ignorance. The soldiers didn't understand how the drug worked in their bodies. A snort of smack on one night usually took a period of time for it to clear the body's system. So while you might feel OK the next morning, the heroin was still in your system. Likewise, if you did some more on the following night, then that added more heroin to what was already in your system. Over a period of time the amount in your system would build up until that one snort put you over the line. The Army, of course, took a dim view of all this and established an amnesty program and treatment centers where soldiers could get care without fear

The makings of a "Number 4," including a $5 vial of heroin, 95–98 percent pure. Heroin could be tamped into a cigarette and smoked with no smell.

6. Dudes, Duty and Diversions: 18th Engineer Brigade

of reprisal. In many cases this helped, but they never got to the root of the problem. If they'd left pot alone, I doubt they would ever have had the problems with heroin.

The worst enemy we faced was boredom with routines broken only by moments of excitement, uncertainty, and whatever activities we could dream up to occupy ourselves when we were not at work or engaged in some other duty. We devised many diversions, but probably the most memorable were the golf tournaments. Bob Wilks was responsible for initiating this activity purely by accident. From somewhere, Bob came up with an old seven-iron golf club and four plastic practice golf balls and one afternoon we found him practicing some chip shots. This was a new diversion for us and the boys in the group began to poke fun at Bob for a while. They soon realized that with a little organization a game of sorts could be put together. Since Dong Ba Thin was one massive sand trap with a lot of "rough," there was no fairway that could be determined and the rough was truly rough. Also, there was no hole to shoot for, so adjustments were made. Initially Bob had just been knocking practice balls around. But now a game had been conceived.

We put our heads together, so to speak, and came up with rules for our golf games. A plastic wash basin about a foot in diameter was our pin and our hole. The course was developed as we went along. The wash basin was thrown out in any direction and wherever it landed was the green. The object was to put the ball into the wash basin but since it was not set in the ground, we found that we could spend all day trying to chip the ball into the basin and never make it. To remedy this, rules were established to govern putting. If you put the ball into the bowl, it was counted as one stroke. If the ball fell within three feet of the bowl, it counted as two strokes. This simplified things and we proceeded.

Since we only had four balls, only four people could compete. The wash basin would be thrown out, a par determined and then we would play that hole. Once everyone had "holed out" the basin was tossed in some random direction again, par computed, and we teed off. The majority of the company thought we were crazy and indeed we must have presented a comical appearance playing golf with one club, four practice balls and a plastic wash basin.

Our course varied with every game as it was never pre-determined. We played down the company street, between the hooches, through the theater area, through the motor pool, the S-4 yard, the bridge yard, and on down the back streets. We would play nine holes, total up the scores, determine the winner and organize a new group of players. There was always time for a couple of quick rounds before the movie in the evenings and it seemed the more we played, the more interest developed in what we were doing.

The spirit of competition was keen. Soon those of our group who thought we were crazy, became caught up in the spirit of the game. However, with only four balls, the number who could play was limited. This was solved this by establishing four teams of two men each. A scorekeeper kept score for each team and our tournaments were off, complete with galleries of spectators and interested on-lookers.

We enjoyed these makeshift games, and a great deal of skill was developed among us but all good things must end, and so it was with our golf games. One by one the four balls were sliced off into the rough, never to be recovered. After all, there were not too many people who wanted to climb into grassy, over-grown concertina wire to recover a golf ball that had inadvertently landed there. Finally, we were down to one club and one golf ball and that seemed to be the end of it since the PX did not carry practice golf balls.

B-Chuck came to our rescue when he went to Hawaii on R&R and returned with a bag full of practice golf balls. At last, we had enough balls so that teams were no longer necessary, and a real tournament could be held. The golf games were revived.

We played games in the evenings, but on Sundays we had tournaments. Playoffs were set up and nine-hole rounds were played complete with referees, official score keepers, ball spotters, and our own sports announcers as well as a multitude of interested spectators mingling with those scheduled to play later games. We had plenty of golf balls but still only one club which limited our play. Some Sundays we spent the entire day playing golf, throwing out the basin, and proceeding to range all over Dong Ba Thin rather than just in our company area. There was a playoff for the winners and one for the losers. I do not recall just who took what honors but that didn't really matter. There were no prizes handed out because it was the enjoyment, the competition, the break in the routine that mattered most.

Interest in the games faded as we lost more balls to the overgrown roadside ditches and concertina wire entanglements. But the games did emphasize that we had a competitive spirit that could be vented in ways other than on the company basketball court. Eventually volleyball games were organized between the enlisted men and the officers and much of the interest that had driven us to develop our own form of sports recreation was diverted to that pursuit. After all, it was much harder to lose a volleyball to the overgrown concertina wire entanglements, whereas the plastic golf balls eventually were sacrificed to the rough.

A more comical sight I don't believe I've ever seen than that group of soldiers playing golf with one club and four plastic golf balls. Perhaps someday, someone will wonder about the multitude of plastic golf balls scattered about the site of old Dong Ba Thin.

7

Heavy Weather

On the night of 20–21 October, the monsoons arrived. The morning of 21 October was cloudy, cold, windy and wet. We struggled to the office covered in ponchos and bent against the wind. It poured in torrents for half an hour, then stop as suddenly as if a faucet had been turned off. Then it would start up again just as suddenly. The rain continued off and on and for the next several days were the same. On 24 October, our radios announced special notices of Typhoon Kate moving in the South China Sea and speculation was it would strike the coast somewhere near Cam Ranh Bay. On the 25th, clouds covered the sky and word was the typhoon was coming and we made preparations to receive it.

October 26 dawned with a high wind and no one needed to be told the typhoon was headed for us. We accomplished very little as the winds blew rain through the open screen windows getting it all over the office. By noon work was suspended as everyone was battening the hatches. Plastic sheeting was brought in and tacked up over the windows.

By 5:00 p.m. the office was secured, and we were released to secure our hooches. Everyone was scrambling around nailing boards and sheets of plywood over the screen windows. Since Ski and Hud and the R&U crew lived in the room next to mine, we were able to get hammers, nails and other tools and Tom Franklin brought a roll of plastic sheeting from the office. The area between our hooch and the neighboring one was flooding due to the accumulation of several days' rain and the walkway between the hooch and the revetment around our hooch was under water. If it rained much more, our hooch was in danger of flooding as there was only an inch or so of clearance between the standing water outside and the top of our concrete floor.

By 6:00 p.m., our room was secured with windows covered and everything in its place.

I had food stashed in my little cupboard, so I chose not to go to the mess hall and settled in for an evening in my own snug little corner. It had been cold and wet for several days, but I had more than my authorized one blanket and was assured of a cozy night's sleep. With the lights glowing warmly, I took my fatigues off, sat on my bunk and relaxed.

I decided to wade through the water behind the revetments to go to Ski's room around the end of the hooch. As I stepped off the wooden front step into the cold water, I saw Hard Dick at the end of the hooch. I started wading through the ankle-deep water but when I approached him, he turned around with a wide-eyed look and began running towards me. "Get out of the water!" he yelled as he came at me. Somewhat puzzled, I jumped back onto the wooden step at the front door of our room. I saw others running down the sidewalk behind Hard Dick and yelling something that I couldn't understand. Hard Dick jumped and landed on the wooden step beside me.

"What's the matter?" I asked.

He looked at me with that wide-eyed look. "There are power lines down by the cook's hooch and they've lost part of their roof. It just blew away." With that he was gone, and I stood there in my shorts feeling a little vulnerable. I decided it might be a good idea to get some clothes on, especially some boots, just in case.

I walked back into my room. Groucho, Franklin and B-Chuck were still at chow, so their corners were dark. I sat on my bed and pulled my boots on. As I was lacing them up, I heard a high-pitched squeak like a nail being pulled out of a board. I looked up at the plywood ceiling we had nailed over the bare rafters above us but nothing seemed amiss. I continued lacing my boots when I heard even more pronounced squeaking. I looked up again as it ceased but when I stood up the squeaking came again. This time it became a loud, clattering noise and my first thought was the roof was caving in! I dove under my bunk to await the avalanche of debris but there was no crash. Everything grew strangely quiet except for a slight, fluttering sound. I crawled out from under the bunk and stood up. The roof hadn't caved in. I looked up to see the ceiling above me vibrating in the wind creating the fluttering sound and I could see daylight through spaces between the panels. The roof was gone!! But where had it gone?

I ran to the screen door and looked across to the hooch next door just as our roof came crashing down on top of their roof. The huge, twisted, squealing mass of corrugated sheet metal and 2 × 4's smashed onto our neighbor's roof and lay there poised in the wind. Great chunks were torn from the twisted mass and flew away. The wind was so strong that the whole jumbled mass slid across the hooch and fell into their courtyard with more debris flying off into the wind. The ceiling fluttering over my head brought me to my senses. I knew I couldn't stay in the hooch now. I rushed to my corner and dressed. As I pulled my pants on the electricity went out, plunging everything into semi-darkness. At that moment Hard Dick came in and hurried to Groucho's corner. "Got to get Groucho's stereo to the bunker!" he yelled as he disconnected the turntable and ran out. When he rushed out the door, Groucho and B-Chuck came in to grab the receiver and speakers. What had been a slight wind-blown drizzle was now falling in torrents with the wind driving it horizontally. I had never seen it rain horizontally before.

The door slammed as they headed for the bunker. I secured my guitar in the wall locker and covered my bookshelf with blankets. As I rushed out the door Tom Franklin hurried in to secure his corner. I stood on the wooden step as the wind howled around my ears and rain stung my cheeks. In the gathering darkness, I could see the guys from the neighboring hooch swarming like ants as they formed a human chain to sandbag their roof with bags from the revetments to keep it from blowing away. Others from the next room were hurrying into the bunker with valuable items and returning to their darkened room to get more. I returned to my room to find my poncho since it was raining so heavily. B-Chuck and Groucho were fumbling around in the darkness as I groped my way to my wall locker. At that instant Hard Dick came in. "Everything OK here?" he yelled. I found a candle on my desk and struggled to get it lit.

"I think everything is secure, Hard" B-Chuck yelled.

My candle cast a feeble, flickering glow over the scene. I could hear water dripping on the concrete floor. A flashlight beam lit our door from the outside. The door opened and a dark figure entered. "Is everyone OK in here?" CPT Calaber yelled. Good old CPT Calaber. It seemed only natural he would be the first to come to our assistance.

"We're OK, sir" B-Chuck replied.

"Where are you guys going to sleep? Where is everybody else?"

"They're in the bunker" Hard Dick said.

"We'll find some place to sleep" Groucho added.

"Lieutenant Thornton and I can sleep others in our room" CPT Calaber replied. "We've got extra bedding. You people get into the bunker and stay there until I get back. We don't want anyone getting hurt. There are power lines down all over." With that he was gone.

I rummaged in my wall locker until I found the flashlight I used for guard duty and followed the group out of the room. It was blowing heavily with rain coming in horizontally. Someone had brought heavy sheets of plywood and propped them up against the open ends of the bunker to keep the rain from blowing in. The night was especially dark with the power out and only a few lights from the airfield glimmering in the stormy darkness. We pulled the plywood aside and entered the bunker. It was a jumble of folding chairs, lawn chairs, people, stereo equipment and even a cot. We weaved our way in and someone pulled the plywood sheet back across the entrance.

Once inside with the plywood in place, the atmosphere changed. It was quiet and the howling wind only slightly audible outside. I sat on a chair beside Hard Dick next to the plywood that covered the opposite end of the bunker. Several flashlights cast a mellow glow and I could see that the entire enlisted contingent of our office was crammed into that bunker. There was a mumbling of voices punctuated by an occasional laugh while a radio played AFVN music. A few bottles of wine passed around and I could see our spirits were high in spite of the adversity.

We sat safely in the bunker while the storm raged outside. On several occasions a flashlight would pierce the interior darkness from the opposite end, and someone would yell "Hey, is so and so in here?" If he was, he'd yell, and if he wasn't, a wave of obscenities rose up sending the flashlight away. Time passed and we were starting to have a good time in that bunker. At one point our gaiety was interrupted when someone pointed his flashlight into the entrance and yelled "Has everybody got their weapons?" He didn't wait for an answer and continued "If you don't you better get them because the west compound is taking small arms fire and we may go on alert at any moment!" That news hit us like a ton of bricks! We knew if we went on alert we would have to man the perimeter bunker line which was not a pleasant thought considering the storm.

The plywood was pushed aside, and everyone dashed for the hooch. Flashlight in hand, I entered my dark room and retrieved my M-16, bandoliers and alert gear. As B-Chuck, Tom Franklin and Groucho rummaged in their corners, I swept the flashlight over the ceiling. Our foresight in putting up that ceiling was a blessing now. Although it was in no way watertight, it did offer protection since water only leaked in through the open seams.

When I returned to the bunker, I could clearly see green tracers trailing off through the storm west of us, leaving florescent streaks in the darkness. They were answered by red tracers from the compound and parachute flares that sailed up and were swept away in the wind. A red flare popped overhead and was rapidly carried off by the wind, followed by another that did the same thing. This was not a comforting sight. Red flares meant direct hostile contact.

The storm appeared to be as intense as ever. We hurried to the bunker and sat quietly, expecting to get word to man the perimeter. With the power out and the high wind, it was questionable whether the alert siren could be sounded much less heard. I couldn't help feeling that it would be a good time for an attack since there was no way gunships could get up to provide air support and with the electricity out the possibility of sapper attacks was very real. The green tracers certainly testified that they were out there.

Time dragged on with no alarms. Eventually the spattering of rain let up, the howling died down and we could hear occasional footsteps outside crunching past in the wet sand. The plywood was cautiously pushed back, and we ventured out into the darkness. It was evident that our disaster was already attracting the curious. Clusters of shadows shuffled through the wet sand around the bunker and hooch while a couple of flashlight beams swept across the twisted wreckage of our roof. I turned my flashlight on and Groucho, B-Chuck and I hurried to our room to check things out. Friends began to stop by to check on us. Most inhabitants of the now roofless hooch returned to the congenial atmosphere of the bunker. Rain fell in a fine mist while we stood on our little front step. A flashlight beam streaked across the bunker followed by a shadowy figure. The beam fixed on our group and the figure approached. "How is everything?" CPT Calaber said. We mumbled a greeting. "Get anyone who doesn't have a place to sleep and bring them to the office."

We talked with CPT Calaber about the roof and he disappeared again. B-Chuck and Groucho went into the bunker as Hard Dick and I went into his room next door. Hard Dick's room looked much different since they didn't have a ceiling and the night sky shown through the overhead rafters. Even in the darkness, the room looked like a tornado had hit it. The door slammed and Willy walked in. "You seen the yard next door?" he asked. "Our roof is over there. It's really a mess." He walked over to his wall locker and rummaged around inside as Hard Dick and I went outside.

B-Chuck and Tom Franklin waited by the bunker. "You going to the office?" B-Chuck asked. We fell in and walked slowly up the company street. My flashlight beam swept across puddles of water in the wet sand and lines were down everywhere. When we got to our neighboring hooch, I stopped and swept the flashlight beam over their courtyard. I was astounded by the sight. The bulk of our roof lay in a shattered, twisted, heap of wreckage extending the full length of their building. It looked like an airplane had crashed there.

The wind picked up again, so we pushed on past the darkened buildings toward the glow of lights in our office which apparently still had power. As we approached, we saw figures moving around inside and, upon entering, found CPT Calaber, MAJ Marks and BG Schrader all decked out in rain gear. We staggered in wet and unkempt with weapons and bandoliers slung over our shoulders. BG Schrader was concerned about his men and promised all kinds of assistance to get our roof repaired in the morning. After he was satisfied the situation was under control, he left and we followed CPT Calaber to his hooch across the street. There we spread a few spare mattresses on the concrete floor, took our boots off, rolled up in dry blankets and slept.

As the light of day crept into the room we roused ourselves. I pulled my boots on, grabbed my weapon and bandoliers and followed Hard Dick and B-Chuck out the door. It was quiet since everyone was still asleep and the sun was just breaking through the clouds promising a little more sunshine than rain which was encouraging. At our neighbor's hooch, we marveled at the mass of wreckage from our roof that lay there to reaffirm the events of the previous night. The glare of daylight made an even greater impact since we'd only viewed it with flashlights the night before.

The bunker where we took shelter was quiet, with the plywood pushed aside, and someone sleeping on the cot inside. The interior was piled with stereo equipment, chairs and assorted trash. The yard of our hooch held large puddles of standing water and one piece of the roof was wrapped around a telephone pole that stood there. Our hooch stood in the morning light with half its roof gone. Only two of the six rooms the building contained remained covered. I walked to our room and put my weapon and bandoliers in my wall locker. I pulled the damp blankets off my desk which remained relatively dry. Our room had taken the blow better than anticipated due chiefly to our ceiling.

The morning after the typhoon blew through as seen from the top of the bunker where we took shelter. Note the indentation on our neighbor's roof where our roof landed on theirs, and the pile of sandbags on their roof holding it down so it would not blow off as ours had done.

7. Heavy Weather

Survivors began gathering outside along with a growing number of curious who showed up with cameras. I entered the next room to see how Hard Dick was doing. His room was a shambles and the sky loomed through the rafters. Magazines and paperback books lay in soggy piles on the floor with wet clothing here and there. The bedding and mattresses were now just big, wet lumps. We gathered outside around the bunker and discussed what to do since the repair job facing us seemed staggering. We wished for some kind of miracle to occur; however, we knew full well that any miracle would have to be created by us. But we were not blind to the fact that we had a good excuse to get out of work for a day or so. Once again, I thought I might have cause to thank my guardian angel.

About 7:30 a.m., MSG Florence and SFC Hagberg put in an appearance to survey the damage. We were informed the general had issued an emergency request for repair materials and we would not have to go to work unless sent for. As they turned to leave, SFC Hagberg informed us we had to police up our shattered roof. We were dumbfounded. The roof was in the next courtyard and strewn clear across our corner of Dong Ba Thin. It might take a full day just to find and gather up the pieces! The R&U boys, who also suffered the same fate, broke out hammers and crowbars and we broke up into groups to begin retrieving our wayward roof.

Several people climbed onto the remaining roof and removed broken 2 × 4's and twisted sheet metal still attached to the intact roof. Another group began tearing apart the wreckage next door while a third group took a truck and spread out in search of pieces that had been blown hither and yon. We spent the morning in a flurry of hammers and crowbars dismantling wreckage that had been our roof, then piling the salvaged material in our courtyard. The group working up on the remaining roof began using the salvaged materials to start rebuilding the roof. By the time lunch had come and gone, we began to see that it might be necessary for us to rebuild our roof entirely out of salvaged material since there was no sign of the general's emergency repair materials.

As the afternoon wore on, clouds gathered, and the imminent threat of rain grew more ominous. Everyone was working on our roof, pounding out bent sheets of roofing tin, fitting salvageable 2 × 4's into place and gradually an uneven parody of a roof slowly spread across the replaced 2 × 4 framing. The pounding of hammers grew to a crescendo as the clouds blotted out the sun and drops of rain spattered our cheeks. We worked with growing desperation as our emergency repair supplies had still not shown up. The resurrected roof progressed until it once again covered my bunk and was continuing to proceed across the framing.

At last, our room had a roof again but there remained two rooms at the end of the building uncovered. The motor pool sergeant produced canvas tops from several trucks to spread over the exposed rooms which provided enough roofing to allow everyone to stay in their own rooms that night. It appeared we had overcome our adversities; that morning I would never have believed I would spend that night in my own bunk or that we would have a roof.

With aching muscles and blistered hands, we climbed off the roof that afternoon and turned in our wet bedding for dry. The roof would never be the same, but we had a roof. It didn't look pretty, was rather wrinkled, bent and ragged but it was a roof. As evening settled in the rains came, but we were snug in our hooches although we still had no electricity.

BG Schrader's emergency requisition for materials arrived the next morning. By this time we'd rebuilt over half the damaged roof, so we had surplus material when we finished. Since building materials were hard to get for hooch improvements, everyone cast covetous eyes on our truckload of brand new 2 × 4's, plywood sheeting and corrugated roofing tin, but it was all ours.

We finished re-roofing the last two rooms and remaining materials were divided among those who'd worked on the repair. Several people installed ceilings in their rooms after seeing how our ceiling had saved us, others partitioned their rooms. The remaining material was bartered off.

We survived Typhoon Kate but as time went on other changes came. By the end of October 1970, most of the old group was gone. In December, Billy Casick extended for six months and made ready to go home on a thirty day leave, then fell from grace with 1LT Burns and was transferred to the 45th Group at Da Nang. Needless to say, Billy was pissed. So much so that when he went home on his leave, he didn't come back and we never learned his fate. But there were big changes in store as the New Year loomed on the horizon.

8

A Temporary Reality

The specter of the Bust hung over us long after the event and 1LT Burns seemed satisfied he had dealt the company heads a mortal blow, but they were not put out so easily as he learned. A big bag of pot was found stashed in the shower water tank at the warrant officer's hooches. The traffic up and down the water tower ladder at all hours aroused suspicions and the discovery, added to the fact a sandbag atop the security guards' hooch had been found to contain pot and not sand, added to the perception that there was still pot smoking going on. All this led 1LT Burns to request the Air Force to bring their drug dog to Dong Ba Thin to check things out.

At morning formation one November day, we received word that on the following morning we formed up an hour earlier. Since the reason was not explained, this spawned all sorts of speculation, but we felt whatever was afoot could only be for no good purpose and fore-warned was forearmed so that evening I concealed my stash under sandbags in the revetments.

The next morning was cool and overcast. We had company formation at 6:00 a.m. and 1LT Burns informed us that our hooches would be off-limits until 10:00 a.m. The only places we could go were the mess hall and our offices. A jeep pulled up with two Air Force MP's and a large German shepherd dog. We knew what this was all about. This was the dreaded drug dog we'd heard the Air Force had in Cam Ranh. 1LT Burns, obviously feeling very smug, explained he was going to walk through our hooches with the dog. We wondered how good this dog was. After all, we had been fore-warned the day before that something was afoot, so if those who needed to take precautions hadn't done so, there was little sympathy. We watched with wary eyes as the dog, its handlers, and 1LT Burns disappeared down the row of hooches.

With that we were dismissed to wander over to the mess hall for breakfast before going to work. There was a lot of quiet conversation during the balance of the morning and everyone speculated on the outcome. Finally, about 10:00 a.m. we were called to another company formation. It seemed the verdict was in. As we gathered, we could see the Air Force MP's playfully throwing a few decks at the dog, which growled and tossed them around.

1LT Burns called us to order and said he'd been pleasantly surprised. In four hours, they had not found any pot!! They had only found what the dog handlers had hidden as bait. There was an audible sigh of relief from the assembled ranks. I could hardly believe this drug dog had not turned up a stray bag. There must be several pounds of grass stashed in and around the hooches, but the outcome seemed to fit the insanity we knew so well.

At lunch we went back to our hooches. Dog tracks in the sand clearly showed that it had walked right past my stash, but I waited until dark before I went to see that it was undisturbed. After this episode, 1LT Burns seemed to feel reassured that any drug problem was under control and there was no further attention focused on the issue.

When I arrived in the company, the smokers were careful and got out of the company area before smoking. There seemed to be a taboo against smoking within company limits and I understood this but there might be places within the company area that would offer concealment.

There were few in the company who would consider, much less attempt, to smoke during the day and go to work stoned. The Bust did a lot toward fostering this sense of paranoia and in its wake everyone kept a low profile. I knew Mike Sanger and John Robards often smoked at lunch or other times during the day. It wasn't that work was so stimulating, but rather that most people felt they would draw undue attention to themselves or not be able to perform properly. I felt that way during my early months, but I felt it could be done. I was well-trained in my job and could do it without thinking. Then there came a turning point in the office.

It was late afternoon and usually at this time the enlisted men cleaned and swept the office and the trash was collected and disposed of. We had a large, galvanized garbage can into which all the trash baskets were emptied; when the can was full, MSG Florence would detail two men to carry it to the trash burning area located near the LZ behind the brigade HQ. This was not a bad walk but with a well-stuffed trash can in tow, it took some effort even with two people. All the clerks in the office dreaded the job and, since you had to ensure that all the trash burned, it took some time as well because you had to stir the fire until everything was consumed.

On this day Ronnie Hard Dick and I were detailed to burn the trash. We each grabbed a handle and hobbled out of the office to the perimeter. In no time we had a roaring fire going in the two metal barrels that served as incinerators and we talked as we tossed wastepaper into the fire. As it burned down, I happened to reach into my pocket and to my surprise found three joints. It was the remains of a deck from the previous night.

8. A Temporary Reality

That morning, I put on the same fatigue jacket and went to work with them in my pocket.

I showed them to Hard Dick and we jokingly talked about smoking a couple. Hard Dick was reluctant and said we would smell like smoke. I said we would smell like smoke anyway since we were standing there burning trash. That would cover any smell on our clothes, and it was late enough in the day that we should be able to deal with the office before quitting time. After a moment's thought, he agreed, and we fired up. Since the incinerator was fenced by corrugated sheet metal walls, no one could see us, and we kept a close watch. Other than the guard on Tower 17, no one was out there and if anyone walked in it was a easy to dispose of the joints.

We smoked the numbers, got enjoyably buzzed, finished burning the trash, collected the empty garbage can and returned to the office. How amazed we were! It was like walking into a whole new world, a new reality, almost as if we had not been there that day. No one suspected a thing. We returned the can to its corner and went to our respective desks which faced each other across an aisle. I marveled at how well we pulled it off. I would look across the aisle at Hard Dick and he would look back at me and grin, then begin to laugh. We both carried on with our work and I knew at that point, I could do my job just as well stoned as I could straight.

A few days later when the trash needed to be burned again, Hard Dick and I volunteered which amazed MSG Florence since he knew no one liked the job. Hard Dick and I burned the trash every chance we got and got stoned every time. MSG Florence was really pleased that we were becoming so mature as to volunteer for such a distasteful detail as trash burning. He thought it was a sign that we were becoming "good troops."

The outcome of this day at the incinerator was that it led to us getting stoned before going to work in the morning. Soon, a few of us were going in stoned every morning. But in the beginning it was a problem finding some place to smoke because there was so much activity in the area with people wandering around, shuffling to the shitters, the pissers, the showers, the mess hall, the water point. I solved this by using an abandoned shower building nearby. There were originally two shower buildings in the area of the enlisted hooches, one located a short way down the street from the other. They both worked at one time, but a malfunction caused one to be shut down.

With the end of the year approaching, we were looking at changing over the office files for a new year. I decided not to perpetuate the disaster that constituted my files. Instead, I developed my own file system that simplified the process, removed the redundancies, used a cross-reference system, and was a streamlined model of efficient filing as far as I was concerned. I could find documents by knowing what the subject was. No need to go to the correspondence log to see where the document had been filed. I then extended the system to the older files and incorporated all the past documents into the new system so that all older material was more accessible. It was an elegantly simple system and even MSG Florence was impressed. From then on finding documents at a moment's notice was a breeze.

November meant the Thanksgiving holiday was upon us. It was monsoon season. We had survived Typhoon Kate a month before and the days were windy and overcast with intermittent rain. The Thanksgiving meal in the mess hall was above average and there was more to eat and a larger variety than usual.

The weather was uncooperative and there were no company activities planned so we made other arrangements. Ralph, JC Arthur and others made plans to go to the beach. It was certainly not beach weather, but we figured on having a party anyway, not to go swimming, but to get away from the compound. As usual, Vinnell Beach was the place for this holiday celebration. The main purpose of the party was to give two of our group a rousing send-off since they were short-timers and going home soon. Although the day was overcast, windy and threatening rain, we gathered after lunch, got a ¾-ton truck and headed out for Vinnell. The truck had no canvas covering the back where most of us sat getting soaking wet.

Vinnell Beach was deserted when we arrived. The wind howled and the waves crashed against the beach. It didn't look as inviting as it did during warmer weather. We climbed up into the rocks but the spray from the ocean and the drizzle of rain drove us to seek shelter under a rocky overhang near the beach. The batteries in the cassette player wore out and we ended up huddling together, smoking joints and sitting quietly, each lost in their own thoughts.

We remembered observances of years passed but who among us would have believed we would be sitting in the rain in Vietnam on Thanksgiving of 1970? As the rain fell harder, we gave it up and headed back to Dong Ba Thin.

After Thanksgiving, Christmas descended upon us. Through early December I received packages from family, friends and even people I didn't know. They had gotten my name from some place and in their patriotic fervor sought to help us lonely soldiers so far from home. The majority of boxes I received were tucked away in my corner for Christmas morning.

The company was not planning a big party, but many little group parties were organized, such as an S-4 office party that CPT Calaber put together. He told us we would go to the beach, cook steaks and we were to be as free as we wished without any fear of reprisals for any deeds done or words spoken during this party. This meant we could smoke if we wished.

8. A Temporary Reality

Now this was a strange turn of events since the enlisted men of the S-4 office knew they had no choice in whether they went to the party or not. We had to go because the good CPT Calaber had gone through a lot of effort on our behalf organizing the event. The thought of us lighting up joints in front of all the junior officers from the S-4 office was rather disconcerting. We decided to make the best of it and take the good captain at his word.

In a later conversation with Ralph and JC Arthur we learned that a group from the personnel office was also going to party at the beach so we extended an invitation for them to join ours since this would give us an advantage in numbers with the personnel gang backing us up. When CPT Calaber asked for suggestions as to which beach, we should go to we offered Vinnell Beach without hesitation. He had not been there before, but he took our recommendation to heart.

A few days before Christmas, CPT Calaber came by our hooch with a newbie captain in tow and we were introduced to CPT Brown, a stateside buddy of CPT Calaber. Brown was a friendly, personable fellow, not much older than some of us and seemed to fit in well with everyone. Having just arrived in-country and having been assigned to the 18th BDE, CPT Calaber was doing his best to see that the newbie captain had an enjoyable Christmas. At that point CPT Brown had not been assigned so he was still a transient. Since he was a friend of CPT Calaber, we assumed he was OK and in the next few evenings the two captains were often at our hooch.

Christmas Eve was spent in Ski's hooch smoking joints, followed by walks around the area. We visited Ralph out on the guard tower and smoked with him celebrating the imminent holiday. As the evening wore on I retired to my room, enjoyed some Christmas cookies and went to sleep with visions of something dancing in my head.

Christmas morning! The sun shone through my screen window and I immediately went to the gifts from family, friends and others that I'd saved for the occasion. Before the morning was much older, CPT Calaber was at our hooch handing out Christmas gifts and dealing with last minute details for our S-4 Office party. Soon the truck was brought around, the chow and drinks loaded, the gang gathered up and off we went.

Cam Ranh was strangely quiet, and we found this same solitude at Vinnell Beach when we arrived there. Our party was set up, the steaks set to cooking, and the suds to soaking, and the officers made for the water to swim. It was a beautiful, warm day and CPT Calaber reassured us once again of our complete freedom to do as we pleased. We managed to discreetly light up a few joints but wound up taking refuge behind a large rock nearby where we set up our own party. Before things progressed too far, we received reinforcements with the timely arrival of the personnel office truck filled with other heads from the company including Ralph, JC Arthur,

Ski and Hud. They established their party adjacent to ours and cranked up their cassettes and toked up on their joints. Everything was in the open now. The S-4 officers seemed a little bewildered by it all, but CPT Calaber just stood back and smiled.

Then came New Years! Our New Year's celebration didn't begin until we got off work on that afternoon of New Years Eve. We were supposed to have New Year's Day off so plans were made and they amounted to the typical day-off plans; loading up a truck and heading for the beach. Once off duty that New Years Eve afternoon, the parties began. Everyone had some party to go to as there was one going on in every hooch. I joined Ski, Hud, Mathison, McGregor, Schives and Hard Dick in Ski's room and we headed out to the Rock Pile at dark to smoke before retiring to Ski's room. There was "coke" to snort, pot to smoke, champagne and wine to drink. Needless to say, we got fairly bent out of shape. I felt good since 1971 was almost upon us and I would be getting out of the Army and Vietnam.

As the evening progressed there was discussion about Ralph and JC Arthur who had gone to Sydney, Australia on R&R spending New Year's Eve in Sydney. We wondered what they were up to and wished we could have been with them.

New Years Eve in Ski's hooch.

8. A Temporary Reality

Precisely at midnight, the whole sky around us was rent with shattering explosions of light and noise as all the guards on the towers around the compound let loose with a multi-colored barrage of flares, machine gun bursts and numerous rounds of small arms fire like they had done on the 4th of July. We could see all manner of similar rejoicing going on as far away as Cam Ranh.

We returned to Ski's room. About 1:00 a.m., Mathison and McGregor had to take the big water tanker to Cam Ranh to get water and we pondered whether we should take our party on the road with them. Everyone was fucked up and wanted to ride with them but in a truck cab where four people would be a crowd, we weren't sure how it would work. We had too many people to fit in the cab. [See Water Truck image, p. 91.]

As we discussed the problem, I decided not to go to make room for those who wanted to. In the end, everyone declined to go since it would require us to stay up longer; we had plans for the next day and the hour was late. Some rest would be needed to meet the New Year. Once Mathison and McGregor got on their way, our party wound down. I stumbled to my room in complete ignorance of the disaster I'd averted by declining that ride with the water truck boys. Once again, my guardian angel was looking out for me.

When I awoke on the first morning of 1971 everything was quiet after all the raucous celebrating of the night before. Hard Dick was sound asleep, and I knew it would be several hours before everyone had recovered enough to get our party rolling again. I dressed and went around to Ski's room to see who was awake there. Much to my surprise, everyone was awake! This was when I got the news of events that had taken place in the early morning hours of 1971 while I slept. Mathison and McGregor had returned just before I arrived in Ski's room and I learned our beach party was canceled and the compound was closed with no one allowed in or out.

During that night military police and Criminal Investigation Division agents had been out in force. They raided the villages of Su Chin and Tanh Tonh since it stood to reason that a large number of soldiers would be celebrating in the villes. The MP's and CID agents surrounded the villages and moved in arresting soldiers. Naturally, fighting broke out as some soldiers objected to being arrested and responded to force with force. It became a wild-west shoot-out in both villes. We heard that several soldiers and CID agents were killed, and a number wounded. A lot of men were rounded up and taken to MP compounds in Cam Ranh. Soldiers who escaped were still being sought that morning which was why the compounds were closed down.

When McGregor and Mathison left for Cam Ranh to get water the night before, they drove right into this chaos. The road was alive with MP jeeps and Mac and Mathison were stopped, searched, and taken to MP HQ in Cam Ranh. The few vials of heroin they had stashed in the dashboard of the truck luckily escaped detection, so they were merely detained and not arrested. It was easy to imagine what our collective fates would have been had we all gone with them the night before, jammed into that truck cab, smoking and toking. There would have been no way we could have gotten out of the mess we would have driven into. As it was, Mathison and McGregor were held at the MP station until 8:00 a.m.; since they actually were water truck drivers, they had a good reason for being on the road that night, so they were released.

They say the Lord takes care of fools and drunks and He must have been looking out for us that night, for we were guilty of being both. In spite of everything, I made the right decision and the others who followed my lead were spared a more serious headache than the one we had from the wine and champagne. New Year's Day was still ours and we compensated by taking our party to the small stretch of beach below the chapel. It wasn't Vinnell Beach but it was a beach, and it was on the compound so we made the best of the situation.

As we entered the New Year, I began thinking about taking one of my R&R's. Ronnie Hard Dick went to Bangkok, Thailand on R&R in September 1970. It was one of those places where guys went to spend seven days drinking, eating and enjoying large quantities of sex. I knew I had an R&R coming but hadn't thought much about it. There were a number of destinations to choose from, including Bangkok, Hong Kong, Taipei, Sydney or Hawaii. Most married men opted for Hawaii since their wives could meet them there. Everyone who served in Vietnam got at least one R&R. If you extended your tour or volunteered for an additional tour, you received additional R&R's. I had no interest in going to Hawaii. I had no one to meet and I started to give some thought to where I would go when the time came. When I extended, I was authorized another R&R so the question became not only where to go, but when. I decided that I would put it off until we got into 1971. With two R&R's to use, I wanted to be smart about how I used them. I'd thought about going to Sydney, Australia. After all, I had two R&R's and Sydney seemed to be the place. Walters had gone there, and I hadn't heard anything bad about it, so pretty well made up my mind. John C. Arthur and Ralph went to Sydney over New Year's and we anxiously awaited their return. When word came around that they were back in the company, I couldn't wait to hear what they had to say. Since we were approaching the Tet holidays, bunker guards had been posted around the perimeter and John C. and Ralph had drawn that duty.

After supper Ski, Hud and I hiked out to the bunker line to find John and Ralph perched atop a CONEX container bunker. We climbed onto the top, fired up some numbers and relaxed as the sun slipped behind the mountains. Ralph and John sat back, filling our ears with wondrous stories of girls, sex, dope and wild times in Sydney. They told us about their New Year's Eve cruise in Sydney harbor on a boat blasting loud, live rock music, girls in hot pants, a city that never slept, and the commune where they stayed. I finally decided to go to Sydney. When I told Ski, he said he'd go with me, so we made a pact to go together at the earliest opportunity.

Changes brought new people into the unit and into our group. Charles W. Stinson came in early 1971. He was a tall, lanky Southern boy from Atlanta and played guitar. He became known as "CW." He had originally been sent to Engineer Command in Long Binh as a courier for the 18th BDE. All he did was take a sack of mail to the airport, meet a courier from Cam Ranh, exchange bags and return and turn in the bag. Because he refused to wear an O.D. baseball cap rather than his boonie hat he was sent to BDE HQ where he was assigned to the mail room. The mail room was located on the end of the S-4 building, and I usually picked up our mail, so CW and I developed a friendship. We had a lot in common and it was obvious he was a head so it didn't take long to become a member of the group.

In January 1971 another newbie arrived in our office. He was a quiet, unassuming, fair-haired fellow with a fuzzy moustache. This was Chris Wilson from Downey, California. By this time B-Chuck had gone home and Hard Dick had moved into my room, so they put Chris in the room with Hard Dick and me. Chris made his stand on drugs known right away. As he sat on his bunk by the door of the hooch one evening, Hard Dick and JC were in Hard Dick's corner snorting some heroin. Chris ran over demanding to know what they were doing. Hard dick looked at him and said they were snorting "Smack." Chris smiled and asked if he could have some. Chris joined our ranks. We initiated him into our little trash burning detail and it soon became a three-way competition to burn the trash since only two could go. He informed us he had 500 hits of pink mescaline available at home and asked if there was a market for it in the Nam. We'd heard this talk before from many newbies who passed through, but we usually never saw any of the stuff.

The Tet holiday in January 1971 saw increased VC activity in our area and during this time Hud and I pulled guard on Old Tower 19. Late that night all hell broke loose when the Air Force compounds across the bay in Cam Ranh were rocketed. We could hear the rockets zooming overhead all night. Strangely enough, we never went on alert. Dong Ba Thin was left alone although there was a lot of activity over in Cam Ranh and down the road at the Korean compound.

One afternoon in 1971 as I took some paperwork into the major's office, I heard the twanging of someone playing an unamplified electric guitar coming from the mailroom behind the wall. I returned to my desk and at my first chance, dashed to the mailroom to find C.W. Stinson playing a Gibson Firebird guitar. In answer to my questions, he told me about his new hooch mate who was also a guitar picker. CW and I had jammed occasionally but this was the first I'd heard about Bo Long. It seemed Bo was on CQ (Charge of Quarters) one night, playing his guitar in the orderly room, when the brigade surgeon, MAJ Stance, walked by. Now Stance was a middle-aged man, short, with a round Elmer Fudd face. The good major liked Bo's playing and hit upon the idea of forming a band to supplement his developing anti-drug program.

MAJ Stance had previously taped an interview with some smack freak from the 299th Engineer Battalion who had turned himself in on amnesty prior to being discharged. The tape was everything the major wanted for his drug education program; the public uproar over Vietnamese heroin had begun and the major wanted to reach out to soldiers in well-intentioned hopes of redeeming their souls from the demon drug. He planned to do this by using the interview as the basis to build an entertaining, yet educational program. Since the majority of the soldiers he wanted to reach were young, he needed a band that could perform relevant music.

There was a band at 35th Group in Cam Ranh that was breaking up because its members were going home, so Doc claimed their special services equipment consisting of two huge Fender amps, a small, beat up Gibson amp, two Gibson electric Firebird guitars, and an assortment of microphones and stands. Doc brought the small amp and the two guitars back to Dong Ba Thin and stored them in the mail room which was why I heard C.W. playing that electric guitar.

When I arrived at the mailroom door, CW was playing one of the Gibson Firebirds, with a big shit-eatin' grin on his face. "I knew this would get you down here" he said. With that he laid the whole story on me about Bo Long and how Doc Stance wanted to form a group and what its purpose was. CW explained that he and Bo were the only ones in the group so far but he figured I could also get in on it. I had not yet met Bo since he had just come into the company, reassigned from the 11th Armored Cavalry when it stood down. He was assigned to C.W.'s hooch. When I met him, I liked him immediately. He was from Virginia and I found him to be an easy-going Southern boy with a fuzzy moustache.

Several days later, I got word that Doc wanted me to come in that night with Bo and C.W. to practice with them. I got my guitar and followed them to the dispensary; a large, solidly built, air-conditioned bunker. Doc met us as we entered and I was formally introduced. Bo, C.W. and I sat along one wall while Doc laid his trip on us. He said he was glad we were devoted

8. A Temporary Reality

enough to sacrifice our free time to his noble cause and he was confident we were starting something BIG!

We unpacked our instruments and sat doodling on the strings of our guitars, each to himself so that we sounded like a music box playing backwards, while Doc continued to talk. We wondered what kind of group we would form. Bo was into folk music in a James Taylor sort of way, CW was laying down some electric rock and roll licks. I was figuratively and literally, in the middle with a blues and jug band tilt. There we were, three people, each from a different part of the music spectrum, hoping to find some common musical ground. Doc talked to me and I played some tunes for him so he could get an idea of what I could do. He then decided that his band was complete. Of course, he warned us that our Crusade was holy and he would tolerate no drug use on our part. We nodded and swore solemnly we were as pure as the driven snow. Doc smiled and said he knew we were all as straight as the day was long. His band turned out to be our mail clerk, C.W. Stinson, his hooch mate Bo Long, and me. We unofficially dubbed ourselves the Dong Ba Thin Anti-Doobie Band. His program was a little too corny for our tastes but to Doc, it all fit together. We played songs like "Yesterday" and "Where Have All the Flowers Gone?" and several assorted ones we thought up that fit the general theme of the program.

After we ran over Doc's repertoire for his show, we adjourned until another appointed time. We walked back to Bo and C.W.'s hooch, climbed up on the big bunker outside their door and settled back. On paper, the idea looked as though we may have tapped into a good thing. Doc said he would get us released from our duty stations and we would work for him. Once we'd gotten the show put together we would travel with him all over Vietnam and perform the show. In our off time we would practice and improve our repertoire. In fact, all we had to do was play guitar. It sounded good, yet it sounded too good.

Since my office was the only one of the three of us that had access to a truck, I volunteered to secure it to move the remaining equipment over from Cam Ranh. MSG Florence listened to my request with his usual air of suspicion but consented since it was for Doc Stance. Hard Dick, Bo and I made the trip to 35th Group one afternoon, loaded the amps and equipment into old #22, and deposited them with C.W. in the mailroom.

We later discovered that the two big amplifiers and microphones were signed out from the Nha Trang Special Services and arrangements had been made with the Cam Ranh special services to assume responsibility. When we obtained them from 35th Group, it was necessary for us to drive to Nha Trang to sign the paperwork to take official possession. Naturally, this, of course, required us to take the equipment there, turn it in and then have it re-issued to us. Typical Army procedures. Once again, we needed a truck for this so I approached MSG Florence. He was even more suspicious this time, going to Cam Ranh was one thing, but all the way to Nha Trang was something else. He finally gave permission on the condition that I do the driving. Hard Dick would do my office job as part of the deal. We made the trip without incident and got the paperwork taken care of and the equipment signed over. Now it seemed the DBT Anti-Doobie Band was ready to roll.

There had been rumors of the 18th BDE being deactivated and suddenly they were more than rumors. The 937th Group, one of three groups that comprised the 18th BDE, had been deactivated in November of '70 and sent home. Now word was that the Brigade HQ would be closed down, effectively deactivating the 18th BDE. This was to happen within a month or two. Doc Stance promised our band would continue and we would be reassigned to him, yet he was failing to make good on any of his promises. We had yet to be released from our duty stations because our section leaders would not cooperate so we continued to serve two masters.

Our practice sessions were strained as we struggled to learn the inane songs that Doc required. One night as we sat on top of the big bunker in front of CW and Bo's hooch passing a pipe around, an NCO came up out of the darkness to tell us that Doc wanted us to collect our instruments and come to his trailer. We grumbled and groaned but gathered our guitars and headed for Doc's quarters next to the brigade headquarters building. As we approached we could see by the glow behind the patio enclosure that Doc was entertaining.

We walked to the entrance and found Doc, MAJ Stiner from my office, who had replaced MAJ Marks, MAJ Baldwin, the adjutant and Chaplain Fix, sitting around a smoldering charcoal grill with an array of liquor bottles scattered over a picnic table. Doc stumbled over to us with liquor on his breath and a slur on his tongue and asked us to run through our repertoire. We hedged a little but unpacked our instruments and sat down to tune up. We were offered drinks but declined. Besides, we were still pretty buzzed from smoking on top of the big bunker before being summoned to this gig. As uncomfortable as the situation was, we did our best, then begged off and departed at the first opportunity. We went back to the bunker, fired up another pipe and sat under the stars. Bo went to his hooch and CW told me that Bo was ready to call it quits since he was becoming very disillusioned.

This did not bode well but we understood from the outset the whole idea was a little "far-fetched" considering the state of affairs as the brigade moved closer to deactivation. The three of us might have pulled it off, given the right support, but there was no support and we could see that

8. *A Temporary Reality*

even if Doc Stance couldn't. Our motivation was to ride this pony as far as it would take us but we had no illusions about how far that would be. For us it had more to do with "passing time" doing something we enjoyed. We knew it was too good to be true, and Bo's departure was merely another indication that our efforts would never bear fruit. For CW and me, we both knew the days for the Dong Ba Thin Anti-Doobie Band were numbered.

9

Duty Calls

Valentine's Day mail call surprised me with a letter from Janet, my hometown buddy's girl friend. It had been so long since I'd had any contract with her, that this letter was a bolt out of the blue. Back in June of 69 when I was home on leave under orders for Vietnam the first time, I'd gathered with some of my high school classmates to bid goodbye to one of our friends, Janet's steady boy who we knew as the Phantom. He'd been drafted and since he was leaving for induction while I was home on leave, we had to see him off in style. Many old high school friends were there including John Criner and Tony Phillips. It was great to see everyone although our pleasure was tempered by the fact that the purpose of the moment was to send another of our group off to the Army, and probably to Vietnam as well.

During this visit, I'd reconnected with Janet whom I'd not seen in several years. My, how she'd changed! She was no longer the skinny, long-legged girl of several years earlier, but had turned into a voluptuous young woman and the looks she gave me were more than those of just a friend. The relationship I'd had with her was more of a big brother and little sister. In the years since I'd gone to college and entered the Army, she'd finished high school and was working and living on her own. Her relationship with my buddy, the Phantom, had gone through ups and downs but they still seemed to be together.

She was distressed about him going in the Army but she was more distressed about me heading to Vietnam. When she learned I was going to Peoria to visit my guitar-playing buddy, Bruce Brown, aka Captain Marvel, she insisted I visit her in Bloomington on the way. I agreed and on the appointed day I stopped at her apartment.

It was a pleasant visit until that evening when the conversation turned to smoking pot. She'd been against it but on that evening she asked me to turn her on since she had never smoked it and it had been a source of friction in her relationship with the Phantom because he smoked. But at that moment she wanted to try it and said I was the only one she would trust to take care of it. She was scared because of what she was asking but I agreed so we sat cross-legged on the floor facing each other while I rolled up a joint that we proceeded to smoke. I thought if she liked it, perhaps she and the Phantom could find common ground on the issue rather than having divided opinions. I'd hoped I was doing him a favor.

After she had gotten a good "buzz" everything seemed smooth then she suddenly lunged across the floor and attacked me with passionate kisses and as we rolled on the floor my mind flashed on a million thoughts. Was this a product of true emotions or released by lowered inhibitions? Was she expressing true feelings or was this a result of her first experience with pot? Was she trying to send me off to Vietnam with a parting gift that only she could give me? I had no way of knowing at the moment but the over-riding thought I could not shake was that she was Phantom's girlfriend. There was no way I could take advantage of her. I was afraid of doing something we would regret. It would be like screwing my sister! I resisted the urge and convinced her we should get something to eat. The balance of the evening was awkward. We ignored what happened and when she went to bed, I slept on the sofa in the living room. When I awoke the next morning we were spooning on the sofa.

I was soon on my way to Peoria but the revelations of that night were troubling and, although she told me she and the Phantom were no longer together, I found it difficult to reconcile my feelings. He was an old friend whom I'd known since 4th grade and we had always been like brothers. I knew more than one friendship had been destroyed by disagreements concerning a woman and I didn't want this to happen to us. But Pandora's Box had been opened and there was no way we could go back to the way it was before.

Our night of stifled passion left unanswered questions and her silence during my time at Hunter Army Airfield did little to provide answers. I accepted what happened as being a fluke and assumed she was embarrassed by it, so I let it drop. Now, after so many months in-country, much of the life I'd left behind back in the World became like it never really happened and I'd all but forgotten about it. Then this letter from Janet.

I was pleased to hear from her but unprepared for what she had to say. The letter was pleasant and she was apologetic for not having written for so long. She was concerned about my welfare and wanted to be a part of my life again. She was living and working in Michigan but was soon to move to Atlanta, Georgia, with a girlfriend. She professed love and concern and promised to write again when she was settled in Atlanta. I didn't know quite what to make of this but she did write me from Atlanta as promised.

A steady flow of letters began passing between us after that Valentine's Day, in which we confided many things we might not have, had we been in each other's presence at the time. I corresponded with a number of young ladies, however, Janet seemed intent on filling that place in my life and I was pleased to have the mail.

The subject of R&R came up. I had two R&R's coming to me, one for my year tour and a second for extending my tour and I was already committed to going on my first R&R with Ski in about a month. We discussed meeting in Hawaii but the fact she was, or had been, my buddy's girl hung over me like a dark cloud. Was meeting her in Hawaii the right thing to do? It could be a disaster, but if all went well … who knew? I might return to the World and then there would be time enough to evaluate our relationship and where it was heading. Going to Hawaii might complicate things rather than clarify them. I finally decided that while I was in-country, letters would suffice until I returned to the world and then we could meet.

That February 1971, I was promoted to Specialist 5 (SP5) after making a favorable impression upon the January promotion board. That brought me a little more money but it also brought me different duties. As a SP5 I would no longer be required to pull guard duty which distressed me. However, I would have the opportunity to pull duty as CQ (Charge of Quarters). In the evenings when the offices closed down and the company rolled up, there were only a few functions that continued during the night. In the headquarters building, the OD monitored communications and functions around the company. In the company orderly room, it was the CQ's duty to stand by and take incoming phone calls, handle minor emergencies, deliver messages, assist in posting bunker guards if we went on Yellow Alert, and anything else that came up. Standing CQ could be nothing more than a long, quiet night or, if the compound was hit during the night, it could be an incredible pain in the ass. It was like being on guard; you didn't get any sleep but you didn't have to stay on a tower.

The CQ went on duty just after supper and stayed in the orderly room until relieved the next morning. A duty roster was posted each week and CQ usually ran itself. The only time this duty could be inconvenient was on Sundays since it was a full day shift and then the following night, which made for a long day. Once I was promoted, I expected to be pulling CQ and my name appeared on the duty roster almost as soon as I made SP5.

On the appointed evening I reported to the orderly room where 1SGT Harris briefed me and left it in my hands. The SOG arrived as the guards prepared for guard mount. I was glad to see that the SOG was Mike Smith from the commo section. I knew Steve as an old-timer who was very much into heroin, so I knew I didn't have to worry about him surprising me in any compromising situations. Guard mount proceeded and the guards were soon on their towers.

Since part of my duty was to patrol the area every so often, I was able

9. Duty Calls

to go to my hooch and other points. After the movie everyone wandered back to their hooches and as the company settled down, I made my way to the shitters next to the transient hooch because they were in sight of the orderly room. No one was inside so I turned out the light and fired up a joint while keeping an eye on the front door of the orderly room. It was convenient to stand in the darkness inside the shitter and smoke while being able to monitor the orderly room.

After finishing my number, I returned to the orderly room and settled back at the 1SGT's desk to read my book. As the evening progressed, I moved out to sit on the front steps. About 1:30 a.m., SOG Mike Smith stumbled up and joined me on the front steps to smoke a joint. So far it had been quiet and we hoped to get through the night without any major incidents.

When Steve left, I returned to my book but by this time I'd abandoned the 1SGT's desk and took up my post in the company commander's office. 1LT Burns was the architect of the Bust and I had no particular affection for him. He was down on the heads, so I decided to extract some small form of revenge. I sat back in his chair, propped my feet upon his desk, pulled out a joint and fired it up. How ironic, I thought to myself as I sat there watching the smoke drift across the office. 1LT Burns, who was so down on pot, who had tried to get the company heads shipped out and almost succeeded. He couldn't get me and now here I was smoking in his office where he had interrogated me during the events surrounding the Bust.

"This one's for you, Mike and John and Glenn and all the others" who fell prey to Burns' witch hunt. The night passed slowly and as the light of morning filtered across the sky, I made one last stroll through the area and returned to the orderly room in time to be relieved by 1SGT Harris. A little bleary-eyed and sleepy I shuffled off to the mess hall to start my day. Not long after my tour of duty as CQ it was decided to only have the middle-ranking NCOs pull CQ, so I was returned to the guard roster which was fine by me.

As we entered the New Year, we were informed that CPT Calaber's friend, the good CPT Brown, was to be our new company commander replacing 1LT Burns! At morning formation, the company was introduced to CPT Brown and he spoke to the assembled group. We had nothing to hide now and if Mike Sanger's photo album had been enough to ship people out of the company, we who had committed these acts directly in front of our new C.O. could not help but wonder at what might follow. However, CPT Brown was no 1LT Burns and was far more enlightened and understanding. It was clear there would be no "witch-hunts" and, as long as we continued to do our jobs and stay out of trouble, there would be no problems under his command.

Guard duty rolled around generally once a week. Ralph and I were almost always on guard at the same time since we always signed each other up for a shift and a tower. We pulled guard on Tower 15, Ralph had first shift and I the second. That day we'd driven down to the car wash and picked up a GI hitch-hiking who turned us on to some O-Jays and before we reached the car wash, we changed course for the ville as our friend took us to his source for the O-Jays. We procured an ample supply and after getting our friend on his way, headed back to DBT. We also found ourselves with a supply of OJ's for a change.

It was dusk and we were smoking with Ralph laid back on one cot and me on the other. It was not unusual for the SOG, or perhaps the OD, to come around but they usually drove in a jeep and we could hear them pull up. As we lay on the bunks, we heard the ringing clatter of someone climbing the tower's steel ladder. Ralph was first shift and it was his duty to yell the customary "Halt! Who goes there?" Not knowing who was coming up our ladder, we fumbled around to hide any traces of smoking while the sound of climbing continued on the ladder. I quickly yelled "Halt! Who goes there?" The climbing sounds stopped.

"The Company Commander" came the reply. I looked over the edge of the tower and sure enough, it was CPT Brown, the new C.O. about half-way up the ladder.

"Advance and be recognized" I said. We knew CPT Brown through CPT Calaber and both officers knew very well where our heads were at.

He came up the ladder, climbed into the tower, made himself at home and visited with us for a while. He must have known we were blasted but didn't make any remarks about it. He was a good person and an

I get an ARCOM for dedicated filing work under hazardous conditions in a combat zone.

improvement over 1LT Burns. He said he was out walking and had never been up in a guard tower before so decided to give it a climb, or so he said. Ralph and I had been lying on the cots so we would not have been visible from the ground and I'm sure he probably couldn't see anyone in the tower when there was supposed to be someone up there that may have had something to do with it.

We had a pleasant visit with CPT Brown and parted on friendly terms. When he left we gave a sigh of relief because we were afraid the gang would be coming out for smokes and tokes and we weren't sure what CPT Brown would say when fifteen other people began climbing the tower. Fortunately he left before they came. Mike Sanger's party photographs had been taken in this very same tower. All the boys were soon collected in the tower blazing away with smoking pipes, not guns.

One night I was doing third shift on Tower 15 with JC Arthur and Bob Wilks. Being third shift meant I didn't have to be on the tower to stand guard until 10:00 p.m. for my two hours. Then I slept in the tower and stood my last shift between 0400–06:00. I always volunteered to put the flags up at HQ which allowed me to get off the tower early and be done with guard. Everyone else had to wait at the towers until the SOG relieved them. By putting up the flags I didn't have to wait to be relieved. I finished my shift and woke Arthur who was first shift, so he could take over while I climbed down off the tower and put the flags up. Once done I headed for the hooch.

It was Saturday morning and I was tired from being on guard all night. When everyone left for the office I settled back with a joint. I didn't have to deal with anything until Hard Dick came in and told me I had to stand for an awards ceremony because I was to receive a medal! This was news to me. I was certain this was some sort of prank but he assured me it was on the level. Almost every Saturday morning, there was an awards ceremony outside BDE HQ where any and all awards were bestowed by the BDE CO or his designated representative. Since the BDE was in the process of standing down, these ceremonies were taking place more frequently. I was too blasted to care much about it once I realized that it was going to interfere with my morning off, so I decided to go to work and take the afternoon off instead.

At the appointed time I joined a contingent from the office and walked to the HQ where we found an NCO arranging all those who were to receive awards and was told where to stand. Spectators arrived as well as JC Arthur and Ralph who began making wise cracks and pointed comments at me as I knew they would do their best to make me laugh during the ceremony. There I was, standing in ranks with all the other recipients, but I had to look at these two pranksters. I pulled my boonie hat over my eyes and fought the laughter that welled up from within. The ceremony began. The awards were given by the full colonel who was running the brigade pending its deactivation. I did my best to ignore JC and Ralph although they tried their best to make me laugh.

I was awarded, an Army Commendation Medal, and my picture was taken. The citation read:

> For meritorious achievement in connection with ground operations against a hostile force in the Republic of Vietnam during the period 1 November 1970–12 January 1971. He distinguished himself by meritorious achievement while serving with the 18th Engineer Brigade, Republic of Vietnam. Through diligence and determination, he accomplished his assigned mission with dispatch and efficiency. His unrelenting loyalty, initiative and perseverance brought him wide acclaim and inspired others to strive for maximum performance. Unselfishly working long and arduous hours, he has contributed significantly to the success of the allied effort. His commendable performance, outstanding achievement, and devotion to duty were in keeping with the highest traditions of the military service and reflect great credit upon himself, his unit, and the United States Army.

While the citation doesn't actually say anything about what I did to deserve the medal, I found out later MSG Florence had put me in for it because of my excellent job at reorganizing the S-4 filing system. He told me my system had been adopted at Engineer Command in Long Binh as it was seen as being superior to what they were using. I didn't care about the medal. It was the fact that MSG Florence had put me in for it that meant more to me than the medal itself, because after all of our head-butting and harsh words, we had come to a level of mutual respect.

During the early months of 1971, a new project was undertaken by the combined commands of Dong Ba Thin. There had been problems with sappers getting into the compounds. This had been demonstrated by a VC sapper who had "Chu Hoied" or switched sides. He was brought to Dong Ba Thin and demonstrated of how they penetrated wire obstacles around installations by passing through our perimeter wire.

I was serving a four-hour shift on Tower 17 at the time and had an excellent vantage point from which to watch this little Vietnamese man in GI underwear with three sticks, about a foot long, pass right through all our wire. We felt so secure behind our perimeter wire, so this little demonstration was unnerving to everyone who witnessed it. After this it was decided to build a chain link fence around the installation and incorporate pressure sensitive cables buried just outside the fence. These sensors would set off indicator lights in towers 17 and 19 if anything over seventy-five pounds walked within three feet of it. Each company would be responsible for fence construction in their areas so we watched as this work crept closer to our corner of the compound.

9. Duty Calls

One group worked ahead of the detail installing the fence digging a trench about a foot deep so that the bottom of the fence could be secured in the ground to prevent crawling under it. Then metal fence posts were installed. The second group laid out the fence and, after a bulldozer stretched the fence tightly, it was secured to the posts and the trench backfilled. When the fence construction reached the Tower 19 frontage, our company took over installation around the 18th BDE area. The work proceeded to the corner at Tower 17 and then turned north continuing down the beach.

About this time I was on guard on Tower 17 and anticipated spending my four hours of daytime duty watching all the work, but that day was wet, rainy and cold so the detail was not sent out. It was cloudy and overcast with wind and an occasional sprinkling of rain and I made the best of my four hours on the tower with sodas, smokes and a book. I was standing at the front of the tower leaning on the M-60 enjoying a smoke and walked to the rear of the platform. Being the kind of day it was, I did not expect anyone to come out to visit The fence detail had passed the front of Tower 17, turned the corner and had progressed a good ways down the beach.

Suddenly, movement caught my eye. There was an older man in an Army flight jacket and OD baseball cap walking around below the tower. Then, almost as if he knew I was watching him, he turned and looked up at me. My heart jumped! It was BG Henry Schrader, commander of the 18th ENGR BDE. "Just wanted to see how they are coming along with the fence" he yelled.

"That's quite all right, sir" I replied. Yes, fine with me as long as he stayed down there. I was pretty zonked. Since the tower was situated directly behind the brigade HQ building, BG Schrader's office was always close by but I had never seen him out back before. No one at HQ ever bothered with the guard tower or the people on duty there. Yes, it was fine if the general wanted to look at the fence. I just didn't want him to climb the tower. Why should he? It was a long climb and he was certainly no youngster.

He walked around for a while surveying the fence and water-filled bulldozer tracks, then looked up at me. I managed a weak smile and tried to act totally at ease. Then he said "I'm going to come up. Is it all right?" What could I say? It was his guard tower and I was one of his troops.

"Help yourself" was all I could reply. He commenced the long climb up the ladder and I was reeling. I had never had a one-on-one contact with a brigadier general before and although my initial impressions of BG Schrader were good ones, I didn't know what he expected of me. Was this a business or social call? I hoped the boys didn't come out for a visit while he was up there!

He reached the top of the ladder and I wondered if there was any chance he could tell I was zonked. He pulled himself over the side and stood up in the tower next to me and smiled. I was so blown away by the whole thing that all I could say was "How're you doin,' Sir?" It never occurred to me to salute him which I most certainly should have done but he seemed to understand. He was a grandfatherly type of man with almost completely white hair, a healthy build and a congenial personality. He walked to the front of the tower and took in the view. I think it was the first time he had ever been up in one of the guard towers, much less Tower 17. We made small talk about the fence being built and security issues. He fooled around with the machine gun, checked out every little thing up there then sat down on one of the cots and tried to put me at ease. Our conversation turned to home and family and the World.

After about forty-five minutes of chit-chat, he decided he should get back to work so we parted. I neglected the farewell salute but again, it was unintentional and for some reason I felt he knew that no insult was intended. He climbed over the edge and descended the ladder, pausing at the bottom to wave before walking back to the HQ. I heaved a huge sigh of relief and sat down. I knew the general was down on heads and felt I had managed to come through this encounter without betraying the fact that I was totally whacked.

About this time old Tower 19 was torn down and new Tower 19 built adjacent to the old tower's location. New Tower 19 was steel and rose about twenty-five-feet. With its construction, all guard towers in our area were now steel. New Tower 19 was a joy in comparison to the old version. It was larger and easily accommodated the crowds of smokers who frequented the smoke-fests that Tower 19 was notorious for. The new tower was part of the improvements being made that included the chain link fence and movement sensors.

One attraction of duty on Tower 19 was that you could fire the M-79 and pop a few grenades into the wire and beyond. If there were ever any questions about this, we always blamed it on the guys in adjacent Tower 20. A grenade fired from Tower 19 sounded just like one fired from Tower 20. Sometimes Tower 19 participated in H&I fire. This Harassment and Interdiction fire occurred when guards in designated sectors around the perimeter were allowed to fire grenades and small arms indiscriminately into the surrounding brush. There was no rhyme nor reason to the scheduling as it was intended to keep the enemy at a respectable distance from the perimeter since they never knew when firing would take place. This would often go on all night so the sound of grenades exploding around the perimeter was a frequent occurrence.

Thus it was that, when the boys on Tower 20 participated in H&I fire,

Tower 19 tended to join in although our participation was unauthorized. Since Tower 20 was situated directly off the right front of Tower 19, they occasionally dropped grenades a little too close to our front, sometimes uncomfortably close. One reason the guys on Tower 19 started joining in on Tower 20's H&I fire was self defense. The guys on Tower 20 became notorious for dropping their grenades too close to Tower 19 and I'd heard others complain about this.

One evening Ralph and I were on new Tower 19 when Tower 20 began popping off grenades. We were smoking when the grenades began falling close by our wire with uncomfortable detonation. I'd finally had enough of their game and decided to take action. Since our telephone lines did not connect to Tower 20, we had no communication with them. I flashed our spotlight at them, which only yielded a reply from their spotlight. Another grenade from Tower 20 fell inside our wire this time. With that challenge I retrieved our M-79 and dropped a grenade in front of Tower 20. This brought a grenade in our wire in reply. I returned two grenades in quick succession in their wire which was replied to by a grenade in front of our tower.

I surveyed the situation. Tower 20 was in a corner of the perimeter and the perimeter road passed through a large, open area behind their tower. I felt confident in my abilities with the M-79, so taking careful aim, I dropped a grenade in the road BEHIND Tower 20, just off the base of their tower. Needless to say, they did not reply to that one and no more grenades were exchanged. Either they thought I was too damned good or too damned stupid, but they chose not to press the issue and we were never again bothered by Tower 20 putting grenades in Tower 19's wire. From that point on, they always kept their grenades to their own front and away from our wire.

New Tower 19 was the scene of other insanity and drama. On another occasion Ronnie Hard Dick, Hud and I were on duty there. At dark, there was a lot of helicopter activity over the installation. The compound had a "cyclops," which were Huey helicopters with immense spotlights mounted on them. They would fly around at night, often with no running lights which made them practically invisible. Then with the flick of a switch, the spotlight came on, illuminating everything below in a brilliant beam of light. From our vantage point all we could see was this large beam of light moving strangely across the landscape with its source somewhere in the dark sky. If the cyclops spotted inappropriate activity it would open up with mini-guns and work the area over before turning off the light and moving on. It was an impressive sight.

On this night, the cyclops was prowling around the perimeter wire barely forty-feet up. It would fly past in the darkness, flash on the light and open up with tracers that bounced in all directions when they hit the ground. It was a strangely beautiful sight when viewed from a safe distance but this cyclops was paying so much attention to our perimeter that it was uncomfortable. It flashed over our wire, past Tower 19 almost at the same level with us. We watched it coming with its spotlight on and, after it zoomed past us it began a quick turn about and looked for all the world as if it was going to make a gun run back toward the tower. We couldn't believe it would open fire so close to the tower but no sooner had the thought crossed our minds than the cyclops came back and hovered over the wire in front of Tower 19, then opened fire with its mini-guns. A staccato clattering and a steady stream of red tracers hosed through the wire. We were shocked! The bullets were ricocheting all around the tower and "pinging" off the steel plates. We ducked behind the steel walls and carefully peered over the edge. The cyclops hovered in our front, spraying the wire with careful precision. It was beautiful and it was scary because we didn't know if they were shooting at something we should know about or just putting on a show for us. Regardless of the reason, we had front row seats whether we liked it or not. As quickly as it came, it disappeared but it proved to be an omen for the night ahead.

Things calmed down. Hud went off duty and was asleep on one of the bunks in the tower. I was second shift so Hard Dick and I were still up smoking a doobie or two. I was sitting in the guard chair looking west over the compound towards an area of Dong Ba Thin where there was an ARVN basic training facility. Cambodian soldiers were trained there by the South Vietnamese Army and as I looked at the twinkling lights of that camp, I saw a bright flash and a shower of sparks over one of the barracks. I knew immediately it was a rocket. I'd seen enough of them while on guard to recognize the flash and the sparks. I told Hard Dick we were going on Red Alert before we heard the sound of five distinct detonations. He was impressed at how I knew that.

The siren blew and the whole compound went on alert. Then mortar rounds began to come down around flight line behind us. They came in groups of ten rounds about ten seconds apart and kept coming. I could see how they "walked" the incoming rounds across the runway and made several large "X's" across our compound. As we watched in awe and fascination, I kept looking to our front, keeping an eye on the perimeter in case any sappers tried coming through our wire. It was one of the worst attacks I'd seen since being there and we started putting up flares to illuminate the perimeter while people began coming to man the bunker line.

By the time the rounds stopped falling, it was time for my shift to end, so I turned things over to Hard Dick and laid down on the bunk to sleep until standing my next watch. I heard officers come up in the tower as they always did during a Red Alert but I slept. They played around in the tower and Hard Dick entertained them until things quieted down. Poor Hud slept through the entire thing and we had to tell him about it the next morning! He didn't believe it. We learned the next day that the first hit on the ARVN camp had landed in a Cambodian barracks and killed five and injured twenty-five others.

We managed to make our runs to the car wash but more times than not only heroin was available. A number of guys who smoked cigarettes began lacing them with smack. I had been fooling with the stuff off and on, being as careful as I could as I'd seen too many others get screwed up on it and I didn't want to go that route. Since smoke was becoming difficult to find, the heroin became my backup. As the rumored brigade stand-down became a reality, work in the office diminished considerably. One afternoon I wandered down to the mail room to talk to CW Stinson who by this time had moved into my room. I mentioned I was going back to the hooch to roll up a doobie and he said "Put some of this in it" and handed me a vial of heroin. I decided "what the hell?" and took it. I walked back to the hooch, rolled me a smack joint and smoked it.

I returned the vial to CW and went back to work, sitting at my desk feeling good. I don't know how long I sat there but I began to get that queasy, nauseous feeling in my stomach. Panic began to creep into my brain as I considered the sight of me puking right there in the office. I had to get to the shitter and in a hurry. No one was paying attention to me so I grabbed my hat and headed out the door. As soon as I got outside it came and I puked right outside the office door. After that I headed for the shitter once again but puked a second time at the end of the personnel building. Once more to the shitters! Again I puked, this time in the ditch alongside the road. I finally made it to the shitter where I continued to vomit.

In a matter of minutes I'd vomited four times and felt miserable but there was also a sense of relief. I sat in the shitter trying to get a grip before I went back to work. From that point on, I vowed "No more smack!" I decided never more would I feel it drop from my nasal passages into the back of my throat and then try to wash the bitter taste from my mouth. I would just smoke my pot and do psychedelics. Once I composed myself I headed back to the office. Having puked at the office door and all the way to the shitter I was sure I would have some explaining to do when I got back but no one had even noticed my absence. I just walked back in and resumed my work.

It was about this time we lost one of our favorite beach destinations. Vinnell Beach eventually obtained such a reputation that it was closed down. One afternoon while we were there and the entire place was occupied with heads, the Army intervened in the person of some unknown full-bird colonel who arrived in his jeep with his driver. He proceeded to walk through the beach and order people out of the area. Since no one wished to confront his authority to do what he was doing, people packed up and left. From our spot up in the rocks we witnessed what was transpiring and not knowing exactly what was going on we evacuated with everyone else. After that day, Vinnell Beach was closed off. We didn't appreciate being denied this little escape from Vietnam.

10

"Who is this chick? Where the hell am I? What am I doing here?": R&R #1

In March 1971, Ski and I were looking forward to our R&R. We'd submitted our requests, and received orders to go on 16–23 March, flying from Cam Ranh to Tan Son Nhut and report at the R&R center at Camp Alpha. We'd decided to go to Australia after hearing it from Hard Dick, Ralph and JC but the same machine that churned out our R&R orders also ground out other orders as the war went on and these influenced events in our lives. Throughout December and January we had message traffic in our offices referring to an ARVN operation named Lam Son 719. In February news broke that the ARVN were invading Laos to cut the Ho Chi Minh Trail. This was Lam Son 719 and U.S. Forces were supporting it including the diversion of a large number of U.S. aircraft to fly support for the ARVN. Regular in-country flights suffered as a result.

We were aware of people in our company who'd missed flights to Saigon for R&R because of the backlog of people requiring flights and the lack of sufficient aircraft for transportation. Since Ski worked in the orderly room arranging flights for new men in our unit being sent to their assigned units, he had some contacts at the airport and reassured me we would not miss our flight departing three days ahead of our reporting date for R&R processing.

After morning formation on 13 March 1971, Hard Dick pulled up outside our hooch with old #22 and Ski and I climbed in and sped off to 14th Aerial Port in Cam Ranh where we bade Hard Dick farewell, grabbed our bags and entered the semi-darkness of the terminal where a varied assortment of crowded humanity stood, sat, or mingled. Groups of newbies in their new, green fatigues and baseball caps looked about with uncertainty. There were old-timers in faded and worn fatigues, battered boonie hats and M-16s slung over their shoulders. ARVN soldiers stood around jabbering to each other while a few Vietnamese women sat nearby comforting wide-eyed children.

We flew out on a C-130 packed with hot, sweaty people that made the air stuffy but we were trapped and no relief to be had. An hour later the landing gear whined, clumped into place and the pilot announced our descent into Tan Son Nhut. After landing we taxied to a point where the engines shut down, and the rear doors opened, flooding the interior stifling with heat.

Buses took us to the terminal where we claimed our bags and waded into a milling mass of humanity. We fought our way through the crowd and made our way outside where we were immediately surrounded by a crowd of Vietnamese lambretta drivers.

They milled around us jabbering and yelling until Ski fingered one and said "OK, get us out of here!" He led us to his lambretta and we climbed in the back while he started it and pulled out into the traffic. "You take us to Camp Alpha" Ski yelled at the driver so as to be heard above the traffic. We sat back and watched the sights pass by. It was obvious we weren't in Cam Ranh anymore. The streets had curbs and there were regular stateside cinderblock barracks as well as the wooden ones and even a swimming pool. The traffic was almost entirely military vehicles with the ever-present Vietnamese lambrettas weaving in and out.

Ski leaned over to me. "There's no sense spending three days at Camp Alpha. Let's go to Saigon." I agreed so he gave the driver $5 to get us off Tan Son Nhut and take us to Saigon. He promised to make good for us but he had to switch vehicles first. We agreed and he took us into a Vietnamese section of Tan Son Nhut that was dirty, trash-ridden and a stark contrast to the military areas. We pulled up to a long building with shuttered windows and a small station wagon parked out front. The driver shut off the motor and went inside. The building hardly looked inhabited but several small Vietnamese children stood in the doorway looking at us.

In a few minutes he returned with another man and we were instructed to get into the back seat of the station wagon, hold our bags in our laps and hunker down. The driver and his friend got in the front and we were off. From inside we caught glimpses of buildings going by and I saw the hangers of the airport and roof of the terminal building as we passed. Then the driver told us to get down and I caught a fleeting glimpse of the main gate as we sped through. "OK, OK," our driver said. "Where do you want to go?"

"A hotel, a good hotel" Ski replied.

The driver seemed to think we wanted a whorehouse and after several stops we finally made it clear to him that we really wanted a hotel and not a whorehouse. He drove on and in a few minutes we pulled up in front of a decent hotel beside a big house that was a USO facility. This was more acceptable and we paid the driver, climbed out, and checked in.

We spent our time at the USO, walking the neighborhoods and visiting nearby vendors. On the street we were besieged by a dozen little Vietnamese boy-sans selling drugs, women, black market merchandise and other products and services. The language barrier was difficult when it came to the word "NO" as it seemed there was no equivalent word in the Vietnamese language.

At the hotel bar Ski met a fellow in Navy dungarees. His name was Rob and he had just returned from an Australian R&R. One thing led to another and Ski invited him up to our room to enjoy a smoke since the people he was with were all juicers. We spent the afternoon in our room digging Rob's music, smoking and listening to the story of Rob's R&R in Sydney. He related stories that were similar to those we'd heard from Ralph and JC Arthur. He told us of a very nice commune he'd stayed at with nice girls in residence and good facilities. We had the address of the place where Ralph and JC had stayed but we took note of the address Rob gave us: 257 Bourke Street. As the afternoon faded into evening Rob left us so Ski and I ventured to the USO one last time before retiring to our room to smoke the last of our stash and going to bed. Tomorrow was our day to report for R&R processing.

That morning we checked out and walked to the main street where traffic was flying past. All we had to do was stand on the curb with our bags and three taxis pulled up. The drivers squabbled amongst themselves before we selected one and climbed in his car. After we settled on the price of the trip and made it clear that we did not want any girls, drugs or black market deals, he drove us to the front gate of Tan Son Nhut where Camp Alpha was located.

We climbed out, grabbed our bags, paid the fare and walked to the gate. We were nervous. The MP by the gate house halted us and asked for ID cards and orders which we produced. He glanced at them, handed them back and told us to proceed. Once past the gate, we hailed a lambretta and were whisked off to Camp Alpha.

There we checked in at the gate and proceeded to a building where there were two windows and a crowd of people milling about. One window was where you checked for flights leaving that day and the other window was for flights leaving the next day. We checked in and were told to meet in front of the building at 6:30 p.m.

Camp Alpha was controlled chaos and reeked of Stateside Army. The buildings and barracks were white painted cinder block, the ground was asphalt with curbs and concrete sidewalks and there were suitcases everywhere with soldiers in all manner of civilian and military dress. The facility was set up in a large square with three barracks forming a "U" and the open part facing the processing building. In the center was a large air-conditioned NCO-EM club that was always crowded. We waded into the confusion.

After lunch we went to the barracks to take a shower and change into civilian clothes. Since we couldn't take our fatigues out of country we had to pay to have them stored. This was handled by a Vietnamese contractor located in of one of the barracks rooms where we stored our fatigues and boots. The air-conditioned club was packed so we didn't attempt to find a seat in there. We did find a bookcase with free paperback books in front of one barracks so we settled back on a bench in the shade to pass the time.

About 6:00 p.m. we joined a crowd gathering in front of the processing building and at 6:30 p.m. a couple of NCOs came out with R&R orders. Everyone fell silent as they spoke up with a barrage of instructions about processing, then began calling off numbers and those whose numbers matched proceeded into the building. Ski and I heard our numbers and joined the procession. Inside we funneled through one of several lines where our orders and shot records were checked. From there we went into a large room filled with desks and reminded me of my high school days. We stashed our bags in racks provided and scrambled for seats.

We were lectured, instructed, ordered, asked and filled out forms, signed our names, and finally we were ready and, as usual, officers and NCOs were allowed to go first. After they had filed through the door into the next room, the enlisted men were released one row at a time.

We proceeded through the baggage search, were metal detected, and I had my wallet and pockets searched, and finally sent to another room where everyone else was waiting. We sat through another lecture and, more instructions before we converted our MPC back into real honest greenbacks. From there we checked our bags and waited for the buses to take us to the plane.

When we heard the buses arrive, the doors were opened and the call came for officers first and since everyone was in civilian clothes and we all looked alike, Ski and I got in line and filed out to board a waiting bus with the officers. Within a matter of minutes we were off past various buildings until we found ourselves on the airfield, rolling down the runway to a Pan American 707 bathed in spotlights. When told to board the plane everyone rushed up the stairs into the plane. We scrambled for seats and staked our claim. Real, live, round-eyed stewardesses walked the aisles and we were all pretty crazy by then.

Once aboard, the engines wound up amid a roar of applause and when the plane began to roll forward, we cheered. We taxied down the runway and we yelled. When we gained speed and zoomed off into the blackened night sky we were screaming at the top of our lungs! The plane rose into the darkness and we watched the lights of Ton Son Nhut drop away below us. The flight was uneventful with the exception of a late night stop at Darwin to refuel and stretch our legs.

The light of Monday morning filtered through my window as the occupants came to life and the stewardesses distributed a hot breakfast. We noticed the increasing number of buildings on the ground below indicating we were close to our destination. Then we saw the Sydney harbor bridge, the opera house and tall buildings reaching up to greet us. The stewardesses prepared us for landing although we were more than ready already. The engines geared down as the pilot announced our arrival and in a few short minutes we were bumping down on the runway and taxied to the terminal.

A man entered the plane to welcome us before we disembarked. When the call for officers came, Ski and I carried off our bluff and strutted off the plane in our best officer style and made our way through the terminal, where we were subjected to a cursory search, had our bags checked and were on our way. We entered a long waiting area with large glass windows where we were directed to put our bags on a waiting bus and get aboard. There was little to say that we weren't actually in the States other than the fact that the bus driver wore Bermuda shorts and he was sitting on the right side where the wheel was located instead of the left.

The drive into Sydney was exhilarating and as we got into the city, the excitement level on the bus increased. Someone would see a car driving alongside whose occupants wore short skirts which caused a rush of soldiers to one side of the bus with much drooling on the windows. Another shout and someone would see several girls in Hot Pants strolling along the sidewalk which resulted in a rush to the other side to the bus. This went on all the way to the R&R center.

We rolled through downtown and up to a large, two-story building that looked like a parking garage. When they stopped we filed out, were ushered into the building for processing and told about the fun things to do in the six days we would be in Australia. We converted our currency then the order of business was hotel reservations. Ski and I planned to get a hotel, rest up, enjoy some good food, then check out the communes recommended by Ralph and JC or Rob, the Navy guy we'd met in Saigon.

When it was over the call came for officers to proceed to the reservation desk in the back of the room so Ski and I followed through with our little ruse and were practically first in line. Our reservations were confirmed and we were instructed to get our bags and board a bus so we hurried down the hall to where the luggage was, grabbed our bags and headed for the door. A driver directed us to one of the buses parked along the curb. We hurried out and boarded only to find that the bus was empty except for the two of us so we sat down and waited.

As I looked out the window of the bus, my attention was attracted by the sight of a lovely, petite young girl about 5'2" with long blonde hair and striking features. She was standing at the corner talking to a guy who was obviously a G.I. finishing up his R&R. In a moment he left her and entered the building. I nudged Ski and pointed her out. As he looked in her direction she looked towards us and yelled "Hey! You guys are freaks! Come here!"

This caught us by surprise and we weren't sure if she was really talking to us. I motioned as if to ask "Who, us?" She motioned to us again and said "Come here!" So we went to check her out. It turned out she was from the commune Rob, the Navy guy in Saigon, had told us about and that the place was only a few blocks up the street. Her name was Janet Carr and she was more impressive up close: small, with an impish smile and a lovely voice that oozed from her mouth. It was not what you expected from one so small. She was quite convincing so Ski and I forsook our hotel for the commune at 257 Bourke Street. After all, we figured we could always find a hotel.

She stepped between us, took our arms in hers and we walked along talking about where we were from and other topics. Janet talked about the commune and all the good dope she had. She'd already been up three nights "tripping" on LSD and couldn't get enough. We came to a main street filled with traffic and since it was the reverse of what Ski and I were used to in the States, I began to blunder across the street since the direction I looked in was clear of traffic. Janet grabbed me and saved me from walking directly into oncoming traffic. She knew this was a GI trait and it wouldn't be the last time she would save me from blundering into traffic.

We arrived at the commune located in two unimpressive townhouses in a section of row-houses. One had a balcony from which flew a home-made Stars and Stripes with a peace sign in the blue field where the stars usually were. We entered and were given a tour. The house was a three-story affair with bedrooms on the top floor, living rooms at street level and kitchen, bedrooms and bathrooms on the lower level which opened onto a small, enclosed courtyard. In back, one wall of the courtyard had a hole broken through it that allowed access to the courtyard and townhouse next door which was similar to the first.

We were introduced to young ladies who were residents of the commune as well as other American GIs who were staying there on R&R and finally ended up in Janet's room at the top floor of the second house. Ski and I needed to talk things over so we went into the hallway to discuss the situation. To stay at the commune would cost us $40 each for the six days

The 257 Bourke Street Commune was composed of the two buildings with orange doors.

and this price included our rooms and one good meal a day. Ski was ready to rumble. Besides, Janet wanted to "trip" with us and I hadn't tripped with a girl in ages, particularly one who was providing the "acid," so we decided to stay there for a few days and if need be, relocate later. With that settled we paid our $40 each and were given a room to share. Janet wanted to treat us to an acid trip so we made a date to trip with her and her roommate that evening.

We then ventured into the city to explore. It was mind-boggling. Used to sand, heat and small wood and sheet metal hooches, we'd been dropped into the middle of a large, modern city in a matter of hours. We made our way up to Kings Cross where we were told "it" was happening.

When we returned to the Bourke Street commune we were greeted like part of the family. I found a guitar and played some tunes. Janet liked that. As she sat at my feet enthralled with my guitar playing, I began to see her in a different way than what I had seen earlier. There seemed to be some "chemistry" there. As I played, she began to sing and I was knocked out by her voice. She had a very unique sound and I was entranced by her singing. We worked well together. As evening fell, there was a cookout planned in the rear courtyard. I played guitar while the burgers cooked and I could tell Janet was attracted to me. At one point I took a break from playing and went to the washroom. She followed me and we made small talk as I washed my hands. When I turned to face her she looked up into my eyes and told me that her boyfriend's name was also Roger and he was also a GI she'd met several weeks earlier. No surprise there. It was a strange coincidence that my relationship with my Janet back in the States had been developing at this same time and I explained to her that my Stateside lady was also named Janet. We both chuckled over this irony. It was at this time that we decided that for the next several days I would be her Roger and she would be my Janet. The pact was sealed with a kiss.

I tried to remain above the situation because I didn't want a R&R romance. My personal love life was confusing enough without further complications. Besides, she told me her boyfriend was a GI she'd met on R&R so I knew there must have been others before me and would be others after I left. I didn't feel like being another one of her guys so she could pin my picture on her wall with the others. I planned to have a good time but "Love 'em and leave 'em" was the order of the day.

I was introduced to Renny Vorsa who was a beautiful, tall, red-headed girl. She was the housemother to the group since she owned the two

Renny Vorsa and her boy friend, Neil, our "house parents" at the Bourke Street Commune.

10. "What am I doing here?": R&R #1

townhouses. Renny had been working as a waitress and hair dresser when the R&R flights began coming to Sydney. Her job brought her into contact with GIs and she began to see that many of them needed something more than a hotel. They needed a touch of home with home-cooked meals and a family atmosphere. With that realization she came up with the idea of the commune. After pooling her resources she bought the Bourke Street townhouse and in no time her endeavor was a success, so much so that she was able to pay off the mortgage and purchase the neighboring townhouse. With her boyfriend, Neil, they ran a tight ship. Neil was very muscular and well-built and could easily take care of any problems that might arise in the house but he was always ready to assist. He kept order and no one wanted to get on his bad side for it was clear he could take care of himself. They were great friends to everyone whether commune residents or R&R personnel.

The cookout went well and Janet's roommate appeared during these festivities. Her name was Sue and she was blonde but a little on the plump side and fell in love with Ski. I could tell he wasn't exactly thrilled with her attentions but at this point he didn't care because the free acid was the biggest attraction. After the cookout we retired to Janet and Sue's room located conveniently across the hall from the room where Ski and I were bedded down. The LSD was some stuff they called "Honolulu" and it was blotter acid that had been carried around in a purse and smelled like perfume and tasted like it too, but we chewed it up and swallowed it.

We collected on the balcony outside their room and watched the traffic. I could feel the acid coming up the back of my neck as it made its

Tripping with Janet the "Acid Queen."

way to my head. Janet decided we should go down to the park and I should bring the guitar and play some tunes. I replied that the park was fine and the guitar idea was too, as long as I didn't have to carry it. Janet readily volunteered to be my "roadie" and carry the guitar so we trooped through the house, out the door and down the sidewalk, feeling good, skipping along, yelling and laughing. By the time we'd walked two blocks to the main street, I was absolutely blasted and I could tell that Ski was in the same condition.

We turned the corner and headed up the street past stores and people on the sidewalk. The traffic noise assaulted my ears and I was fast losing touch with reality. I felt so obvious, almost as if I had a neon sign on me reading FUCKED UP AMERICAN GI ON R&R. My better judgment told me to go home and go to bed but my better judgment had to compete for my attention. I looked at Janet and my mind kept screaming "Who is this chick? Where the hell am I? What am I doing here?" Ski was just as blasted, but I knew him and he was my grip on reality. It was a total mind-fuck because hours ago we were in Vietnam and now, thanks to the wonders of modern transportation, we'd been dumped in the middle of a modern city with its lights and noises and people. Needless to say we were unprepared to cope.

Janet grabbed my hand and we crossed the street to the park. By this time, it looked like an entirely different place than the park Ski and I had visited that afternoon. It was now a land of shadows and trees and bushes and dim lights and fountains and faceless people in the dark. There was an eerie silence in comparison to the city noise a few yards away. We sat on the steps around a lighted fountain and I struggled to make my fingers play the guitar. I no sooner played one song when Janet and Sue wanted to go somewhere else. I was content to sit and play the guitar but they could not sit still. Sue took the guitar and dragged Ski off into the shadows. I stood up to face Janet and she kissed me. My system was pulsing with LSD and I hadn't been with a woman in some time so I was taken off guard. She smiled at me and took my hand. "Let's find Sue and Ski."

We wandered off through the darkened bushes until we found a dimly lit pathway. As we followed the path we could hear Ski and Sue in the darkness and almost ran right into two drunken old, men. One was tall and thin with shabby clothes on while the other was short and plump and dressed much the same way. They were hobbling along arm in arm and singing rather loudly when we ran into them. We must have surprised them as they jumped back when they saw us. We stood there warily eyeing each other and my heart sank as I anticipated trouble. Suddenly they both grabbed the hats from their heads and shakily bowed in unison. "Good evening my lady, good evening young man" they chorused in unison.

"Good evening to you, kind sirs" Janet replied as she bowed to them.

10. "What am I doing here?": R&R #1

"Hope you will excuse us" the tall gentleman said. "I'm seeing that Maurie gets home OK."

"Beautiful evening, isn't it?" Maurie spoke up.

"Certainly is" I managed to respond, somewhat shocked at this turn of events.

"Are you visiting in our fair city?" the tall man asked me.

"Yes I am. I just arrived today."

"I thought you might be an American serviceman" he went on. "I hope you enjoy our city and country."

"Thank you, I am." I replied.

"We must be on our way now. Have a good evening." they said as they linked arms and wandered off down the path singing their song.

I was blown away by this little encounter but I didn't have much time to dwell on it as Ski and Sue came up at this moment and before I knew what was happening, we were off again up to Kings Cross which never seemed to close. The sidewalks were crowded with American GIs stoned out and drunk, prostitutes, women and people of the night. Janet carried the guitar, strumming it and singing loudly even though she didn't know how to play the thing.

She'd saved my life several times as I blundered into traffic and she pulled me back before I was hit. She could see how freaked out I was and I kept asking to go back to the house. Janet finally told me to loosen up. "No one is going to mess with you! You're on R&R. You've earned a week to blow off some steam and we all know it so let it blow!"

This bit of common sense calmed me. "Look…." I told her. "Ski and I have been living a completely different reality and overnight we are in a whole new place. It's a little too much to handle all at once!" She could understand that. After we'd wandered all over Kings Cross, we finally went back to the house. I felt better as we neared the familiar ground at 257 Bourke Street and since hunger was starting to gnaw at our stomachs, we stopped to buy a bag of hamburgers, French fries and some sodas before going back up Bourke Street.

We went to the kitchen where we ate. When finished, Janet and Sue dragged us into a bedroom off the kitchen where the walls were covered with aluminum foil and a strobe light pointed upwards presenting quite a sight. Ski and I collapsed on the bed. More people began trooping into the kitchen and the noise level grew as residents returned. Janet and I went upstairs to the living room where we collapsed on a couch. She fell asleep almost instantly and I lay there wide awake watching the cartoons in my head as the residents slowly found their rooms and silence eventually fell over the house. It was 4:00 a.m.

I laid there thinking about my first night in Sydney. It had been a real blow-out. I didn't know where Ski and Sue were as I lay there and watched Janet sleep. She was like no lady I'd ever met. She was pretty much "on" all the time. Sleep for me was impossible because my mind was wide awake, and while my body cried for sleep, my mind was not interested. It was getting light outside and I watched the sun come up over the city. It was a beautiful Tuesday and Vietnam didn't even exist. Gradually the house residents awakened and when I heard people thumping around in the kitchen I left Janet and ventured downstairs. Sandy, a rather large girl, and Rhonda, who was far more attractive, were making coffee. I visited with them while enjoying a cup of coffee that put new life in me. I washed up and went out to the rear courtyard to find Ski coming through the hole in the wall. He survived his night and was ready to face another day.

He'd slept with Sue but had his eye on Rhonda although she was with a big, burly GI at the time who would be returning to Vietnam soon so Ski planned to pick her up. He was willing to continue with Sue if it would help me with Janet. I told him whatever Janet and I had shouldn't be contingent upon his relationship with Sue. I knew Ski would not stay with Sue with so many other good-looking and available young ladies around.

Sue had to work that morning, so left as we ate breakfast. Janet also had to work but she decided not to go in order to stay with us. We then went downtown and followed our route of the night before up to Kings Cross. The Cross was full of head shops, stores and hippies and we explored everything. There were young hippie girls hawking for various head shops and handing out literature and flyers. This was Janet's job since she hawked for one of the head shops.

The day passed and I had to admit that I found her more attractive the more time we spent together. Gradually I learned that her parents were French, having left France when she and her twin sister were three. Her mother had passed away and her father at that time was operating an auto parts business in Perth. She had sung in the Australian production of "Hair" and done some vocal work with various groups that eventually brought her to Sydney.

That night we stayed straight because Janet had been tripping for four consecutive nights. Such were the hazards of living at the commune. By this time the GIs in the commune were becoming better acquainted, as one group would depart and another arrived. They were all great guys and we sat around the dinner table and talked about the World, Vietnam, life in general and the benefits of Vegemite. Some of them were infantrymen while others flew helicopters.

Several were just back from flying cover missions for the ARVN operation Lam Son 719 in Laos.

A few had been shot down in Laos and one fellow had been shot down three times in one day!

Janet, Sue, Ski and I made our way to a coffee house in the Cross called "The Ball Pants" where we sat in the smoky, darkened interior and listened to a variety of live music; it was nearly 3:00 a.m. before we got back to the house. Ski and I trudged up to our bedroom headed for bed. Janet and Sue were in their room next to ours and as I got ready to turn out the light, Janet crawled into my bed and beckoned me. Ski smiled as I turned out the light and slipped into bed.

Wednesday morning Janet went to work. That afternoon we walked up to the Cross. We were still little burnt out by all the activity of the past few days, but we explored the head shops, talked to girls on the street and finally walked to a small park at an intersection where there was a large fountain. We sat to rest and while there we could hear faint, far away voices yelling "Hey! You guys!" We looked around but could find no source of the voices. Finally we looked up. The building on the corner to our left had apartments in the upper floors and about eight floors up we saw two girls hanging out of the window waving. Once we determined they were indeed yelling and waving at us, they began to motion and yell "Come on up!" We decided "what the hell?" counted floors and went across street to the building.

We took an elevator to the eighth floor, stumbled around the hall until we determined the door we wanted, then knocked and entered. Two girls were there. One was a regular knock-out lady, but as always seemed to be the case the other was rather plump and plain. The apartment was a typical head palace with day-glow posters, black lights, etc., all over. They put on some music and we learned they had some real pot to smoke so Ski and I enjoyed a joint which was a nice change. They also had some acid to sell so we purchased some of that. After an hour or so of talking and smoking we made our departure and went to find Janet and Sue as it was time for them to get off work. As we walked to Bourke Street we talked. Ski was very interested in the one girl at the apartment we'd just left and he was itching to latch on to someone other than Sue.

That night after dinner the four of us sat in the living room contemplating our evening.

The whole group was gathered since there were new people in the house as another R&R flight had arrived and there were new GIs and new girls in the group. Now that her latest GI boyfriend was gone Ski had made inroads with Rhonda. He talked her into tripping with him later. Ski, Sue, Janet and I did up our acid and planned on spending a nice evening at the house but the demand for acid grew as others also wanted some. Janet wanted more and Ski and I knew we could get some at that apartment so we decided to pick some up there. It was about 11:00 p.m. and since the acid we had ingested was not quite coming on we piled into a cab and went to Kings Cross.

At the fountain we climbed out of the cab and could see lights in the apartment eight floors up so we zipped up on the elevator. When the door opened we stepped out and found the apartment door standing wide open with black lights shining forth and George Harrison blasting from the stereo. We entered and were greeted by several girls and found the plump girl we'd met that afternoon. She directed us to the bedroom down the hall.

The bedroom light shone brilliantly at the end of the darkened hall and we entered to meet another R&R GI. He recognized that we shared this connection and an immediate rapport was established. While I talked to him, Ski was talking to the girl he had the eye for. While this was going on, Janet and Sue waited uncomfortably in the living room.

Once the deal on the acid was concluded I returned to the living room. Ski followed me and pulled me aside. The girl he was dealing in the bedroom wanted to trip with him and he wondered what to do about Sue. I told him it was his choice and to play it the way he wanted. He returned to the bedroom but when I returned to Janet, she sensed that something was afoot and immediately began to argue with me about what was going on. Somehow, she knew that Ski was going to dump Sue and accused me of helping him. I realized that our little conference in the hall probably reinforced that idea in her mind but I tried to explain that I had no involvement in Ski's actions. However, logic did not appeal to her and she grabbed Sue and they promptly left.

Here I was waiting for some acid to come on and she was flipping out! I felt there was a point of honor involved and I followed them onto the elevator to plead my case. Janet could not be moved but Sue seemed absolutely mystified by the whole affair so I tried to reason with her. She didn't mind if Ski didn't want to be with her and she didn't understand Janet's attitude. We left the building and Janet sat on the curb. I tried to reach her but she tuned me out. Finally, I gave up. "OK, Vick" I said "Be that way. Come on Sue, let's you and I go to the Ball Pants." Sue was agreeable and begged Janet to come with us. She obliged so we walked to the Ball Pants.

That place was jammed when we got there. A fellow was playing guitar and singing and we squeezed through the smoke and people to find a place to sit down. No sooner did we get settled than Sue met one of her friends. This guy was all right and when we left there he came with us. He soon invited Sue to go somewhere with him and she happily went with him. This turn of events lifted the pall of gloom from Janet since Sue was happy and I was Mr. Wonderful again so we marched up the street arm in arm as the acid came on.

A few minutes later she spied Ski climbing into a taxi with his new girl and another couple. "Ski!" she yelled and fairly dragged me to the taxi before I knew what was happening. Ski looked uncertain as we approached but I explained developments to him. They were off to the beach so we climbed in the taxi with them and sped off into the night.

At a darkened beachside park we climbed out of the taxi and could hear the ocean rumbling and splashing nearby. By this time we were pretty zonked as we scrambled down the steps and onto the sand. Everyone was having a good time. Ski and his group took off for some rock ledges along the edge of the beach and disappeared. Janet tackled me and we rolled in the sand and made love on the beach while an old man sat on a nearby bench oblivious to it all.

When we had spent ourselves, we waded in the surf then headed for the rocks to find Ski and his group sitting up on a pile of large boulders making cosmic designs in the sky with the glowing tips of their cigarettes. We stayed until Janet wanted to leave, so we left the group, climbed down out of the rocks and headed across the beach for the parking lot. My mind was muddled by the acid but I felt that I was lost. My watch said 2:00 a.m. and there was no traffic on the road let alone the sound of any nearby. I had no idea where we were or which way to go. We trudged up a long, sloping road past silent houses. Janet wasn't bothered by our predicament so I took heart in that. When I inquired as to how we would get back to the house she said we would hitch-hike as if the lack of traffic hadn't impressed her.

We plodded on until the headlights of a car approaching from behind illuminated us. We stood back and Janet stuck out her thumb. The car was a French Citron that looked like an old 1934 Ford sedan pulled up and stopped. The door opened and we climbed in the back seat. In the front were two long haired freaks and in the back were two girls. We slammed the door and were off. We talked with them for a moment and a brief friendship developed, sealed by the glowing joint that was passed back to us. One fellow in the front seat had some pot and this friendly and familiar item made me feel better. I was also able to negotiate the purchase of a matchbox full that I stashed away for later use. About a half-hour later we reached a busy street where they let us out. We thanked them and hurried to the corner where we flagged a passing taxi. In no time we were back at the Cross.

We wandered to the Ball Pants where I did a little guitar playing on a borrowed guitar. The folks in attendance appreciated my music and the manager asked me to come back and play on another evening which I consented to. I talked to Janet about singing with me and she agreed, providing we could work up some material.

Eventually we walked back to Bourke Street and retired to my bedroom. We were still wired and I suggested we do a toke or two of the smoke

I'd purchased earlier. Janet got a pipe and we settled back on the bed. I learned she'd never really done much pot smoking. She'd gotten strung out on acid, but she was much nicer smoking pot than doing acid. Soon Ski wandered in. His deal hadn't worked out so we got him buzzed and carried on until the wee hours of the morning.

Janet went to work on that Thursday. She'd received several boxes of flowers from her other Roger but I felt secure. That afternoon Ski and I walked to the Cross and ran into Janet on the street. She was hawking for her store and looked like a fairy wood nymph prancing up and down the sidewalk in her bare feet, long flowing dress, and her black hair falling about her shoulders. She hugged me and immediately took us to her store where we met her boss. After exchanging courteous conversation we headed to the street where Janet went back to work. I ran an errand to another store while she and Ski sat on some steps. When I returned she was ready to finish up work so Ski and I headed for the house.

Ski acted as if he knew a secret and with a little prodding on my part he was induced to tell me about the conversation he'd had with Janet while I'd been gone. It was mostly about me and how much she had come to care for me, even love me. This was news to me and I wasn't sure just how real her feelings were or if she was just playing the role. Ski insisted that she was really flipped out and wanted to come to the States to be with me. I let it pass, not wishing to become overly involved in something I felt was a passing fancy on her part rather than a true emotion.

When she came home that afternoon she was more mellowed out than she had been since we'd met and, although she was very sweet, she did not betray any of what she had confided to Ski. That evening we went to the Factory for music, tunes and fun. When we got home she came to my bed and we slept the first good night's sleep I'd had since arriving in Sydney.

Friday was the day of a big outing Renny had planned for us and we were up early and ready to go. The plan was to go horseback riding in the country, then picnic on the beach with a few things in between. Everyone chipped in money and Neil rented two station wagons. It was early and we were all like a bunch of kids as we waited on the sidewalk outside for the cars to arrive.

Janet was in her full glory and we were planning to trip again as I had two hits of blotter acid.

When the cars arrived we piled in and off we went. By this time Ski was making his move on Rhonda and the two of them with Janet, Sue and I were in one car with Eddie, a new guy. As we zoomed off through traffic and out across the harbor bridge, I could sense an uneasiness with Janet. She was gradually befriending Eddie and although I knew he was attracted to her, he remained quiet because he associated her with me.

10. "What am I doing here?": R&R #1

She asked Eddie if he wanted to trip with us and he said he did but he had no acid. Ski was also in a predicament because Rhonda wanted to trip with him but he only had one tab and needed another. Janet was determined that Eddie should trip with us and when I offered to split a hit with her and split my other hit with Eddie and Ski, she got mad! This was beyond me. She got mad and clammed up. I tried to explain but she said if she couldn't have a whole hit she didn't want any. She was acting like a spoiled child, pouting and getting an attitude because she couldn't get her own way, because she couldn't have a whole tab.

Undaunted, I declared that I would do my hit by myself and sell the other one to Ski, which I proceeded to do. She rode in silence until we reached the ranch where we were to go horseback riding. The place looked like portions of northern Arizona I'd seen with rocky hills and scattered woods. Since there were so many of us, we rode in shifts. Ski, Janet and I went in the first round.

When we got back we waited while the others took their turns. Janet was friendlier and even kissed me but she was not the girl I'd gotten into the car with at the beginning of the day. She talked to Eddie trying to use the old "jealousy" routine on me but I maintained. She finally wandered off and Ski and I got back in the car. Eddie soon joined us and I decided that, since he was a GI, we had more in common with each other than either of us did with Janet, and that it was better to be his friend since Janet seemed intent on using him against me. Ski and I talked with Eddie, explained the deal with Janet, and he understood. He was a decent guy and he had a matchbox of pot and some hash so he offered up a number which we accepted. The three of us crept off and got a buzz on, which cemented the bond between Eddie and me.

When we returned to the car, the horse riding was drawing to a close and Janet came running up to us. She told me she'd secured two hits of acid from someone in the other car and she was happy again. We took off for the beach. In the car the acid was divided up and Janet assumed the role of "ring leader," supervising the whole show. Our spirits soared as we sped through the Australian countryside. The ocean loomed up before us and we zoomed along the streets and past stores that lined the beach before pulling into an open area to park and everyone piled out to scatter down the beach. There were others swimming and a few surfing but the place was far from crowded. The picnic lunch was spread out and we hungrily devoured it.

As the sun dipped lower in the sky, we prepared for the return trip to Bourke Street. Janet had come down somewhat and her attitude was more tolerable. When we got home we all collapsed in the living room. There were new people at the house and one girl in the crowd was a new face. A short visit with her revealed that she was from Peoria, Illinois. Far out! I used to live there, had family there and my buddy Captain Marvel was there and, as it turned out, she knew my cousin! A small world indeed.

That evening we mellowed out in the living room. Janet still played her game and I was growing tired of it. If she wanted to be with Eddie then be with Eddie. If she wanted to be with me then be with me. This playing both ends was growing old fast and I got tired of waiting to see which way she was going to go and quietly left the room. I walked out into the backyard, climbed through the wall and entered the other house. I trudged up the stairs and stood wearily by my bed when my ears heard the sound of someone rapidly coming up the stairs. In a flash, Janet appeared rushing in from the stairs and grabbed me in a flying tackle. We tumbled upon the bed. She looked deeply into my eyes. Nothing was said. We curled up together.

She had come through! I expected the whole deal to be done with after the weird vibes of the day and when I left to go to bed without her, I'd left the decision to her. She could sleep with Eddie, she could sleep alone or she could come with me. In the end, she followed me. That was a surprise, yet it was still troubling. If she was really playing a game, why continue it when presented with the opportunity to end it? I began to realize that perhaps

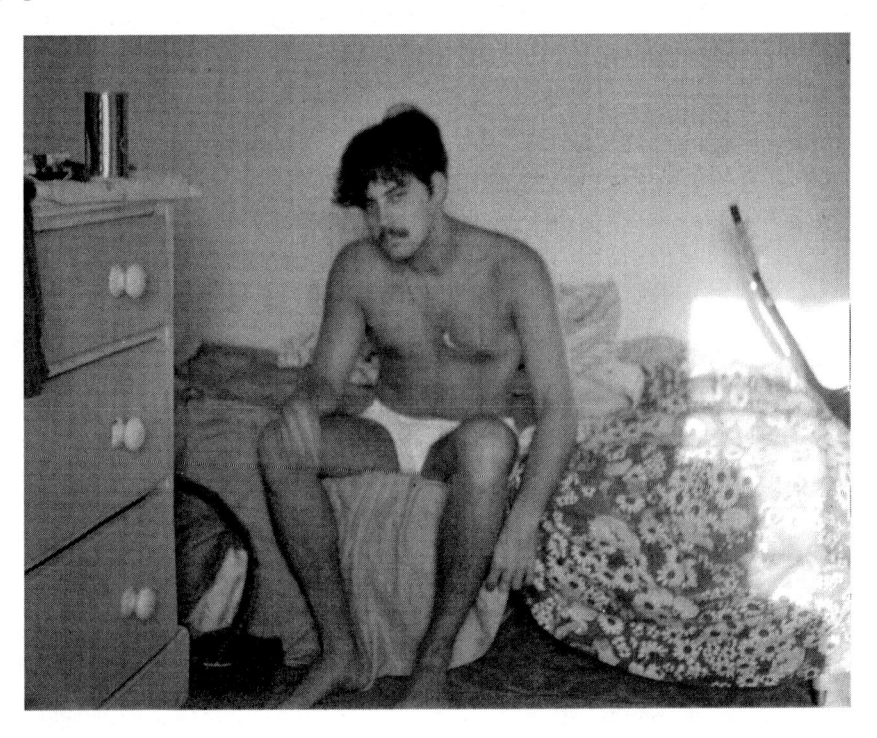

This image gives clear evidence to the fact that I only got about 12 hours of sleep the entire week I was in Sydney.

10. "What am I doing here?": R&R #1

I had been right about some things and wrong about others. Maybe she wasn't playing a game. Maybe she really felt something for me as Ski had said.

Saturday and the realization sank in that our R&R was drawing to a close. Ski and I were working in different directions now and Janet was more herself. She persisted in her Samaritan attitude toward Eddie and insisted he come with us when we wandered up to the Cross and bought some fried chicken at a Colonel Sanders' Kentucky Fried Chicken. We ate in the little park by the fountain where Ski and I had met the girls in the eighth floor apartment several days earlier. The day was anti-climactic and we ended up in the kitchen for supper and a long talk over hot coffee.

We walked to the Cross again where we made our way to the Ball Pants. When an opportunity presented itself, the proprietor asked me to play some tunes and I accompanied Janet on several songs. It was a sweet moment for both of us. From there we walked back to the house where we found Eddie. He suggested we retire somewhere quiet and smoke some of his hash. We went to my room. I found Janet's pipe and Eddie filled it with tobacco and hash. Ski wandered in blasted on acid and talked to us for a long time. He and Rhonda were tripping again and Ski was fucked up but she was blasted and ready to rape Ski but he was hiding from her. He left and then Rhonda came in, with tears on her cheeks. She was hunting for Ski and we denied having seen him. She left and Ski returned. We smoked some more Hash while we played card games, listened to the radio and casually let the night pass. Ski and Eddie eventually disappeared and as the streaks of dawn filtered across the sky Janet and I slept.

Sunday was our last full day of R&R. It was hard to see it all come to a close and it felt as though I'd always been there. Vietnam was so far away, like a dream I'd had. Almost as soon as I'd opened my eyes Ski was in the room sitting on my bed. His hair was wet and he was laughing and wanted to talk. Rhonda had caught up with him in the living room where he'd been talking to the blonde from Peoria. She wanted to trip too, so Ski tripped with her and Rhonda. The two girls eventually took Ski to task and fucked his brains out. That led to the three of them taking a shower together and he'd just gotten out of the shower.

It was quiet because it was Sunday. Janet had an errand to run and while she was gone, Ski and I with some other GIs from the house went for a walk to take some pictures. We walked all over the city, up to the Cross, visiting places where we'd spent good times but would probably never see again and spent time with buddies who we would never see again. People who were complete strangers a few short days ago were now old friends. I loved them all but I had to go. I'd found a new fondness for Australia and its people.

When we returned to the house, Janet was there smiling and quiet which was a different side of her than I'd seen that week. Ski and I collected all of our belongings and were ready to go when the time came. We then gathered in the living room to watch TV. Janet and I lay on the floor and she curled up in the crook of my arm. I felt a sense of sadness in realizing that our last day was closing around us and on the morrow we would fly back to our raggedy hooches in Dong Ba Thin.

She looked up at me and I was surprised to find tears in her eyes. She looked intently into my eyes and spoke quietly. "I love you, Roger, I really do. Please stay with me. I don't want you to leave." She lowered her head to my shoulder and sobbed softly. This freaked me out! It was not what I expected. She was no longer the hard-core Acid Queen I'd met that first day. She was a warm, soft-hearted woman and I knew that she was indeed feeling everything she'd said.

Now I was perplexed. She loved me. I could love her. I'd found it easy to do so, but had kept my emotions in check. She wanted me to stay and now that I knew she loved me, I wanted to stay, to forget Vietnam, the Army and just stay. I could do it, just stay AWOL until we had come to some conclusions and then go back. There was so little time left to make a decision of such potential importance. I felt awed and a little afraid. The immensity of the decision and all of its repercussions flooded my mind.

Once I recovered from the shock I could realistically weigh the matter. Regardless of how much I wanted to stay, I knew I couldn't. I had to go back. There was only one right way to do it and several wrong ways. I told her I loved her too, but I couldn't say more. I had planned on having a good time with her and leaving. I did not want to write her or try to hold on to anything that could never be. But now she was saying that she loved me and wanted us to be together. We spent the night in a quiet understanding. I felt she understood what I was thinking and although we both felt a sadness, we were happy on the outside.

As the evening wore on everyone gathered in the kitchen for another long discussion of anything and everything that came up, interspersed with liberal applications of smoke, and coffee.

We laughed until our sides hurt. As the evening drew to a close, Ski and I said our farewells to everyone and retired to our room where we collected our belongings for the last time. We went to bed early partially because we were pretty strung out but also because we had to be up early to report for processing at 10:00 a.m.

I felt sad to see Monday morning sunshine pouring in the window. I felt like a condemned man realizing the end is near. Ski woke up and got dressed. I watched Janet sleep and remembered that first morning I had lain on the couch downstairs watching her sleep. Was it only a week ago? It

10. "What am I doing here?": R&R #1

felt like ages. As I watched, she opened her eyes. There was sadness in them and we kissed and made love.

I got up and dressed while Janet went to her room to do likewise and then I took my bags to the other house before meeting Janet in the courtyard out back. She was quiet, restrained, yet smiling. We sat in a swing and talked. There seemed to be so much to say and yet neither of us could find the words. I felt like we were at a funeral. Ski and I said our goodbyes, promised to come back and gathered our bags. Janet placed her arm in mine and we silently walked down the same four blocks the three of us had walked up only a week ago.

When we arrived at the R&R center, it was swarming with soldiers and girls and waiting buses. If ever there was a scene from a million war movies, this was it. The GIs, hung over, fucked up, burnt out, milling about with dazed, glassy eyes, awaiting the call; the girls, some crying, some happy, but all attached to someone who was about to depart. People were hugging and kissing and crying and I could hardly believe that I was actually a part of it. My mind felt like I was sitting in a movie theater watching the whole thing on screen. Janet and I barely had a chance to speak to one another before they called us inside to begin out-processing. She said "I'll see you when you come out" and kissed me.

The processing was brief and simple. We changed our money back to greenbacks and were briefed. They called the officers to board the buses so Ski and I continued our farce and filed out with them. I half-way expected her to be gone. It might have been better, but she was still there. She grabbed me as I came out and we walked silently following the crowd. The bus drivers were counting off numbers as the buses filled and we walked until we were at a bus that I could get on.

The moment had arrived. I turned and kissed her. She said "Write to me, please write to me." This was unexpected as we had not discussed corresponding. I did not want to be another of her "pen pals" and was satisfied to leave her to be a pleasant memory. But in light of recent developments between us, she was asking me to write to her rather than the other way around. I agreed. We kissed and hugged before I boarded the bus. She smiled and her face slowly blended into the crowd of faces around her. I found a seat next to Ski who was in a pensive mood. I could see her through the window. She waved and mouthed the words "I love you" and was then swallowed up in the sea of female faces that had turned the buses into islands.

The engines started and we began to roll. We sped up the street we'd just walked down and past the commune at 257 Bourke Street. Janet's flags still fluttered from the balcony of her bedroom. We sped silently through Sydney while everyone sat lost in thought. It was such a contrast to the bus load of loud, noisy GIs who had come in a week earlier. I knew there was probably more than one broken heart in the bunch. We were a bus load of wasted, burnt out GIs returning to our war while all around us Sydney was awakening to another Monday work day.

At the airport we unloaded, boarded the plane and in no time were in the blue Australian sky zooming northward, happy, but tempered with sadness. Vietnam would look good to us after a mad week loose in Sydney. I realized that Dong Ba Thin was becoming my "home." I hated to admit it to myself but it was true and I had only just come to that realization. I felt like I was going "home" and it would feel good to get back to my own little corner of the hooch.

The return flight was uneventful. We stopped in Darwin for an hour then headed into the evening sky bound for Vietnam. It was dark when we were informed that we were close to Tan Son Nhut and we watched the city lights below and flares drifting in the sky. When we landed there was no doubt about where we were. The smell of Vietnam greeted us when the door was opened and there was no denying that it was all over now. We were hustled onto waiting buses and sped into the night, past the same lights, hooches and buildings we'd passed a week ago.

We arrived at Camp Alpha, unloaded into the same building we had processed out of, exchanged our greenbacks for MPC, then went through customs. We had everything from our pockets to our bags searched and were then turned out into the night. Ski and I got a bunk in a barracks. Everyone was subdued. We left our bags at our bunks and then went out for a walk. We were both still blown away by it all and took some comfort in the fact that we experienced it together and could reassure each other that it all really happened. When we returned to our bunks, I climbed into bed. It was very anti-climatic to climb into an Army bunk in a barracks after a week in Australia. As I lay there thinking I couldn't help wondering if Janet was leading some other stoned GI around Sydney at that moment.

The next morning we were rolled out of our bunks early, retrieved our fatigues from the shop where they were stored and changed clothes. It felt good to get out of civilian clothes and back into the familiar comfort of our faded fatigues and scuffed boots. I pulled on my boonie hat and I felt at home. It was hard to admit it, but it was good to be back. We collected our bags and headed for the front gate with visions of beating the rush to get an early flight to Cam Ranh. We got a lambretta, zoomed to the airport and were disappointed to find that flights were still scarce due to the ARVN Laos operations and everything was booked except the evening flight at 6:00 p.m. We booked that flight then wondered what to do to kill the day.

We left the airport, hired a lambretta and as we drove off, Ski flashed a $5 MPC note in front of the driver and promised to give it to him if he would get us some smoke and drive us around. He agreed and took us to a run-down area of Tan Son Nhut where we scored a deck of Sin Tan Jins. These were regular commercial cigarettes that had been packed with pot instead of tobacco and repackaged. The balance of the afternoon we drove around in that lambretta getting stoned and trying to comprehend Australia.

The flight back that evening was no big event. In no time we were at the 14th Aerial Port again. The terminal was bustling as usual. We grabbed our bags and tried to call our company for transportation but as to be expected, we couldn't get through. It was dark and almost 9:30 p.m. The main gate to Cam Ranh would close at 10:00 p.m. and we would be trapped in Cam Ranh until morning unless we got through the gate before it closed and it was several miles away. We could never walk it and carry our bags so we took the situation in hand and hiked out to the road hopefully to hitch a ride.

A van stopped. He was going to Cam Ranh Army on down the peninsula but he could take us to Myca Bridge which was near the checkpoint. We climbed in and arrived at the Cam Ranh side of Myca Bridge at 9:45 p.m. where we got out and I began to feel we wouldn't make it out of Cam Ranh before the gate closed. We were so near and yet still so far. At that moment a civilian jeep pulled up with a Korean fellow inside. He could take us through the checkpoint to the highway but from there he was not going our way. No sweat! The guards only checked our orders and waved us through. We drove into the night with the sound of a machine gun chattering in the distance and flares drifting over the hulking shadows of the mountains beyond.

I was a little frightened since we were loose, unarmed and at the mercy of whoever or whatever might be lurking in the shadows of the night. At the highway intersection we tried to persuade our Korean friend to take us to Dong Ba Thin, only a few miles down the road, but no amount of pleading or money could convince him. He left us on the side of the road in the darkness, we watched his tail lights fade as he sped off into the night heading south. During the day, the place where we stood swarmed with Vietnamese and lambrettas but now it was deserted. We waited until we spied a light approaching from Su Chin. It was a lambretta and we flagged him down. A little cash and we were off. The lights of Dong Ba Thin never looked as good as they did gleaming ahead of us that night. At the main gate to our compound we unloaded our bags.

There was only one security guard on duty and he was not familiar although we knew most of them. We fearlessly approached the gate. The security guard was a newbie and very young. He was uncertain about our arrival and asked where we had come from and what our business was. We exhibited our ID cards, our orders, and convinced him to his satisfaction that we were legitimate. It was barely past 10:00 and the newbie guard agreed, motioning us through.

As we started to walk the long distance to our company area, a ¾-ton truck pulled up with Bob Mathison driving and a load of guys from our company in the back. He was a former hooch mate of Ski's and a former water truck driver, was now one of the security guards and were we glad to see him. We exchanged greetings, climbed in the back of the truck and rode to the 18th BDE area. Now it was really over. We were "home." Upon arrival at our hooch, we found no one around but succeeded in tracking the group to Ralph and JC Arthur's hooch where we walked in and surprised everyone. They gathered around us while we tried to find the words to condense a week's worth of insane events to a few minutes.

I felt like I'd never left Dong Ba Thin. Sydney, Janet, and the Bourke Street Commune were all very far away at that moment almost within the realm of fantasy. Things at Dong Ba Thin were the same except that the brigade stand-down was progressing, and in my absence, old Ronnie Hard Dick had gotten a chance to go home early and took it. I didn't even get to say "good-bye" to him which saddened me. I would miss him but I was happy for Ronnie.

Australia Janet continued to haunt my thoughts. She'd asked me to write her, so I did. I figured a letter to Janet might help so I poured it all out on paper and mailed it. I took heart in the fact that I still had another R&R and intended to take it as soon as possible. But how did this affect my growing relationship with Stateside Janet? She still wanted to meet in Hawaii. Could I go to Australia again, and how could I explain it to her if I did?

11

Stand-Down, Let Down

Rumors had circulated about brigade deactivation and in November 1970 one of the brigade's three groups was deactivated and sent home, leaving only two groups in the brigade. By spring of '71, word was that the 18th BDE would be deactivated which came as a shock to many of us, but the reorganization demanded by U.S. efforts to disengage in Vietnam meant the 18th and 20th brigades would be deactivated. Remaining engineer groups would then be incorporated under the direct supervision of Engineer Command in Long Binh.

The attitude at 18th ENGR BDE HQ Company was very loose as stand-down loomed on the horizon. Men were shipped out for new duty assignments almost every day; others sent home. As a result, the company population dwindled and that meant guard duty came around more often. It appeared that no one wanted to rock the boat so a "live and let live" attitude prevailed. The nightly walks continued although the group was reduced.

Beyond the theater area, where C.W. and Bo Long's hooch was located, there was a large open area where a volley ball net had been strung following the decline of the Dong Ba Thin golf tournaments. This was adjacent to a large bunker that looked very much like a beached whale. At night this bunker was the gathering point for the remaining heads in the company and after dark it was alive with activity. We would get buzzed, sit and play guitar, sing or just lay atop the bunker staring off into the clear, cobalt blue night sky. Other times we sat and watched helicopter gunships work out around the perimeter. Occasionally we could see the ARVN compounds under attack atop the mountains to our west. They were too far away to hear the detonations, but the tracers, parachute flares and flashes from explosions could be clearly seen.

On my return from Sydney I found letters from Stateside Janet in my accumulated mail while I still had Australia Janet fresh in my mind. I went back to work, but everything was changing due to the stand-down.

At this time, Doc Stance was trying to sell his idea of the Dong Ba Thin

Anti-Doobie Band. As a sort of official kick-off, he arranged for his program to be presented to BG Schrader and the officers at the officers club on the night of 16 April 1971. Bo Long had quit the group a short time before and CW and I carried on. We practiced and toked up at the big bunker, then went and performed in grand style for the general and his staff. They loved us. We were smash hits! The officers were very appreciative of such talent in their company, however, hanging over it all were two facts: (1) the company was dying as stand-down approached, and (2) we had no idea what would become of the group.

The most notable effect of this stand-down was another empty bunk in my hooch since my hooch-mate Chris Wilson, had been sent to 35th Group in Cam Ranh. The most startling news of all was that the pink mescaline he'd had spoken of had arrived! Chris told us he could get a load of it from his California connection although no one put much stock in his claim. We'd heard this before from others but we never saw any. However, Chris got 250 tablets, in the mail before he was sent to 35th Group and it was premium stuff. People seemed to be eating them like cookies and they produced an experience of cosmic proportions, they became known as "cosmic cookies." We gathered in Ralph and JC Arthur's hooch and mellowed to the music. The party eventually moved to the top of the big bunker where we settled back with a few pipes.

In the office the following day, I learned my job was being phased out and I would become the driver for old #22 since Ronnie Hard Dick was gone. After work, CW and I had to practice music with Doc Stance. It was decided there was enough time to do some cosmic cookies and be on the downhill side before going to practice. It was 4:00 p.m. when we did this and we had to be at the dispensary to practice at 8:00 p.m. But at 8:00 p.m. we were still utterly zonked despite it being time to practice. Neither of

The "old-timer" with 11 months in-country.

11. Stand-Down, Let Down

us wanted to go, but we could not fail to show up either. We had to face the Doc, stoned or not.

We put on our "straight" faces, and went to the dispensary while the Mescaline continued to work its magic. We planned to beg off and explain that we'd already been practicing and were rather burned out and hoped we could get in and out before we blew our cover. Doc was sympathetic, though our explanation was rather implausible. However, he had things to discuss with us and he kept us there while he talked on and on. We sat there hallucinating and trying not to look at each other. We were on the verge of uncontrollable fits of laughter the whole time and, if our eyes met, we got the giggles. It seemed like hours, but Doc finally let us go. If he had any idea of our true state of mind, he never let on. By this time, however, we didn't much care anymore.

Not long after this, C.W. Ralph, Bo and I went to the mailroom and plugged in the electric guitars and amps. We were all pretty zonked on Chris' cosmic cookies and proceeded to turn the volume up as high as it would go. This was quite effective in our altered states but it eventually led to blown fuses which crippled the group since replacement fuses could not be readily obtained.

We still had acoustic guitars but the electric guitars were prime implements for live performances.

With stand-down progressing, we had little confidence that the group would continue.

The brigade stand-down gave us a lot of idle time and our numerous perversions ran amok. The fate of the Dong Ba Thin Anti-Doobie Band seemed uncertain but Doc assured us he was going to the 35th Group and we would go with him, therefore the band would carry on. Although he had yet to do anything about our duty assignments, we continued to practice as he had hopes of presenting us to the command group at 35th Group to convince them to support the idea and allow us to carry on. We had little faith that the idea would continue much longer.

As the official stand-down date approached, Doc told us he was actually going to 45th Group in Da Nang but that he had arranged everything with the 35th Group and we would carry on with their surgeon but 35th Group had no interest in supporting the band and the Dong Ba Thin Anti-Doobie Band died a slow death through neglect and lack of interest. It was in its final death-throes at this time but all the equipment was still stashed in the mailroom. Since we had blown the fuses in the big amps and there appeared to be no chance the band would survive the stand-down, CW, Bo and I ended up loading the disabled amps and equipment into old #22 and drove madly to Nha Trang one afternoon to turn them in to the special services. And so, with that, the 18th ENGR BDE Dong Ba Thin Anti-Doobie Band faded away.

Stand down of the 18th ENGR BDE had a profound effect on us at Dong Ba Thin. It meant our company was deactivating and some people found themselves short-timers before they knew it since the time they had left in-country didn't merit their being reassigned there. Thus, they were sent home early. For those who remained it meant being reassigned to another engineer unit to finish their tours. I was in a unique situation because I had extended four months to get an early out from the Army. I already had eleven months in-country at this point which made me eligible to go home with the brigade. However, if I did that, I would still have almost a year of my enlistment to finish stateside before I could get out of the green machine.

What a situation! I could leave the Nam early, but stay in the Army for my full enlistment, or stay in Vietnam and get out of the Army five months early. I didn't look forward to doing stateside Army time after having lived all those months in-country, and I clearly remembered those Nam vets back at Hunter Field who all wanted to go back to Nam rather than stay in the stateside Army. I did consider the possibility of going home, if I could go back to my old duty station at Hunter Army Airfield in Savannah, Georgia, but when they couldn't guarantee this I decided to stick it out where I was. Besides, I was almost ashamed to admit that this place had become "home" to me so I made up my mind to stay and do my time. My family would never understand my decision, so I never told them about my opportunity to come home early.

The next step was to figure out who in our little circle would be leaving. Hard Dick had already gone and it appeared as if almost everyone was going home, including Ski, Hud, McGregor, Mathison, Arthur, Schives and others. Only Ralph, C.W. and I were hanging on, but we were in a good position since we were allowed our choice of reassignment. We could go to Long Binh and work at Engineer Command Headquarters with the starched fatigues and stateside Army attitudes; or we could go to 45th Group at Da Nang, although that transfer would be made by convoy over VC infested roads, and ending at a place we did not know; or we could go to 35th Group in Cam Ranh. The choice was easy. Cam Ranh was only about ten miles from us and we were already familiar with both the area and 35th Group, so we decided to request assignment there even though it was considered to be the worst choice.

So we were bound for Crusader Switch, the telephone switchboard name for the 35th Group phone connections. Although we had dial phones, they didn't work. To make a call you picked up the receiver and talked directly to an operator, giving them the number you wanted to call, or the switchboard you needed to connect into. Crusader Switch was the 35th Group switchboard.

Before Ski, Hud and Schives departed, we headed out one Sunday to Market Time Beach for one last blow-out. It was just like old times, made

11. Stand-Down, Let Down 171

even better thanks to the supply of cosmic cookies. I hated to see them go but I was happy for them as well. I would miss Ski since he and I had shared many things during our time together.

As stand-down proceeded through April 1971, certain jobs ceased to exist; the people working those jobs were moved to other jobs or shipped out. Since our manpower was steadily declining, we could not continue pulling guard duty, so permanent guards were brought in to man the guard towers. We'd volunteered to render this service nightly on a permanent basis and the lifers attributed this to our highly motivated sense of duty. But this request was denied.

My job at S-4 was one of the first to fall victim to the stand-down; almost as soon as the schedule went into effect, my files were packed and shipped to Long Binh. With my files gone, so was my job. Since Hard Dick had already been sent home, I was assigned to be the S-4 driver. This was acceptable since all the driver did was maintain the vehicle and drive S-4 people wherever they wanted to go. It wasn't long before I found that Ralph had inherited the personnel office driver's job after JC Arthur left so we carried on.

The biggest equipment turn-in I was tasked with was turning in all of headquarters company's weapons since I was an armorer. As stand-down continued, and with permanent guards on the towers, we were told to turn in our weapons. This was not reassuring since we'd pretty much lived with our M-16s since the day we arrived in the unit. We loaded several hundred M-16s and two 81-mm mortars in a truck, the unit armorer provided paperwork, directions, and Willie, from our office, was sent with me to assist. We drove to Cam Ranh Army where we unloaded the weapons, checked all serial numbers, reconciled the paperwork, and reloaded them in the back of the truck. From there we took them to another point where we turned them in, checking off the serial numbers again.

Our company area looked like a ghost town. Hooches of many old friends stood empty and forlorn. Only a skeleton crew existed and we smoked openly in broad daylight in our hooches, and on top of the bunkers. The big bunker across the road from the officers club was still considered to be the place and remaining heads gathered there to smoke, play guitar, lay back and watch the war.

As stand-down progressed, CW moved into my hooch amid the accumulated debris and leftovers from many former hooch-mates. My corner was fairly clean but the rest of the room was cluttered with Army gear, three beds, tons of comic books, magazines, paperback books, clothing, towels, assorted furniture, junk and trash. It had become so trashy that you could not walk from the door to any part of the room without walking on or over something. It remained a mess until we left and then it was up to the aviation unit occupying our area to clean it out.

Of course any good stand-down was not complete without a formal ceremony to mark the passing of the unit. The 18th ENGR BDE was no exception. The ceremony usually consisted of a lot of generals and high ranking VIP officers in attendance, speeches given, and the emotional furling of the banner. The upper echelon of the dying 18th BDE wanted a big send-off complete with honor guards, color guards and the like. Since no one else wanted any part of the honor guard duty, those of us remaining in our company were detailed to provide it and, since our company was merely a skeleton of its former strength, this meant practically everyone would be in the honor guard. Thus, we were mustered and drilled and practiced until we knew what to do.

The day of the ceremony was 24 April 1971; the event was set for 10:00 a.m. That morning I put on clean fatigues, grabbed my gear and made ready for the ceremony. As an after-thought I popped a tab of mescaline. I figured that, after the ceremony, I'd have a good day since we were supposed to go to the beach and have a party. At the proper time we formed up at the orderly room. It was hot already and it would be a killer to stand in the heat and squint into the sunlight. But off we went. We faced a platform filled with generals, colonels and assorted minor ranks while the speaker rambled on about accomplishments, heroic deeds, patriotism, and duty.

My problem was not the heat although I stood there sweating profusely while the weight of my helmet on my head felt as if my neck was being slowly driven into my shoulders. My eyes hurt, my head hurt and I became aware that the mescaline coming on. I could feel it coursing up the back of my neck and into my brain. I was glad when we were called to attention and the brigade's flag was furled. With that, after 68 months of continuous service in Vietnam, the 18th ENGR BDE was no more.* We were called to attention and marched off toward the company formation area, passing the mail room where CW stood grinning at us as we passed.

We were on our own for the remainder of the day. The officers gathered at the officers club for lunch, drinks and more speeches. For the enlisted men, there was a planned trip to the beach but there were so few of us and we had such a lack of enthusiasm that most declined. The heads ended up gathered on top of the large bunker across from the officers club where we smoked. There was something about all of us sitting on this bunker smoking pot in broad daylight while across the street all manner of officers were wandering in and out and all about their club.

Once the stand-down ceremony was finished, we were on our last bit of time at Dong Ba Thin. The skeleton crew was at its barest minimum, the company area was strangely quiet and yet haunted by the memories of so

---

*Schrader, BG Henry, Personal Papers Collection, US Army Heritage and Education Center, Military History Institute, Carlisle Barracks, Carlisle, PA.

11. Stand-Down, Let Down

many people who had once made a barren piece of nothing livable for one another. Many hooches were sadly empty and lifeless, all but the one where CW and I lived. About this time a fellow from the 10th Aviation moved in with us since his unit would be taking over our area. He didn't say much and we didn't see him often but we assumed he figured all the junk in the room was ours. We surprised him. It wasn't ours. It was his.

BG Schrader commanded the 18th Brigade for a year. In preparing a summary of the Brigade's activities during his period of command, he noted: "The Brigade Headquarters did not have a sufficient number of senior staff officers and did not have the strength or functional scope to properly manage a decentralized, technically oriented organization of more than 14,000 officers and men.... The Headquarters did not have sufficient personnel either in the S-1 or the S-4."*

He noted further that the unit commanders at all levels:

> ... are faced with deep-seated problems which have their origin at the national level.... I suggest the unit commander needs more specific guidance in how to control drugs, cope with racial problems, and deal with dissenters, especially at the company level.... Battalion and company commanders need additional training and guidance in these matters. The theater position of trying to eliminate persons with unacceptable habits and traits as rapidly as possible is sound. The USARV policy permitting the unit surgeon to substitute for the psychiatrist in certain instances speeds the process. Additional facilities were recently provided to take the 'bad actors' off the hands of small unit commanders quickly and to hold them until AR 635–212 or other appropriate action could be taken. Everything possible must be done to identify and eliminate the undesirables quickly ...
>
> Lack of 'communication' between officers, non-commissioned officers and enlisted men is often cited as a basic problem in the Army today.... The young men of today will not respond blindly. They want to know what they are doing and why they are doing it. If leaders appreciate this fact and take the time to explain their actions, the vast majority of our men will respond willingly and effectively. The relatively small percentage of dissenters who cannot or will not cooperate must be identified and eliminated from the service ...
>
> The Brigade drug program was pursued vigorously, emphasizing the amnesty program, showing approved drug movies, and inviting drug specialists to meet with officers and men to discuss the drug problem. In January 1971 a program of Brigade/Battalion level drug rehabilitation centers was established employing carefully selected 'contact' men in each company to counsel and work with individuals who desire help. This program had begun to show encouraging results at the time of this writing."†

---

*Schrader, Personal Papers Collection.
†Schrader, Personal Papers Collection.

I'm sure that trying to accomplish his mission while President Nixon was drawing down troop strength was a challenge. No wonder BG Schrader never had "sufficient personnel."

As the end of April 1971 approached, the convoy to the 45th Group departed Dong Ba Thin and I bid farewell to the good CPT Calaber who was going there. At this same time we were notified as to our own dates of departure for 35th Group. Ralph would be the first to go on the 26th and I would follow him on the 27th. C.W., being the mail clerk, would be the last to leave. We three found solace together and spent our last evenings at the Pond smoking joints and watching the sun set behind the mountains. The gang that once trooped out to this location to smoke in the evenings was now down to the three of us.

The following day we hitched a ride over to the west compound to kill a few hours at the PX. While we were walking back to the east compound a flatbed truck pulled up with a bleary-eyed dude in civilian clothes hanging out the driver's window. It was none other than Dan Brozic, an old 18th Brigade vet who had been a security guard before going to work at the west compound NCO club. It was good to see a familiar face from the old times so we climbed on board and he took us to the hooch where he lived.

His room was a cosmic mind-fuck with stereo, black lights, black walls, posters, day-glow paint, etc. But, the biggest surprise of all was finding Ski and Hud there! They were to have left the country over a week ago but had gotten restless at the 22nd Replacement and left, ending up staying in Brozic's room. It seemed there was an Australian band playing at the club where Brozic worked and they were also staying in his building. As usual, this band had two round-eyed girls and the nights held the possibility of lots of parties. So, in honor of our little reunion, plans were laid for a big party that night.

That evening we returned to Brozic's. There was lots of smoke, mescaline and music; we sat back and talked until the Aussie band arrived. Then the party picked up speed. In no time we were barreling along, hell bent for leather, until a faintly ominous sound managed to permeate the volume of music and chatter in the room and sank into my brain. It was a faint thumping that had a strange regularity to it, more felt than heard. "Listen!" I yelled. Everyone hushed and the music was turned down. Then it was clear we were taking mortar rounds! I ran out of the room and my fears were confirmed before I was out of the hallway. I stood in the doorway of the building as CW, Ralph and the others joined me. Mortar rounds could clearly be seen walking down the airfield runway in the east compound, giving off brilliant flashes of light and sparks as they exploded and this was just across the highway from where we stood.

Suddenly their trajectory shifted and the rounds began coming in our direction. Everybody scattered and the Aussies, taking no chances, headed

11. Stand-Down, Let Down

for the nearest bunker while we ran into the hooch until the incoming rounds shifted. The sirens blew red alert in both compounds. C.W., Ralph and I climbed up onto the back of the flatbed truck to watch. We knew things could be hairy in the east compound since it was practically devoid of people and weapons and we could not get to our alert stations since we were in the wrong compound, plus we had no weapons anyway. I never felt so vulnerable in all my life. We figured that we would be missed but we couldn't help it.

There was no way we would be able to get to the east compound until the sun came up.

The M-60 machine guns on the guard towers along the north edge of the two compounds began firing. This was unexpected and usually not done unless in a dire need because the village of Tanh Tonh was only a short distance downrange. The guard towers behind us opened fire with their machine guns and we became even more nervous because we had no weapons. Brozic appeared with a shotgun and a bandolier of ammunition. Then the .50 caliber machine gun at the east compound gate opened up as more mortar rounds dropped into that compound. The .50 caliber continued banging away in ragged bursts, sending red tracers arcing into the night while we began to feel very vulnerable on that truck while the Aussies cowered in the bunker.

Finally, the rounds stopped falling and the machine gun fire ceased. Cobra helicopter gunships were circling overhead and working out around the perimeter. Nothing else occurred so we returned to Brozic's room to continue the party although the Aussies spent the night in the bunker, refusing to come out. The party could not be revived to its pre-alert level so we smoked more smoke, talked about the great send-off that Ski, Hud and Schives were getting and then found ourselves a piece of the floor to crash on.

At first light, CW, Ralph and I said our farewells to Ski, Hud and Brozic and headed for the east compound where we expected a rough reception due to our absences during the alert. But once there, we were surprised to find that no one had missed us. Ralph collected his gear and prepared for his departure to 35th Group. We smoked a good luck number and he was on his way. CW and I watched him leave, feeling ever so lonely now, but my time was also drawing nigh. That evening we walked forlornly to the Pond where we smoked and watched the sun set and we wondered how Ralph was making out on his first night at 35th Group. We knew Chris Wilson was there and Bo Long and a few others, and were sure that he wouldn't be as lonely as we were.

The next day was much like the others. I played around in the supply room which was about the only administrative function of the now defunct 18th BDE. I packed my things, no small chore since I had accumulated a lot of material in eleven months. Once packing was complete, I faced the challenging task of transporting three duffle bags, and a guitar and I wasn't sure how to manage that but wasn't worried since I had only ten miles to travel. The convoy to 45th Group in Da Nang was well on its way and the 18th BDE survivors were on their last gasp. We learned later the convoy to 45th Group was ambushed three times before they got there.

That afternoon I was pleasantly surprised to find that I was to drive a ¾-ton truck to 35th Group and turn it in there which solved my transportation problem. No sooner was this information given to me than MSG Florence told me to get my stuff together and get my butt to 35th Group since the group commander had been inquiring as to my whereabouts. I gathered up my things and headed for the dispensary and personnel office to pick up my records. The personnel office was strangely quiet with only one clerk in the building. I barely knew him through mutual friends. He pulled up my file and looked through it. "I see you took an R&R last month" he said to me. "Got another one coming for extending your tour, eh?" I answered in the affirmative. "Here, you want your R&R back?" he said as he pulled several papers from my file and tossed them in the trash basket. I realized without those papers in my file no one at 35th Group personnel office would ever know I'd already been on R&R. Thus, I still had two R&R's coming to me. Australia was on my horizon again and maybe even Hawaii. I thanked him profusely, took my personnel records and left the office.

This fellow was doing what had been done when I left Hunter Airfield in April 1970 when the personnel clerk removed the records of my two weeks of leave after basic training, effectively restoring that leave to me. I thought nothing of it at the time because I knew those clerks since they were in my company. But here, this fellow didn't know me from the next guy who walked in the door, yet he volunteered to remove documents from my file.

My heart pounded as I went to pick up the ¾-ton truck I was to take to 35th Group and was mildly surprised to find that it was old #22, the S-4 truck in which I'd spent so much time. I signed out the truck, drove it to my hooch, loaded my baggage, said my goodbyes to C.W. and headed down the road turning my back on Dong Ba Thin and all that had happened there.

12

Crusader Switch: 35th Engineer Group

As I drove down QL-1 heading for Cam Ranh I decided to take precautions against being caught without smokes. Cam Ranh, situated on a great peninsula of land, had restricted access, so I had no idea how the boys over there obtained their smoke. As I approached the Myca turnoff, a stop at the old car wash was in order so I pulled onto the shoulder of the road opposite the car wash, pulled out my camera and pretended to be taking pictures. A Vietnamese lady came out of a hooch, scampered across the road, climbed up on the running board and stuck her head in the window. I told her I wanted thirty decks. She hurried back to the hooches and I sat there as traffic whizzed back and forth. Then she returned. I snapped a photo of her as she ran back across the road. It didn't look like she had anything, but when she climbed on the running board of the truck again she began pulling decks out from under her blouse and tossing them in my lap. I put them in a paper sack and handed her the money.

I gunned the engine, shifted gears and took off. I passed the main checkpoint at the entrance and headed for Cam Ranh Army, following the road along the bay, past the supply depot entrances, past the village, and to the only stop light in the whole area at an intersection known as "Times Square." Large, rocky, mountains loomed up in the background with high sand dunes, fields of sand, and sand everywhere. Even from the stop light, I could see the high ridge known as Engineer Hill where 35th Group HQ and affiliated units were located. I drove old #22 toward South Beach and at a small PX turned off to the left on a sandy road leading up a spine of the ridge to the buildings.

Off to my right as I drove up the road was a large, open-air theater and stage built into the downward slope of the dune, creating a natural amphitheater. The backdrop of the blue water and distant mountains was impressive. As I approached the top the first thing that caught my eye was the chapel, an A-frame building to the right, similar to the one at Dong Ba Thin. Behind this was a cluster of graying, weathered wooden frame, single-story

Times Square, downtown Cam Ranh Army. The only stoplight in the whole place.

buildings with large screened windows and corrugated tin roofs. There was a guard house with a guard who ushered me through and then I was in 35th Engineer Group country. My immediate impression again was of an old western mining town in the Arizona desert. The weathered frame buildings, wooden duckboard sidewalks, sand, rocks and activity helped carry off the impression.

I headed for the S-4 office where I'd been instructed to report, parked the truck and went inside. The first person I saw was Chris Wilson, my old hoochmate. He was smiling as I entered and I stopped to speak with him before going to see the NCO in charge. I was informed I would begin work the following morning and was then introduced to SP4 Mark Fritzo.

Fritzo was a likeable fellow, tall and thin with blonde hair and a boyish look. It seemed I was to take over his job as he was being assigned other duties. After introductions and conversation I was taken to one of the hooches and assigned a nice, big corner room where only one other person was staying then left to myself. I unloaded the truck, hauled my stuff inside and made myself at home. Then it was time to turn in old #22 at the motor pool below the dune where we were located.

When I returned to my hooch I was surprised to find that my

12. Crusader Switch: 35th Engineer Group

The entrance to 35th Engineer Group area.

roommate was Chris Wilson. We visited while I unpacked and settled in. Chris said there were a good many heads in the company and it seemed to be the same type of scene we'd had at Dong Ba Thin. I asked about Ralph, and Chris said he was there somewhere, living in an adjacent hooch. I was anxious to find Ralph so Chris directed me to his room. Since it was just past quitting time and everyone was wandering back to their hooches, I walked over to find Ralph's room and see if I could turn him up but his room was locked.

I walked around straining to see a familiar face without any luck. Finally, Chris and I went to eat. Figured I'd find Ralph there, but no Ralph. On our way back to the hooch who did we see gliding up the duckboard walk but Ralph. He'd been assigned to the civilian personnel office and worked with hiring and supervising the Vietnamese employees used in the company for KP, house girls and shit-burners. He said some of the boys would be going out to smoke before the evening movie and he would get up with us after he ate.

When he got back we headed out. I wondered where everyone went to get clear of the area and feel safe while smoking. It wasn't like going for a walk at Dong Ba Thin. Things here were far more confined since the entire company was on top of this big sand dune. As a back drop there was a huge, rocky mountain that rose majestically behind us, seemingly close enough to reach out and touch. However, it was separated from us by a deep valley. The terrain was shaped like a large "V" with the sandy dune side of Engineer Hill forming one leg of the "V" and the rocky mountain forming the other. They joined at an apex overlooking Times Square.

We walked along the duckboard walk, past the theater area, the dayroom and onto a road. Across this road there was a large, open area where the showers were located. Fortunately Cam Ranh had a water system so the shower had a steady supply of water—no more water trucks or showers without water. Up beyond the showers were the shitters. They were a good hike from the company area and seemed very inconvenient. To the south side of the shitters was a large clump of sand covered with small scrub trees and brush. The other side of the shitters had another, smaller clump of brush. These were the remains of the original contours and vegetation of the huge sand dune that had been here before Army Engineers leveled it and reshaped it.

We walked up by the shitters and casually slipped behind them, following a faint path in the sand to an opening in the brush. We continued

The mountain behind 35th Group. There is a valley between us and the mountain is not apparent in this image. Enemy rockets headed for the storage facilities on the other side often hit this mountain if they were not high enough to get over them.

12. Crusader Switch: 35th Engineer Group

through a little tunnel made by overhanging limbs and foliage until we came upon a whole group of guys in fatigues passing around some pipes. The first person I saw was Mark Fritzo. Ralph and Chris knew a few of the fellows and I was introduced. We sat and I pulled out a few joints to contribute. I chatted with Fritzo, or "Frizzle" as they called him, and was glad that we had more in common than just the S-4.

We clustered in a wide spot where someone had cleared the brush so we could look out over the deep valley behind us. We were virtually on the edge of the dune. The huge mountain across the way lent itself to the scenic aspects of the spot that was known as LZ-1 (Landing Zone 1). The open area in front of the shitters was supposed to be the company chopper pad hence the designation, but it was rarely used as such. The large, brush-covered remainder of the dune provided cover for smoking but I didn't feel comfortable. It was too easy for someone to sneak up on us. A path wound through the dense brush and came out by the officers club. There seemed to be little or no way out of the trap this area could become, but I felt these guys must know what they were doing since we were on their home turf, or sand.

As it grew darker we made our way out in a large cluster around the shitters and back down across the open field. We were in full view of everyone in the theater waiting for the evening movie. Could this many people have been occupied in the shitters at the same time? We hurried down the hill and gathered on a revetment to watch the movie.

The following morning I went to formation with Chris and Frizzle and the folks from the S-4 office. We conducted police call but since the movie-goers here were not as rambunctious as those at Dong Ba Thin, there was not as much trash to pick up in the movie theater area.

I worked in the S-4 office with Frizzle and by this time we knew we were brothers and were better acquainted. He was a young man from Detroit, Michigan, who seemed crazy at times but this was due to his youthful exuberance. He had come to the Engineers from the 1st Cavalry Division when it was sent home and he had been awarded the Bronze Star for rescuing wounded under fire while serving with them.

Work routines at of 35th Group HQ were different than what we kept at Dong Ba Thin. They started at 7:30 a.m., took a half-hour break from 9:00–9:30 a.m., followed by a return to work until lunch at 12:00 noon. We returned to work at 1:00 p.m. and worked until the afternoon break from 3:00–3:30 p.m. Work resumed until 6:00 p.m. after which the offices closed. The half-hour breaks in mid-morning and mid-afternoon were something we'd never observed at the 18th BDE.

For us, these breaks were just another time to go smoke a number. However, because everyone was off for a half-hour the activity in the company made smoking in the hooches or the company area risky. This meant we had to get away to smoke and the only place available at the time was LZ-1, up in the brush behind the shitters.

    I met Ralph at morning break and we trudged up to the shitters trying to look inconspicuous, ducked into the brush and hiked in to the smoking spot. There was no one else there when we arrived so we sat down and fired up. While the view off the back of the dune was beautiful, the scrubby trees and brush offered little protection from the sun so it got

The infamous picnic table, gathering point and scene of much outrageous and inappropriate behavior.

12. Crusader Switch: 35th Engineer Group

warm very fast. It was also evident that no one else was accustomed to smoking much during duty hours or we would have had company. In the course of that first day I had occasion to wander back to LZ-1 again by myself. By 3:00 p.m. it was hotter than hell in there. I felt there had to be a better and more comfortable way to enjoy a smoke but was at a loss as to how and where. I determined to find a less conspicuous and more comfortable smoking spot.

That evening I met more company heads congregated around a shabby plywood and 2 × 4 picnic table on a concrete slab. We made the move up to LZ-1 about dusk looking like a herd of cattle going to the shitters. I did not like doing it that way but the old timers seemed to know what they were doing. We returned to take in the movie and once it was over and everyone scattered, we collected at a point of sand behind a large bunker across the street from our hooches. From this vantage point we were fairly secure and the view at night, across Cam Ranh village, the docks and the bay, was breath-taking.

I worked for two days in the S-4 office with Frizzle until much to my surprise, I found out I was not supposed to be there! When I walked into work after lunch the second afternoon, there was my old boss, MSG Florence. He looked at me and said "What are you doing here? You're working in the wrong office!" For a minute I thought he was kidding but I'd worked for him long enough to know he was not kidding. He said I was supposed to be working in the S-3 office and the colonel there had been calling Dong Ba Thin looking for me!

So I walked to the S-3 building, around the corner from S-4 and adjacent to the group HQ building across from the chapel. I walked into the building and up to the desk of a Master Sergeant. He looked up at me and I said: "I hear you're looking for me. I'm SP5 Durham."

"Indeed we are" he said, directing me to a SFC sitting at a desk near his. I was introduced to SFC Forrest. He was a big man, well-built but with a gentleness about him. I liked him right away. He introduced me to two other enlisted men. These two clerks and SFC Forrest comprised an entire section in the S-3 office. One clerk was a short timer and I was to take his place. The other clerk, a newbie PFC was the typist. They seemed agreeable people and I set about learning what this section of the S-3 office did.

The S-3 was divided into sections, such as the Intelligence Section, Admin section and a Flight Operations Section that handled the aviation assets assigned to the group. Then there was my section, the Construction Projects Section. We kept track of the costs of the various projects the 35th Group had in progress all over central Vietnam. Projects ranged from major construction to simple asphalt road paving. We processed requests for materials, kept track of expenditures and handled accounts for their funding. Each project was suitably authorized, assigned a number, granted a specific amount of money, and turned loose. We then kept records on each project and its expenses, issued orders, revisions to those orders, and moved a mountain of paperwork.

I was assigned to take the place of the clerk who kept the files. He was about thirty days short when I got there so I had to learn fast. There was a typist in our section but he was a newbie and no help to me with the files. My job took much of my attention as I worked with the fellow I was replacing; after about two weeks I'd pretty well gotten the hang of my responsibilities.

But every month there was a computer print-out that each battalion sent us with information we had to transfer to an updated print-out from Engineer Command. It was as big as a Chicago phone book! Our information was provided from the four battalions under us so we had to have that data to update the report. The updating process involved laying the print-out all over a large table, penciling in corrections and changes, compiling two updated copies, one for our files and one forwarded to Engineer Command with all of our data to back up the figures and changes we'd submitted so they would have the most current data for their records. This was a major headache for my little section and usually required a week to make it all happen, only to be repeated the next month. It was no fun and I knew I was going to dread the end of each month.

With the revelation that I was working in the wrong office came the revelation that I was also living in the wrong hooch. This meant I had to pack up and haul my stuff to the hooch next door. They told me I could choose between a small, single room, or move in with a SP4 I didn't know. I felt fortunate to have the choice of my own private room so I took that and moved into what had been a lifer NCOs room. The walls of the tiny room were plastered with fold-outs from various girly magazines. They certainly added a dash of color to say the least. I put my stuff in my new cubby hole with a bunk and wall locker, and barely enough room to turn around in.

I'd just gotten settled when Ralph came to ask if I'd be willing to sell a few of the decks I'd purchased at the car wash. One of the company heads wanted to score some smoke and Ralph knew I had a stash. Since this was for one of the crowd I was joining, I agreed. A short time later Ralph brought Pete Simpson to my room. Pete was from New York. He was stocky, well-built, rather quiet and I sensed he was the kind of man you would want on your side if the going got tough. Pete worked in the personnel office and lived with Tom "Dusty" Dustman. Their room was next to one of the Head Havens, a room at the end the hall of a neighboring hooch, known as "Stigg's Room," because that was where Mike Stigg lived. It seemed there was a scarcity of pot and my arrival with a stash was looked upon as the

12. Crusader Switch: 35th Engineer Group

My hooch for the last five months I was in Vietnam at 35th Engineer Group. Considering the fact this was an engineer unit, the condition of the hooch amazed me.

means of tiding things over. I decided it was best to provide some to Pete to pave the way for my inclusion into this group of tokers.

It wasn't long before I met Pete's roommate, Tom "Dusty" Dustman. He was from Ohio and was a short fellow with black horn-rimmed glasses and a thin, youthful moustache grown to handlebar lengths, very much in violation of Army regulations. We hit it off right away. He was funny and had my kind of attitude; with his boonie hat and loose-fitting fatigues, he was described by Ralph as looking like a "shuffling laundry bag." Pete and Dusty made an interesting pair, Pete being big and husky while Dusty was small and wiry.

13

Like There Was No Tomorrow: R&R #2

After I'd gotten trained up on my job, I looked to take another R&R. When I arrived at 35th Group and processed through personnel I let them know I expected to take an R&R at the end of May and started the wheels turning to get my orders. After my first R&R to Australia and the questions it left unanswered, I felt I had to go back to Sydney to get things straightened out with Australia Janet. My Stateside Janet could wait because I felt if we were ever to get our relationship sorted out, then I needed to devote myself to her and not have any lingering doubts or regrets about Australia Janet. However, since Australia Janet had not answered any letters I was looking to go to Hawaii in late May to see Stateside Janet. Then I received a letter from Australia Janet stating she'd written several times but her letters all came back to her unopened so she was wondering what had become of me. Just to get that letter from her gave me hope. She'd received my letters and wanted to see me again. I knew I had to go back to Australia on my second R&R.

I knew mail coming and going out of the old 18th BDE had been screwed up in those last weeks as many of my friends back home, to include Stateside Janet, had written to say that some of their letters had been returned. Since 18th BDE was standing down at that time and people going home or being reassigned, a lot of incoming mail was returned rather than being forwarded. Thus many of Australia Janet's letters were returned to her. Once I got settled with a new address, my mail began again. With these developments I had to explain to Stateside Janet that I would be unable to make the trip to Hawaii. Then I changed my R&R destination.

Shortly after my arrival at 35th Group, Chris Wilson received another 250 hits of that pink mescaline. With my second R&R approaching I started collecting a stash for the occasion and by the time my R&R date was approaching I had accumulated twenty-seven hits.

On the appointed day one of the S-3 boys drove me to the 14th Aerial

13. Like There Was No Tomorrow: R&R #2

Port to catch the flight to Tan Son Nhut. Within a few hours I was at the terminal, caught a lambretta to Camp Alpha and checked in for the Sydney flight that evening. I spent the day walking around, visiting the PX and sitting on the upper porch of a barracks reading my book. After supper I headed to the processing building and when the flight call came I was ushered into the processing room with the group composing our flight. Once completed, we went to customs for the moment of truth. I popped a hit of mescaline to mark the occasion.

In no time I was on the bus flying along the streets of Tan Son Nhut toward the airport and the Freedom Bird sitting on the tarmac. We boarded and were soon rolling down the runway and cruising into the night. We landed at Sydney Airport at daylight, hurried through customs and on to buses waiting to drive us to the processing center. As we drove I kept thinking about the last ride I'd taken on that bus a few short months ago. The whole trip with Ski that March seemed like a movie I'd seen and now I was re-visiting the scene

We arrived at the processing center and once finished, made my way out of the room while others filed their hotel reservation cards. I already knew where I was going to stay and retrieved my suitcase, guitar, and walked out to the street. My mind flashed momentarily on the first sight of Janet, of her standing by the corner of the building talking to a GI. That corner was empty now. Only a bare few months ago she had walked with me to this building where I left her, never expecting to return. Now here I was again. I could still see her in my mind's eye, her face disappearing in the crowd as I boarded the bus.

The sun was shining and it was late May but it was COLD with temperatures in the mid–40s. I'd forgotten winter was approaching in Australia and had not packed accordingly, so I stopped in a shop and purchased a wool sweater before walking up the sidewalk toward the Bourke Street commune. I couldn't help thinking about the last walk I'd made up that street with Janet and Ski and the tearful return down them a week later. But I was feeling good. My mescaline trip was coming down, it was a beautiful day coming on, and I had a whole week ahead of me, a suitcase full of mescaline and, hopefully, Janet.

I arrived at 257 Bourke Street. It looked just like the place I'd left a few months earlier. I knocked on the door. It was still early morning but I felt as though it could be mid-afternoon as I had no sense of "time." There was a stirring inside, then the door opened and there was Renny in a housecoat. She didn't recognize me at first and I didn't expect her to with the constant flow of GIs spending their R&R's there. But it only took a short conversation to refresh her memory and then I felt like the prodigal son returning home. Since it was early, only she and Neil were awake, having breakfast in the kitchen. I left my suitcase in the front hall and followed Renny to the kitchen where I saw Neil. He remembered me right away. As if to prove to me that he really did remember me, he asked about Ski and how he was doing. I enjoyed a hot cup of coffee with them while Janet was in my mind.

Renny remembered quite clearly the relationship Janet and I'd developed and she asked if I'd heard from her. I told her about the letter I'd received and then Renny said "You don't know then, do you?" My heart sank. I didn't know what she was going to say but I could tell from the tone of her voice that it wasn't good. She told me Janet had been depressed after I left but had cheered up after receiving a letter from me. She'd talked about plans and looked forward to my return on R&R. But then, only a short time before, she learned she was pregnant! With that her entire mood changed. She ended up stealing money from her employer and left town under a cloud of suspicion and rumor. So, she was gone and I was not the only one looking for her. This news only raised more questions in my mind. What had happened and where had she gone? More importantly, how could I contact her? Was she really pregnant and if so, whose child was it? I counted the weeks and months and realized that it could be mine but the timing was so very close and I knew there were other GIs she'd been with to include the other Roger she'd said was her boyfriend at the time Ski and I arrived. No one knew where she had gone or how to contact her.

I sat there with my coffee and mulled over the news. I had to reevaluate my R&R since its purpose was gone. I had a fist full of mescaline, a couple hundred dollars and good friends so I was damn well going to have a good time!

Renny told me to go look at the basement room in the house next door as they had converted it from a bedroom to a party room. I walked into the courtyard, haunted by visions of Janet, and through the hole in the brick wall, into the adjacent courtyard, then walked into the other house. The basement room had been totally remodeled. The walls were covered with aluminum foil, black light posters and a few couches and mattresses were placed around the room. A black light hung overhead and a large cable-spool table sat in the center covered with ashes, incense, matches and candle wax. I put some records on the stereo and laid back to relax, then passed out and slept.

When I awoke I knew I was in Australia. The sleep greatly refreshed me and I went for a walk downtown and up to Kings Cross which was as active as ever. By the time I made my way back to the Bourke Street house, the place was jumping. I met other GIs who were staying there and made my way to the party room where there was a party going full blast.

Before the pipe they were smoking had passed much further, I knew everyone in the room. For the majority, it was merely the fact that we had

13. Like There Was No Tomorrow: R&R #2

Vietnam, the Army and smoke in common. I never got much farther that day. We ate supper there and listened to tunes. It was a trip just getting stoned with some round-eyed girls.

The next day I went downtown to run errands. When I returned to the house I found a group gathered at the kitchen table as there usually was about that time of the day. There were a lot of GIs from all different areas of Vietnam there and we all eventually retired to the party room. I noticed some new faces in the room. The guy sitting next to me seemed totally freaked out. I felt like he must have just arrived in Sydney but he didn't look like a GI since his hair was much longer than was acceptable to the military. I struck up a conversation with him and found he had indeed arrived that morning, had wandered around town for a while until he met one of the girls from the house. She brought him to Bourke Street. His name was Pat Morrison and as he related his story to me, I was amazed.

He'd been a civilian employee working in Saigon for Pan Am Airlines for the past three years and apparently having a good time. Then he began taking an interest in the Vietnamese employees he worked with and it became apparent they were being screwed over by Pan Am, so he helped them create a union. Pan Am took a very dim view of his activities and he was fired as a result. They offered him a one-way ticket anywhere in the world and Pat decided to go to Sydney. He didn't exactly know why since he'd never been there before but decided that was the place; Pan Am put him on an R&R flight and he'd arrived that morning.

He was only just getting a taste, but he was starting out on the right foot. We took an immediate liking to one another and I explained some things about what the house on Bourke Street was all about since he was still a little uncertain as to what was going on. As a repeat visitor I reassured him he was among friends and he decided to stay there until he could get situated. He had a good bit of cash and wasn't too badly pressed financially. I talked to Renny about him. She'd met him since she always knew who was staying in the place but she knew he wasn't a GI and didn't know why he was in Sydney. I explained his situation and introduced them. She welcomed him and told him that the house on Bourke Street would be his home from that point on and he became a member of the Bourke Street family.

As the evening wore on I laid some mescaline on Pat and a few others, then Pat and I hit the streets as the night was young and it was his first night in Sydney. We made our way up to Kings Cross and I took him to the Ball Pants, the coffee house that Janet, Sue, Ski and I frequented on the previous R&R. The whole scene there looked much the same as it had when Ski and I had been there. The bare bulb hanging over the entrance cast a glare across the doorway as we entered the dimly lit interior. There was a fellow playing guitar and a small crowd clustered around the stage but we found a table near the door where we sat talking quietly and listening to the music. Pat was really freaked out. It was his new situation and the mescaline and I could empathize with him since I'd experienced much the same sensations the first night of my first R&R when Ski and I tripped with Janet and Sue.

As we sat talking, a group of people came in and sat near us. I suddenly recognized one girl in their party as Janet's roommate, Sue, who had been a part of that first R&R. For a moment my heart jumped. She and Janet had been very close and if anyone in Sydney knew where she was and how I could reach her, it was Sue. I moved over beside her and asked if she was who I thought she was. It was Sue but I didn't expect her to recognize me so I refreshed her memory. However much to my disappointment she didn't know where Janet was. She did know about her disappearance and reaffirmed her pregnancy but had no idea how to find her now.

Pat and I sat there quietly for a while as we both had lots to think about. Before we left I talked to the manager about coming in to play my guitar. He remembered me and the set that Janet and I had played there on my previous trip and gladly consented to playing at my convenience. Then Pat and I stumbled on our way, making a stop at a Colonel Sanders to buy the biggest bucket of fried chicken we could find before returning to Bourke Street. We stayed at the house for the rest of the night as all the residents eventually wandered in and the festivities retired to the party room. I had gotten a room by this time and it turned out to be the large master bedroom at the top floor of the second house.

On the third day the entire household went on a picnic. This was a weekly event since they usually made an outing somewhere. We bundled up as it was a brisk day and drove out of Sydney in two rented vehicles and went to a park in the country.

The outing was a success and we dragged ourselves back to clean up and look to the evening. After a session in the party room, I grabbed my guitar and Pat and I walked back up to the Ball Pants where we spent several hours and I played music and met a number of fellow guitar players. Pat and I spent the better part of the night there before returning to Bourke Street.

The following days were something of a blur but just when I thought this R&R was going to be a smooth ride with no female excitation, I met Gypsy. It was late in the afternoon while I was walking through Kings Cross. There were lots of girls on the streets hustling for the various head shops, hawking and distributing leaflets trying to get people to visit their establishments. I'd seen Gypsy before on the first R&R and I didn't know her by name but I remembered her face and smile. She was small, with long, curly light brown hair that framed the smiling face of a little girl. She looked

13. Like There Was No Tomorrow: R&R #2

barely a teenager but she was older and much wiser than she appeared. As I walked up the street that day in Kings Cross, I saw her just ahead of me.

I had seen her in the past few days but always across the street or talking to people. On this day she stood there alone, bundled up in an oversized fur coat with a scarf around her neck. I could not avoid her as our paths crossed. I knew what would happen because she watched me as I approached. She had a bundle of leaflets in her hand and she offered me one. For a brief moment our eyes met. She began to lay her sales pitch on me and I replied that I'd already been to the shop, which was true. She said she had seen me before and asked if I hadn't been with Janet Carr a few months earlier. I was surprised by this especially that she remembered me. We talked about Janet for a moment but only enough to find that she, like everyone else, only knew of her recent hasty departure under a cloud of suspicion and had no idea where Janet was. But at that moment, as I watched her talk, with her cheeks rosy red from the chill, I didn't care where Janet was.

She introduced herself as Gypsy Kent which was the first time I had a name to go with her lovely face. I gave her my name and out of the blue she asked me if I knew where she could get some LSD. I replied that I had no idea where any acid could be obtained, but I did know where there was some mescaline. Her eyes flashed. It seemed mescaline would be even better so I told her I could get it. She had to work until 4:30 p.m. so we made plans to meet later and walk to her house. I departed to retrieve some of cosmic cookies from the Bourke Street house.

She was waiting for me on the corner when I got back. We walked and talked about each other and topics of mutual interest. It was dark when we reached her apartment. She fired up a heater to take the chill out of the place and then fixed hot tea. I gave her the mescaline and she became so very excited that she wanted to do some that instant. It was R&R and I was having a good time so we did a couple hits together. She explained that she wanted to take the mescaline over to some friends and she wanted me to go with her if I could. I had nothing better to do.

We bundled up and took to the streets. It was dark and I followed her as we walked up one street, across one, down an alley and by the time we arrived at our destination I knew all about her. Surprisingly, she was from California! Her father had passed away when she was fourteen and her mother took the family to Australia. She had a number of brothers and sisters, most of whom were in Australia although one brother was still in California and she had a married sister, who, with her husband, owned a sheep ranch in the Outback.

We arrived at an apartment building, entered and climbed several flights of stairs before halting at a door. She knocked and we entered a room where several people were lounging about. A girl Gypsy knew, named Elaine, was living there with her three-year-old daughter, Tara. By the time we sat down in the living room we were pretty well buzzed. Gypsy gave the mescaline to a fellow there and introduced me as the source for which I was roundly thanked. After a while a number of people departed leaving me with Elaine, Gypsy and another fellow who turned out to be a GI named Bob. I had been introduced to him when we arrived but we hadn't really talked until the crowd thinned out. It turned out he had come in on my R&R flight and was stationed at Long Binh. We visited like old friends who had just reconnected. He had run into Gypsy on the street and she'd led him to Elaine's. He'd been staying with friends he had come on R&R with but they had been getting into things he didn't want to be involved with, so he'd left. I laid some mescaline on him before Gypsy and I left.

We walked back to Bourke Street where we found the group around the kitchen table. Gypsy knew most of the residents and I introduced her to Pat Morrison and explained his situation to her since he was not a GI on R&R. We spent the better part of the night there before Gypsy had to leave. In the early morning darkness I walked her back to her house and left her on the doorstep with a goodnight kiss and plans to see her in Kings Cross the next day.

I slept the better part of that next day since daylight was on the horizon when I finally got to sleep and quit watching the cartoons in my head. Once I got moving again, it was late afternoon and I wondered how Gypsy was doing since she had to get up and go to work very early. Much to my surprise, when I ventured up to the Cross, she was there on the street. We hugged and kissed and went to a nearby restaurant to get coffee. I saw a great deal of Gypsy in those last days and nights of R&R #2. I enjoyed her company as she wasn't one of those pretentious girls who were out merely for your money and a good time. She wanted me to write to her and come back for a visit if the opportunity presented itself. I told her I would write and a return visit was probable and asked her to help Pat Morrison get situated if she could, to which she agreed.

Before I knew it, the end of R&R #2 was approaching and I would be flying back to the Nam again. That last night we had a big party around the kitchen table until the wee hours of the morning. I finally collapsed into bed and slept like a log until the alarm woke me. Since the return trip was an early one I had to be up early. My suitcase was packed and Renny and Neil were having breakfast when I entered the kitchen. I had a cup of coffee with them while we talked. They asked me to come back if I could and I told them I had another R&R coming and would try to return and bring friends with me the next time. Somehow it seemed fitting that I had started this R&R with Renny and Neil having coffee around the kitchen table in

13. Like There Was No Tomorrow: R&R #2

the early morning daylight and was concluding it in the same manner. I had come to find answers and I had found them although many answers only raised more questions. I hit the street for the walk to the processing center. It was early and cold enough to see my breath in the morning air. I arrived and blended into the flow of GIs and their girls. I went through processing and was soon on the buses headed for the airport. In the confusion of boarding and finding seats, I found myself sitting next to someone who looked vaguely familiar. It was Bob, the GI I'd met at Elaine's house the first night I'd been with Gypsy. I'd forgotten he was on my R&R flight however circumstances put us in adjoining seats. We enjoyed the flight back, finishing the last of the mescaline I'd brought with me.

Rather than stopping in Darwin on the way back, we flew into Manila. I enjoyed the stop and introduced Bob to the ploy Ski and I had used of getting off the plane with officers when they were called. He thought that was pretty slick so we continued doing it. It was dark when we circled Tan Son Nhut and Bob suggested I go with him and spend the night at his company in Long Binh. At Camp Alpha the place where our fatigues were stored would be closed due to the late hour and he said he could get me back early enough in the morning so I could get my stuff and catch a flight out. I decided this would be better than bunking at Camp Alpha.

The plane landed, we were bused to the processing center at Camp Alpha and went through de-briefing, customs, etc., before being turned loose. Camp Alpha was closed with hardly a light showing nor anything moving. I asked Bob how he was planning on getting us out to Long Binh from Camp Alpha and he said we could catch a ride on a courier chopper that operated from the neighboring helicopter pad so we gathered our suitcases, walked out the main gate and caught a lambretta around to the helicopter operations building.

The buildings were dark and closed except for one second story room showing a light in the window. We stumbled to a covered waiting area where we set our bags while Bob went to the illuminated office to check on the courier. He returned with news that it would be about an hour before the next flight and we were to wait until paged. We relaxed on the benches in the darkness until we heard the helicopter warming up on the pad, before the word came over the PA system. We grabbed our bags and hurried out. The Huey was sitting there barely illuminated by distant runway lights, and there were several people milling about as we approached. One man took our bags and stowed them under the back seats as we climbed into the darkened interior. We sat there waiting for the "go" signal when the co-pilot in the front leaned back and said "When the general comes, you'll have to get out of the chopper until he gets in."

Bob and I looked at each other in the darkness and replied in unison

"What general?" The co-pilot explained that a general and his wife were riding this chopper to Long Binh. I didn't catch the name of the general in question but I figured it was no big deal. A short time later we saw two shadows approaching and a man came to the door of the chopper and told us to get out which we did. The general and his wife entered from the opposite side and, once they were situated we were given the OK to board so we climbed back in and sat down. I found myself sitting next to the general and his wife although in the dark I could not make out their features or see the nametape on his uniform. Since there were no interior lights other than the gauges on the instrument panel, we were all merely faceless shadows to each other.

The engine revved up and we rose over the pad, gaining speed and altitude. The lights of Tan Son Nhut spread out below like a crazy quilt of black and light. The general began talking to me asking where Bob and I had come from and where we were going. The noise of the helicopter made it difficult to hear but Bob and I both related our story of returning from an Australia R&R.

A bright gleam on the horizon gradually became a large cluster of buildings. It was Long Binh and we circled until we were above a large open asphalt pad next to a bunch of well-ordered pre-fabricated buildings. Bob leaned over and said "Main Army Headquarters Long Binh" indicating where we were landing.

As we set down, the landing pad was illuminated by the headlights of two jeeps. Once on the ground we climbed out and I grabbed my suitcase before hurrying out from under the whirling rotor. Bob came up and then realized he'd left his suitcase on the chopper and went back to retrieve it. As I stood there in the light of the jeeps a figure approached from the other side of the chopper. I looked up to see it was the general. Since the chopper was running, he had to lean down to speak to me with his face in mine. "Do you fellows have transportation?" he asked. For a moment all I could see were the three stars on his baseball cap. THREE STARS!!! General Schrader was a BG, a one-star. I was speechless since I'd never seen a three star general before much less talk to one. Then he repeated the question. All I could say was I didn't really know where we were going because I'd never been there. I indicated that Bob knew our destination and directed him to speak with Bob. He walked away and talked to Bob before they separated.

The helicopter revved up and took off and quiet descended on us. Bob came over to me and said "Do you know who that was?" I replied that I did not. "It's General McCaffrey!" McCaffrey was the Deputy Commander of the U.S. Army in Vietnam! He was second in command to General Creighton Abrams, the Commander of U.S. Army forces in Vietnam. Moments later LTG McCaffrey came back and told us to stay at the helicopter pad

13. Like There Was No Tomorrow: R&R #2

and he would send his jeep and driver back to take us where we were going since it was so late. Then they were gone, jeeps, general and helicopter as Bob and I stood alone in the darkness. A short time later we saw the headlights of the general's jeep returning. It arrived and we climbed in.

We visited with the driver as he drove along the streets. The place looked to me like any installation with hooches, fences, etc., but it was much cleaner in appearance and there was grass everywhere. This wasn't the Vietnam I knew. We pulled up to a dimly lit guard house by a gate where we climbed out. Bob said that technically the company compound was closed since it was so late but he figured the security guard on duty would let us in. The guard came out of the guard house as we approached and Bob knew him so there was no problem.

We walked down an illuminated asphalt street lined with neatly built cinder block hooches. It looked very much like a Stateside Army post rather than the Vietnam I knew. It was a far cry from the weathered wood and sheet metal roofed hooches I lived in and the concrete sidewalks and grass contrasted greatly with the sand and duckboard walks I was familiar with. We walked in a hooch to find a lot of activity and a number of people still up. I was introduced to Bob's friends before we joined a group in another room listening to music. It seemed that another member of their group had just returned from an R&R to Thailand and he had also brought a visitor back to the company to spend the night except that his buddy was a captain. This was kind of freaky but as it turned out the captain was a decent guy and smoked pot with the best of them.

We retired outside to lounge on folding chairs while various pipes and joints were passed about. There was a chain link fence behind the hooch and the road we drove in on was on the other side. It was a clear night and we relaxed while smoking, drinking sodas, beer, and trading war stories. To these fellows I was "out there" at Cam Ranh Bay. While I couldn't agree with that estimation, I could understand their perspective since they had never seen or done many things that were ordinary experiences for me. They hardly ever went on Red Alert. We all finally turned in for the night and I slept in a vacant bunk.

The following morning I showered in a facility that reminded me of a school locker room compared to our ramshackle wooden shed. I cleaned up and Bob changed into his fatigues which were starched and pressed and his boots spit-shined. No boonie hats here, everyone wore baseball caps. It was a far cry from what I was familiar with. In my civilian clothes I felt like I stood out and was anxious to get into the comfortable anonymity of my fatigues and back to Cam Ranh.

Once we were ready, Bob got a jeep and took me where I could catch a bus to Camp Alpha.

We said our farewells and promised to keep in touch. With that he was on his way and I joined a group of other GIs on the corner waiting for the bus to come. No one paid much attention to me although I was the only one in civilian clothes. I couldn't help but think that I was back in the States surrounded as I was by starched fatigues, spit-shined boots and baseball caps. The bus rolled up and we boarded. It drove past the Long Binh officers club, the bustling main head-quarters area, and the infamous Long Binh Jail. We drove down a highway that teemed with Army vehicles and Vietnamese on bicycles and in lambrettas. I recognized my surroundings when Camp Alpha came into view. I climbed off the bus, hurried to where my fatigues were stored and no sooner had I put them on than I was gone. I caught a lambretta to Tan Son Nhut, booked an early afternoon flight and arrived at Cam Ranh airport an hour or so later. I hitched a ride down to Engineer Hill and was back in time to eat supper.

I was surprised to find a letter from Australia Janet waiting for me when I got there. My heart jumped. She was lost but now she was found. It turned out she was in Melbourne but she didn't go into any details about what I knew her situation to be. With high hopes I promptly wrote her back but never heard from her again. All subsequent correspondence disappeared into the mail box and I never found out what became of her.

Regardless of the outcome or any regrets I may have harbored, these developments cleared the way for whatever relationship was developing with Stateside Janet. But then again, now there was Gypsy in Australia and, while I didn't sense the same type of emotion for her that I'd had with Janet, she still presented an intriguing question in my mind. And to top it all, there was apparently a child in Australia that might be mine. Who knew? It was beyond my control.

After I arrived back in Cam Ranh, I got a letter from Bob in Long Binh. He'd done some of the cosmic cookies I'd taken to Australia and wrote to ask if he could obtain some. His letter contained a money order for the purchase and instructions on how to get it to Long Binh. We'd made a tentative agreement to this effect on the flight back from Sydney but I hadn't anticipated he could put together the money so quickly to procure the amount he wanted. I cashed the money order and made the transaction. I was not certain how to get the little package of cosmic cookies to Bob in Long Binh because I hated to mail it but didn't see how else I was going to get it there.

When I returned from R&R, I focused on my job responsibilities and had been learning the ropes of my job in the S-3 office from the fellow I was replacing. He soon departed, leaving it all to me. I had no problems with that, but not long after he left, the newbie typist got an early-out to go back to school, so he left too, leaving me to do typing as well as filing. Then after the typist left, SFC Forrest, the NCO in charge of our section, went

13. Like There Was No Tomorrow: R&R #2

home on emergency leave because his wife had gone into the hospital so he departed, never to return. Now, practically overnight, I was the only one in the office who had any idea at all about what our section did and how it functioned and I'd barely been there a month.

One of the biggest challenges in front of me was that monthly Construction Project Status Report. When the first report was done after I'd arrived in S-3, I merely observed and had it explained to me. The next one I had to do myself but managed to get it done. I submitted the final copy changes for approval before it was sent on to Engineer Command. Just when I thought this report was done I found out it wasn't, but this development also provided an answer as to how I was going to get Bob's cosmic cookies to him.

The day after I submitted the report to the lieutenant, he told me I was to HAND CARRY the report to Engineer Command in Long Binh so I could go over it with them and get a better grasp of the procedures and purposes. I was completely stunned by this development because it meant going to Long Binh. While I was not exactly pleased, it would provide a break in the routine and give me a chance to visit Bob and get his stuff to him. However, I did not look forward to going into spit and polish country at Main Army HQ. Long Binh was far too Stateside for me and my faded fatigues, shaggy hair and boonie hat. I was to fly down on a chopper with the group commander so I sent a note to Bob and told him when I would be arriving and that I'd call him once I got free in Long Binh.

The appointed day arrived, I went to work and learned we were to leave after lunch. I got my gear ready, stuffing camera, toiletries, towel and other essentials into a multi-colored haversack I'd acquired in Australia back in March. After lunch, I threw my haversack over my shoulder, put the massive report in a brown paper bag and met the group at the S-3 office. We were driven off the Hill in a three-jeep convoy to a small airfield located down on the bay on flat land adjacent to the docks. This landing strip was used primarily for helicopter and small, fixed-wing aircraft flights.

There were quite a few newbie passengers on our flight as well as the group commander and his aide. I'd met him previously through work in the office and we spoke about my mission to Engineer Command while waiting for the helicopter to arrive. That was when he explained that the flight was going to the Group's main industrial sites and then on to Long Binh as the last stop. This wasn't the express flight to Long Binh.

The thumping of helicopter blades brought us to attention as the chopper approached from over the bay and settled on the runway. Several of the newbies flying with us were on their way to Don Dzom while another fellow was heading back to his company at Phan Rang. Everyone and everything was stowed aboard and we stood by for takeoff. I was lucky enough to be assigned to an outside seat right on the edge of the open door with the door gunner behind me.

The chopper took off and rose like an elevator. I held tightly to the paper bag with the report in it lest we lose it out the open door as the chopper tilted forward and sped down the runway toward the docks, rising steadily. Once at altitude the chopper leveled off and we zoomed across the blue water of the bay toward the mountains in the distance and Goodview Pass.

We were soon high overhead looking down on rocky peaks and mountains. We left the coast behind and surged over the rugged ridges and mountains eventually coming down amongst the big hills. Soon I could see a settlement of some kind ahead on a hill and realized it was the Army installation at Don Dzom. We approached, hovered overhead, then descended to a landing pad beside a large, grassy hill that I realized was an immense earthen dam with the entire Army installation situated in front of it.

We thumped to a landing and a group of officers greeted the colonel and his aide. They disappeared into a building while newbies dragged their duffle bags off the chopper and wandered to an office beside the LZ. I got out and stretched my legs while the pilot, crew and passengers headed to find a drink. The LZ was quiet and deserted except for me so I walked around stretching my muscles before returning to the chopper to fire up a number and pull out my book.

The pilots and crew soon returned and the colonel and his aide were not far behind. While the chopper warmed up, he said farewells amid a flurry of salutes and handshakes before getting aboard. Then we were on our way again following a valley out of the mountains until we were flying over a flat plain and leaving the mountains behind. In the distance we could see the South China Sea glistening on the horizon and soon were out over the water with the surf below and the beach etched as a fine white line between the deep blue of the water and the dark, rocky brown of the land. We followed the coastline south for some distance before the chopper banked inland. I could make out an installation ahead that I knew must be Phan Rang.

We descended over the city and the chopper slowed over a landing pad. I could see a jeep below hurrying out to the LZ. We settled on the pad just as the jeep arrived. A lieutenant got out and saluted the colonel as he and his aide exited the chopper. They all climbed in the jeep and took off down the road. Our last passenger, who was bound for this place, gathered his gear and left. The pilot and crew climbed out and disappeared. I pulled out my book and settled back. Phan Rang was where the 299th BN was located and whatever business the colonel had to attend to was taken care of in a hurry as the jeep returned about fifteen minutes later, deposited him with us and we were off again.

We turned southeast toward the coast, again following QL-1. The land was lush and green and we flew high over a vast plain that stretched below us with mountains visible to the west. Far ahead I could see one large mountain peak thrusting up defiantly from the surrounding plain. It was the only notable elevation for miles around. It looked like a battleship floating down the middle of a broad, green river. I'd heard its name many times before, but this was the first time I'd seen it. The colonel nudged me and pointed to the mountain in the distance. "Whiskey Mountain" he said. And so it was, Whiskey Mountain Industrial Site, 864th Engineer Battalion. It was the location of an asphalt plant, gravel pit and rock crusher that supplied material that went into paving QL-1 and other roads.

Whiskey Mountain grew larger and details became clearer as we approached. It had two peaks, one smaller, sort of on the bow, and the top one in the center. From the top, a spine led downward and I could see a guard post at its top peak and another on the lower peak. I thought about the guys manning those towers and the magnificent view they had. I could see the industrial site as we approached and a compound at the bottom,

Whiskey Mountain Industrial Site.

nestled in a hollow against one side of the mountain. I was taken with the small size of the place and was almost disappointed. This was the Whiskey Mountain that had seen rocket and mortar attacks and other assorted mischief. This was where CW Stinson had been sent from the 35th Group after we'd left Dong Ba Thin. From here he had been sent to LZ Betty, to the east.

It looked like what it was, a gravel pit, rock crusher and asphalt plant with associated machinery. As we hovered overhead I could see the compound situated on two different levels with the industrial works below and buildings, hooches and offices on a higher plateau. Several jeep loads of officers awaited our arrival beside the perimeter wire as we set down on the landing pad. The colonel and his aide got off and were taken to the buildings on the plateau above.

I climbed off the chopper to stretch my legs and look around. There didn't seem to be much going on although I could hear the rattle of machinery. The hooches down near the landing pad were built into the ground and so heavily sand-bagged they were virtual bunkers. One bunker I noticed was actually the PX as a crude sign attested. I stood by the chopper taking pictures when the pilot came and said they had to go to LZ Betty to refuel and I could either stay there or go with them. I decided to take the ride to LZ Betty so I climbed aboard and we took off cruising just above the trees as the ground passed below us in a blur.

We reached the coast and banked south to follow it. I could see a large city ahead of us which was Phan Thiet. As we passed over the city I could see a small cluster of black fuel tanks with a landing pad situated next to a tiny compound. This was LZ Betty. It was incredibly small, situated on a bluff overlooking the South China Sea. The hooches appeared to be bunkers and there were guard posts situated around the perimeter and miles and miles of wire obstructions.

We settled on the asphalt pad nestled among a cluster of fuel tanks. Refueling regulations called for us to disembark so with my gear in hand I climbed out and walked to the edge of the pad. I could see the compound a short distance away and figured CW Stinson was probably over there somewhere and considered hiking over to find him, but I could tell there would not be time enough to cover the distance both ways and have any time to locate CW much less spend more than a few minutes with him if I did find him. I figured it best to stay by the chopper.

When refueling was completed we were on our way, heading west. We followed a road northward. Whiskey Mountain soon appeared on the horizon and grew steadily larger as we approached. The cluster of vehicles at the landing pad told us that the colonel was waiting on us so we auto-rotated in over the perimeter and set down. The colonel and his aide climbed aboard and with a final salute and a wave, we were off again. Whiskey Mountain disappeared behind us as we continued southward towards Long Binh. As the sun sank into the western sky it disappeared behind a wall of dark, foreboding clouds moving toward us. The air got noticeably cooler and it was clear there was rain coming. The elements quickly became a threat as rain started and grew in intensity. We descended, flying lower in an attempt to stay under the cloud cover and fly visually. We dropped down to find QL-1 and there were a few anxious moments as we flew around, each of us looking to spot that black asphalt ribbon of highway. Then the colonel saw it. We dropped to treetop level and cruised along following the highway below as the traffic sped through the rain.

I noticed an increasing amount of military vehicles on the road below us indicating we were getting closer to Long Binh. The rain slacked off and the visibility cleared although the cloud cover still kept us close to the ground. Soon we passed over the perimeter of Long Binh and approached the installation. I recognized some of the buildings below like the Long Binh officers club and the main Army Headquarters complex. We approached the same landing pad I had flown in to with Bob and LTG McCaffrey that night we'd returned from R&R a month before. It was still cloudy when the chopper circled overhead and auto-rotated down, settling on the asphalt.

The engines shut down and I gathered my things and climbed out.

There was a jeep and driver waiting for us and we were taken to one of the buildings near the pad. I followed the colonel Inside. The wide hallway seemed to stretch forever and the gleaming waxed tile floor almost blinded me. Everything looked regulation and stateside. We walked down the hall past offices although the place was practically deserted since it was so late in the day. We entered an office where the colonel was greeted by three men inside. I was introduced to a young NCO who I was to see in the morning to review my report. I left it with the NCO so I wouldn't have to worry about it anymore. After arrangements were made, the driver was told to take me to Engineer Command HQ Company and see to my billeting. The colonel told me to be at the landing pad at 4:00 p.m. the following day or I would be left behind.

I followed the driver out of the office and down that gleaming hallway toward the parking lot where we climbed in a jeep and headed down the road. He told me I should keep a low profile tomorrow because my faded fatigues and boonie hat, not to mention the outrageous multi-colored haversack on my shoulder, were all invitations for the wrong kind of attention in Stateside City Long Binh. I thanked him for his advice and told him I would keep it in mind. I'd flown there with the group commander and he never said a word about my appearance. If it didn't bother him then it shouldn't bother anyone else. After all, I was doing my job.

We drove down barracks-lined streets and pulled up to a building that was obviously an orderly room. "Check in there" the driver said. "Most of the old 18th Brigade are in this company." I thanked him for the ride, and climbed out of the jeep. It was almost 5:30 p.m. and I knew the orderly room would be closing. I walked in to face a burly staff sergeant sitting behind a desk.

"I'm from 35th Group. Supposed to get a bunk here." I said. The sergeant grumbled something to me as he got up to yell at someone in another room. I was told to stand by while he walked into the next room. I stood there for a moment before I heard the door open behind me and I turned to step out of the way. Much to my surprise I found myself facing SFC Sparks from the old S-4 at 18th BDE! He immediately recognized me, shook my hand like I was a long lost friend, and inquired as to how I was, where I was, and why I was in Long Binh. I explained my situation and he said he'd get a bunk for me since many of the old 18th BDE personnel were residing in a nearby barracks. When the other NCO entered the room SFC Sparks said he would see to getting me bunked, which suited the other sergeant.

Sparks led me to a nearby barracks where we climbed the stairs to the second floor. The interior was arranged with a long central hallway and rooms built on either side of it. I followed SFC Sparks down the hall. There were the usual noises emanating from the plywood walls, of off-duty GIs laughter, joking, loud music and such. We entered one door and I suddenly found myself in 18th BDE Old Home Day. There were a bunch of the old S-4 and others from Dong Ba Thin. They all jumped when I was recognized and greetings were exchanged all around. I noticed their fatigues were starched and pressed and their boots spit-shined and there were no boonie hats among them since they were taboo in Long Binh. I, by contrast, looked more than a little raggedy-assed. SFC Sparks explained my plight and a spare bunk, linens and blankets were produced in no time. After some catching up on where we'd all been since the breakup of the 18th BDE, I followed them out for the supper at the mess hall. After that we wandered back to the barracks where everyone drifted off to do whatever was their routine. Since I knew none of them were heads, I knew they wouldn't be going out for any walks so I made my way outside for a stroll.

The next morning when it was time to go to the headquarters I followed the group down the street to a bus stop where we joined an ever increasing group of starched and spit-shined GIs in baseball caps. They looked like so many green penguins and I stuck out like a sore thumb in faded fatigues and my boonie hat slouched upon my head and my multi-colored haversack slung across my shoulder. Everyone seemed to be carefully scrutinizing me as if trying to figure out just what the Hell I was doing there and where I had come from.

13. Like There Was No Tomorrow: R&R #2

The buses finally arrived and we crammed in and the bus rumbled down the street. We made our way to main headquarters where I scrambled out with everyone else. The others headed in different directions and I headed for the Engineer Command building I'd left the evening before.

When I entered I found the hallway, which had been devoid of activity the afternoon before, was now teeming with life as officers of different ranks walked here and there while enlisted men and NCOs entered and exited from various offices. I entered the office where I'd left the report and found it filled with clerks. Everyone glanced at me momentarily and then I saw a few familiar faces of the men I'd met there the day before. They led me to a desk where I sat down with them and for the next three hours I was embroiled in the report, answering questions, and explaining my material. I felt like I was being interrogated and I was greatly relieved when the last piece of paper was put away and my mission was complete.

Since the colonel was not leaving until 4:00 p.m. and it was about 11:00 a.m., I had a few hours to myself so I borrowed a phone and called Bob. He was surprised to hear from me so soon and pleased that I was in Long Binh. I was unsure on how to get to where he was and he replied that he would meet me on the corner by the helicopter pad in ten minutes. I said my farewells to those in the office and made my way into the hallway trying to look as if I knew where I was going so no one would bother me.

Once outside, I casually walked to the designated corner by the LZ. My official obligations were finished, Bob was on his way and, I was starting to really feel like a short-timer. I'd spent a whole year in-country and was what was termed a "double-digit-midget" since I had less than ninety days to go. I would soon become an "Incorrigible."

Down the street in the distance I could see a jeep approaching. Since there was nary a soul on the LZ, I assumed it had to be Bob. The jeep pulled alongside the curb and at first glance I hardly recognized the driver behind the sunglasses. His starched fatigues and spit-shined boots made him appear like all the other GIs I'd seen around there, but it was Bob. He didn't recognize me either but I was the only one waiting at the designated corner. I'd seen Bob in his fatigues before but he'd not seen me in mine until that moment when we looked hard at each other to make certain of our identities. I climbed into the jeep and we shook hands. "Wasn't sure that was you" Bob said. He looked me over and shook his head before laughing.

We drove down the street and visited as we drove. I explained how my job had provided a purpose so I could deliver their cosmic cookies in person. Bob agreed it was perfect timing and was most happily surprised at the fast service. He and his gang were off to Vung Tau for some fun at the in-country R&R center's beaches there for the upcoming

4 of July weekend. They had plenty of smoke but the cosmic cookies would make their trip memorable.

We approached a familiar gate and drove in, parked the jeep, and walked to Bob's hooch. I saw familiar faces of guys I'd met there a month earlier. It seemed everyone was aware of the mescaline purchase but word had only just gotten around that it had arrived. Since it was a warm, sunny day we retired out behind the hooches to sit in folding chairs in a circle in the shade of the trees while joints were rolled and fired up. I dug into my haversack and pulled out the metal film canister where I had placed the mescaline and with no further ado, turned it over to Bob. He opened it and everyone gathered to inspect the little pink tablets it contained. Since it was securely in hand, they decided to divide it up amongst those who had contributed toward the purchase.

With that, my other mission was complete.

The last time these fellows had seen me I was dressed in civilian clothes but now I was in my fatigues and I did look a little rough around the edges compared to their baseball caps, starched fatigues, and spit-shined boots. My faded fatigues spoke eloquently of a long time in-country and my faded, boonie hat spoke of being just outside their Mickey Mouse Army. They began asking me about where I was assigned and what my life was like there.

As lunch time was upon us, I followed them to the mess hall where I ate as a guest of the company in a gleaming mess hall filled with clean, starched fatigues. After lunch we returned to the area behind the hooches where we sat smoking, and enjoyed good conversation until about mid-afternoon. As 3:30 p.m. approached, I nudged Bob and said I needed to be getting back to the LZ as the colonel was leaving at 4:00 p.m. I said my farewells to everyone and invited them to return the visit anytime they wanted to come to Cam Ranh, and then followed Bob to the orderly room where he obtained a jeep and we were off down the street. I was ready to get back to my own ground, er, sand, at Cam Ranh.

We pulled up to the LZ at the main headquarters. There were several Huey's scattered across the large hard-stand but I knew which one was mine because it hadn't moved from where we'd landed the day before. Bob and I said our farewells and he thanked me for taking time to deliver the cosmic cookies so promptly. I climbed out and waved as he sped down the street, turned a corner and disappeared. I never saw or heard from Bob again.

The LZ was deserted with no sign of crews or pilots anywhere. I fired up a joint while I waited. As it burned down I could see the pilots walking out from the headquarters building, heading for the hard-stand so I tossed the roach away and climbed into the helicopter. The pilot and crew arrived and began warming up the chopper. As the engine began to whine loudly a

13. Like There Was No Tomorrow: R&R #2

jeep arrived with the colonel and his aide. In a flurry of salutes and handshakes the colonel said his farewells and boarded the chopper. He smiled at me as he sat down and asked if I had accomplished everything I had come to do, to which I nodded and said "mission accomplished." He questioned me momentarily about the report and when he was satisfied that everything was ready he put on a set of intercom headphones and told the pilot to get it in the air. The engine picked up speed, the tail lifted off and we rose, then zoomed off into the sky.

The weather was clear and sunny and the flight back uneventful. We made a stop at Phan Rang and then on to Cam Ranh. As the sun settled over the mountains to the west of us, we were hurtling along the flat coastal plain toward Cam Ranh. Soon we were cruising across the blue waters of the bay toward the familiar docks of Cam Ranh. Then the airfield was below us and we auto-rotated in, settling upon the runway. A jeep arrived as we unloaded and were soon back atop Engineer Hill. I was glad to be back among the familiar surroundings of sand, duckboard walks and weathered frame buildings.

We arrived in the company about 6:00 p.m., just in time for supper. I enjoyed a reunion with the guys and took up my spot for the after dinner festivities. My short trip to Long Binh had been like a trip into fantasyland. However, it did reinforce my feelings that all over Vietnam there were many little groups of heads doing their thing. Bob and his friends were just one such group. It was like we were interchangeable parts.

But now I was back on the Hill and back to work at the S-3. For a while I led a charmed life and managed to run the Construction Projects Section, processed paperwork, kept the files up, did the typing and no one bothered me. I expected them to find an NCO to replace SFC Forrest but the days dragged into weeks. No one complained since I kept the show rolling and came and went as I pleased. As long as my work was done, the paperwork processed and, everything ran smoothly, no one had any reason to bother me and they didn't. Although I had my hands full, I couldn't complain since I was left to my own supervision which suited me just fine. And the approaching 4 of July holiday meant a company party and a day off from work.

14

Dudes, Duty and Diversions: 35th Engineer Group

I got better acquainted with heads in the HQ Company. During my first weeks, prior to going on R&R, I had gotten to know who was who and where they worked. Of course, Ralph was my "touch-stone" from the old days at Dong Ba Thin and CW Stinson joined us briefly when he came over from Dong Ba Thin after 18th BDE deactivated. However he was not assigned at 35th Group HQ and resided in the transient hooch up the street for a time before he was sent down the line to 864th ENGR BN where he served as a courier between Phan Thiet and Cam Ranh. While our paths parted, we did see each other when courier duties brought him to Engineer Hill.

The company heads had several after dark smoking spots; after the evening movie was over they usually congregated at that raggedy plywood and 2 × 4 picnic table on the concrete patio near the theater. During the day it was hard to find someplace to smoke. LZ-1 seemed to be the accepted spot although it was hot and bright in there on sunny afternoons and not comfortable. As near as I could tell at the time, Ralph and I appeared to be the only ones in the company who were smoking all day. I kept my eyes open looking for a more perfect daytime smoking spot. It had to be shady and cool, relatively secure and close by where one could enter and leave without drawing undue attention. It was a perplexing puzzle but, the answer was right under my nose and the reason I overlooked it was the reason no one else considered either it. It was too obvious.

As I stood on the duckboard walk at the end of my hooch during lunch one afternoon pondering this problem, I found my answer. As I looked about, my eyes fell upon the large bunker directly across the sandy street. It was a typical bunker, built out of lumber and sand bags and meant to shelter a large number of people during rocket attacks. It was shaped like a large "I" with a fat shank. There were four entrances, one at each corner but built in such a way that no one could look directly inside. It caught my attention once before but I envisioned the interior to be dark and littered and infested with cockroaches since it was virtually never used. But I had never taken the time to actually go in the bunker so it was time to check it out.

Struggling through the ankle-deep sand, I crossed the street, approached the bunker and entered. To my amazement, the interior was like a cool oasis! There were no bugs, no litter, only clean, white sand, plank walls and the sunlight shining through the entrances providing enough indirect light to illuminate the interior. It was so inviting that I was surprised no one had investigated it before. It was like a cool, shady spot under the boardwalk on a beach somewhere. I walked in. It was situated on the slope of the hill so you could stand up at one end but the sand sloped up towards the other end closest to the street so you had to stoop over up there.

I sat in the doorway and fired up a joint, sitting where I could see the street from the entrance but no one could see in. It was cool and shady and a constant breeze blew through the entrances. It was close to the company area and could be entered quickly and without drawing attention. If someone approached, you could see them before they arrived if not hear them coming.

The "bunker," seen to the left in this image, with one entrance visible. There was one in each corner.

A pipe or a joint could be quickly hidden in the loose sand and four entrances provided quick exits. I figured if we did nothing to attract attention, the bunker could be used as a convenient, comfortable smoking spot. I knew Ralph and I could share the spot but felt we should be careful with whom we gave the secret to since too much activity and too many people might attract the wrong attention as had happened with Ski's enterprise at Dong Ba Thin.

I returned to work and when the afternoon break rolled around at 3:00 p.m., I hurried over to the civilian personnel office where Ralph worked and immediately showed him my discovery. He was impressed. We sat back with a couple of joints to christen the place. The loose sand inside the bunker would also be a good place to hide our stash cans. These cans, with plastic tops, were recycled from the numerous cans used for candies, cookies, crackers and other munchies purchased in the PX and they made ideal containers to stash our smoke and paraphernalia in. I had been burying my stash can behind the revetments of my hooch but it was out of reach during the day since it was too exposed. The bunker solved this problem since I could bury the can in there where it was available at any time.

The bunker was the answer. It could be used all day at any time, and by the time it was too dark to see inside the bunker, it was dark enough to

The convoy security gun truck "Bounty Hunter" passes by the bunker seen from the end of my hooch located across the street. 610th Engineer Battalion.

smoke on the revetments, the picnic table or any of the usual night time smoking spots. We kept the secret to ourselves. It was like our secret clubhouse. However, the other heads began to notice our absences during the morning and afternoon breaks and wondered just where we disappeared to. One day during lunch, Dusty tracked us down. Ralph and I had just gotten into the bunker and fired up a joint when suddenly there was a shadow in the entrance opposite to where we sat. We held our breath then Dusty peeked around the corner.

"So, this is where you guys disappear to!" he said with an air of authority as he entered the bunker. "I thought I saw you guys walk out of the hooch but didn't see where you went to and you couldn't have gotten out of sight so quickly" he explained. Dusty sat down and shared joints with us. We already knew Dusty but our friendship was further cemented in that bunker at that moment.

Once the bunker was no longer a secret, it became a secret that was hard to keep. Shortly after, Dusty brought Mike Stigg into the bunker to join us. Mike was a big, husky, well-built young man from Kansas. His room, the Head Haven next to Dusty and Pete's room, was the spot where most of the company heads congregated. The room had been created by combining two rooms at the end of the hall into one large room. Mike had been the longest resident of the room when Ralph and I arrived and he lived there with Andy Davidson from Florida, known to one and all as "Andy," Tommy Tomason from Michigan, and Dave Friday from Wisconsin.

Along two sides of the room a large desk and bookshelves had been built while their bunks occupied the other two walls. Somewhere they obtained a window air-conditioning unit, installed it in a window, and boarded up the rest. Thus, Stigg's Room was an oasis of cool air. A major stereo system and huge speakers gave us outstanding tunes that sometimes made the whole hooch shake. They also purchased a small refrigerator that was kept stocked with drinks. Black lights and day-glow paint and posters everywhere added to the atmosphere.

Stigg was impressed with the bunker and its potential and laughed at those who'd been in the company so long and not thought of it before. After Stigg and Dusty had been initiated into the Loyal Order of the Bunker, it was virtually impossible to keep it to ourselves. The next thing we knew, the whole group had been brought to it or figured it out and it quickly became THE SPOT during the day. However, for a while Ralph and I had the bunker to ourselves. Most folks managed to maintain during the day by catching a smoke at lunch so the bunker saw heavy use during the lunch hour and after work at 6:00 p.m., but Ralph and I had been into a daily stoned routine since Dong Ba Thin and the bunker made it simple for us to maintain that routine.

For the months we were at 35th Group we started each day about 6:00 a.m. when I met Ralph in the bunker for a pipe. Breakfast followed, then morning formation at 7:00 a.m. and police call. Then we'd hit the bunker for another pipe before going to work at 7:30 a.m. Morning break came at 9:00 a.m. and we had a half hour off. Again we met at the bunker before returning to work at 9:30 a.m. Noon was kicked off with a pipe in the bunker with the gang before lunch in order to let the chow line go down. After lunch we went to the bunker for a pipe before returning to work at 1:00 p.m. Afternoon break was at 3:00 p.m. and for another half hour we enjoyed another pipe before getting back to work at 3:30 p.m. We knocked off at 6:00 p.m. and then it was a rush to the mess hall but we made it to the bunker before getting anything to eat.

Ralph and I shared the same pipe. I had a communal cookie can filled with loose pot and another can filled with pipes, rolling papers, etc. We figured out one day that the pipe we used would hold four joints of loose pot, so by using that yardstick, we measured our consumption level between the hours of 6:00 a.m. and 6:00 p.m. which amounted to an average of thirty-five joints a day for the two of us. This does not take into account the amount consumed during evening hours which could easily have doubled that amount. This is no exaggeration.

Hooch girls doing the laundry.

14. Dudes, Duty and Diversions: 35th Engineer Group

The bunker brought us together and in a very short time old LZ-1 fell into disuse and there were no more mass migrations to the shitters after supper. Even the morning and afternoon breaks that had been only Ralph and me were soon a busy time. The bunker made it convenient and safe and all the gang were soon out there burying their stashes in the bunker and smoking up at all hours of the day. It wasn't long before the daily sessions that Ralph and I had enjoyed were now group sessions with the whole group starting at 6:00 a.m.

After the sun went down and night descended there was no need to sneak off to the bunker. Once the movie was over and things quieted down we gathered at the old picnic table outside of Stigg's Room to lounge on the table and revetments while pipes and joints passed around.

Since Engineer Hill was rather isolated, being on a large peninsula, pot was not as easy to obtain as it had been at Dong Ba Thin where one could take a drive down to the car wash or into the ville. But if we couldn't get to the pot, the pot usually managed to find its way to us. The most logical and most utilized source were the Vietnamese laborers who worked on the Hill as mama-sans or other jobs. Many lived in Cam Ranh village down below the Hill that had been there long before the U.S. Army had come.

Other Vietnamese who worked in Cam Ranh took a ferry across the bay from Su Chin, thus pot and other black-market items arrived on the peninsula, made their way through the checkpoint searches and got to us. Some mamasans would smuggle bags of Pot stuffed in their bras.

My mamasan was a small, thin, wrinkled witch of a lady named Ba-Ta. Her voice was harsh and loud and she had the attitude of a Pit Bull, but she took good care of me. I didn't smoke tobacco, so I gave her my cigarette ration. She gave me money and with my ration card I bought her cartons of Salem cigarettes, which made her very happy. She would flash her black-toothed grin at me and tell me I was "Numba One G.I." As a result of this act of kindness, Ba-Ta brought me pot in return and I could usually count on her to get some for me when necessary. She was reliable and in addition to keeping my boots polished, fatigues washed, and my room swept, she kept me supplied. Every noon she and the other hooch girls would get together, hunker down on their haunches and cook and eat their lunches of fish heads and rice and other delights that always imparted a very distinct odor.

About twice a month we had convoys come in from the outlying industrial sites and the soldiers who drove these big rigs were usually brothers one and all. In company with the convoys were a large number of heavily armored and armed convoy security trucks we knew simply as "gun trucks." They were interspersed throughout the convoys and provided suppressing fire when they were ambushed on the roads. Sometimes these convoys were in our area for several days and many of their drivers were billeted in the transient hooch which always gave us a chuckle since the newbies there were usually intimidated by these rough and tumble guys who hadn't shaved, needed haircuts, wore faded, oil-stained fatigues and had no respect for authority. We got to know many of these convoy drivers and gun truck crews and they always brought smoke and other forms of refreshment. Since almost everyone had nicknames, we usually got to know these guys by their nicknames and in many instances never knew their real names.

There was heroin on the Hill, although I had ceased messing with it by this time. The abuse that some people put themselves through was beyond me. Across the hall from me was where the S-3 driver lived. He was an eighteen-year-old fellow from California named Dennis Mayaguez. He was a likeable kid with yellow curly blonde hair. After high school he joined the Army and was exuberant about life although he didn't really know where he was going. When his roomie departed, he invited me to move out of my cubby hole and move in with him. His room was larger and more comfortable, so I moved in with Denny. He was strung out on heroin pretty badly and couldn't get it through his head that it was no good for him. He would sit on the revetments with some other guys and smoke heroin joints all night and by 11:30 p.m. every night was puking his guts out prior to collapsing in bed. It was a nightly ritual.

No two gun trucks were the same. This one has the body of an armored personnel carrier put in the back of a 5-ton truck.

14. Dudes, Duty and Diversions: 35th Engineer Group   213

Denny was usually well-intentioned, but he had a quick temper and a loose tongue which eventually cost him his job at the S-3. He clashed with the MSG in charge on occasion and shot off his mouth once too often. They finally shipped him out to a battalion, and he was gone from 35th Group HQ. I didn't see Denny for quite a while and then one day he was there sitting on the revetments at the end of my hooch. I was surprised to see him and we talked. He was on his way home as he'd been given an administrative General Discharge from the Army. Seems they considered him unable to adjust to Army life so they sent him home. I don't think any of us were really able to adjust to Army life but we all coped in different ways.

Heroin became a major problem for the Army, not just in Vietnam, but on the home front as well. They had not considered the impact of sending boys strung out on heroin, home to their families where they went into withdrawal "cold turkey." It was a self-inflicted wound the Army took measures to correct.

The most obvious method was a urine test to check home-bound troops before they left. Heroin traces remained detectable in the system for two weeks or so, and this meant any soldier going home who had consumed heroin would be detected and could be diverted to medical facilities where they would be detoxed before being sent home to the folks.

Word of this newly implemented piss test meant that every departing

Ralph investigates the "Investigator."

soldier would have to pass that test before going home. That development did not sit well with many troops until it was learned that this test was only for heroin and no other substances. The pot heads heaved a huge sigh of relief. Pot heads did not go home to mom and dad and OD in the living room or go into withdrawal. For smack heads, it was another story. The new piss test resulted in a large number of troopers who failed and required detoxification. This strained the system, so the Army instituted an amnesty program so men could get medical attention without fear of judicial punishment, before they faced the piss test. One of the in-country detoxification centers was constructed at South Beach, below the Hill for those taking voluntary detoxification. It was a nice setting for such a facility. Ironically, it turned out to be the last project I processed.

When Denny left 35th Group, I had the room to myself and I enjoyed the peace and solitude of my own room for a while. Then I met Freddie Warren. Fred was one of the more memorable characters I came across while living on the Hill. I'd seen him at various times in the company and assumed he was either a convoy driver or from the field somewhere as he was not a member of our company. He was an unforgettable sight, standing about 5'8", thin, deeply tanned, blonde hair, deep blue eyes and his upper two front teeth missing. Dressed in his faded fatigues with scuffed boots, shaggy blonde hair and deep tan, Fred looked as if he'd always been in the Nam.

He'd spent two years in Vietnam and when finally sent home he was twenty and not yet old enough to drink or vote legally in his home state of Illinois. Fred was a "home boy" and Ralph and I took to him instantly. He had a certain hardness about him that you could sense in his bearing and speech. Having been born and raised in South Side Chicago may have had something to do with it. In Vietnam Fred served with a well-drilling detachment assigned to the 497th Port Construction Company. It was part of the 35th Group and had its headquarters at the other end of Engineer Hill. This detachment consisted of a lieutenant in charge, an NCO and three enlisted men, one of whom was Freddie. In his two years in the Nam, Fred had been all over the country and seen a lot. With stand-down, the well drillers were called in from the field and deactivated as part of the 18th Brigade's deactivation. Since Fred and the other two enlisted men, Tony Valdez from New York and Pete Mendez from New Mexico, were technically assigned to the 497th PCC, they went back there. Fred didn't know anybody because he'd spent more time in our company when he was on the Hill. Somehow, the 1SGT of the 497th PCC missed that Freddie was assigned to their company and Fred found himself forgotten, having slipped through the cracks.

After Denny Mayaguez departed and I had the room to myself, Ralph and I got to know Freddie. Because he was from Illinois, just as we were and

14. Dudes, Duty and Diversions: 35th Engineer Group 215

since he hung out with all of us, it wasn't long before Fred was in the bunker with the rest of us. Late one night as things broke up I offered Fred the empty bunk in my room so he wouldn't have to trudge back to the 497th. Fred soon became my regular roommate and with my consent moved his meager possessions into my room. Since he was actually assigned to the 497th but had been overlooked there and since he was not assigned to our company, he was just "loose." No one questioned his being in our company area or in my hooch or in our mess hall because he was a familiar figure in the area. That being the case, Fred didn't have to make morning formations, pull any details or go in to work so he lived a life of relative ease. It was always his day off. He slept all morning, ate in our mess hall and for all practical purposes was a member of our company.

As always there were work details we had to pull in the company and one I hated at first was company police call. Our company alternated this duty with another company so we performed it every other month. This duty consisted of taking a detail in a truck down to Times Square intersection in Cam Ranh, to police up all the trash along the roadside all the way to the little PX at the bottom of Engineer Hill.

Viewing off the back of Engineer Hill toward Binh Bah Island and the entrance to Cam Ranh Bay. Transportation units located on South Beach.

Our company consisted of four platoons and each platoon provided one man to pull this duty each day. This police call was conducted after morning formation and again after lunch. I did not enjoy the detail when first detailed for it. It seemed unreasonable to me because our platoon was the smallest and the personnel platoon had over three times our number. If each platoon provided one man for the detail, our platoon got hit especially hard since each man pulled the duty several times whereas in the personnel platoon some people never pulled it.

One day in July, I became curious because every time I was picked for the detail, I noticed that Dusty was always the selectee from the personnel platoon. I didn't understand why in the largest platoon with the most soldiers, the duty always fell to Dusty. When I questioned him he replied that he'd volunteered to pull it permanently. Then, his logic dawned on me.

With two other fellows in the back of the truck and a driver from the R&U section in the front, we drove to Times Square and began police call, spreading out on one side of the road and firing up a couple of numbers while we picked up trash. I followed Dusty's lead and volunteered for permanent duty for our platoon, but our platoon sergeant said I couldn't do this because I would deprive others of the "privilege" of doing their duty. I couldn't see why the Personnel platoon could do this and ours couldn't, so I checked with the others in my platoon and they said it would be fine for me to take the duty permanently. So, we had an agreement that when their names came up on the roster for police call duty, they would go to work and I would pull their duty. This worked fine since I was a short-timer and no one ever missed me if I came in late to work. So Dusty and I pulled police call when that duty came around.

While everyone else went to work at 7:30 a.m., we reported for police call, took the ride to Times Square, smoked a number, and returned to the company where we headed to the bunker to smoke a pipe before returning to work about 8:15 a.m. At 9:00 a.m. came the morning break, so it was back to the bunker for another pipe until 9:30 a.m. when we returned to work. At 12:00 Noon came lunch and we went back to the bunker for another pipe, then back to the bunker after lunch. When everyone returned to work at 1:00 p.m., Dusty and I reported for the afternoon police call, riding to Times Square again and smoking another joint while we picked up trash. When we returned to the company area, we'd head for the bunker for another pipe until about 2:15 p.m. when we returned to work. At 3:00 p.m. came afternoon break so we headed once again to the bunker for another pipe with the guys. We returned to work at 3:30 p.m., and when the shop closed up at 6:00 p.m., we were released from duty. This meant it was time for our usual evening activities. We kept this schedule for the month our company had this duty.

14. Dudes, Duty and Diversions: 35th Engineer Group

But Dusty and I did our duty far beyond what was expected of us because we insured that many a newbie was properly initiated. The group transient hooch was just up the street, where all newbies coming into 35th Group were housed as they passed through the Group HQ. When they had an abundance of transient newbies there, we were authorized to pick some helpers and this we enjoyed immensely. The driver would pull the truck up outside the transient hooch and have the NCO in charge of the transient newbies fall them out in formation. Dusty and I would survey them from the back of the truck and tell the driver who to pick. The newbies always stood anxiously by the road, not sure just what these weirdoes had in store for them. We could usually tell by the presence of "love beads," peace signs, wire-rim glasses or the cut of a moustache among the collection of bright new green fatigues that there were a few heads in the group who could use a buzz. Usually, they were pissed at having been snagged for a work detail but we knew they would change their attitudes once we had them down on the road.

The selected newbies climbed in the back of the truck with us and we sped down the road to Times Square making small talk as we went. Once there, Dusty took a couple of them off to one side of the road and I would take the rest to the other side. While we walked along picking up trash, I'd break out a few joints and offer them up. They always jumped at this development and by the time we reached the PX at the bottom of Engineer Hill we were good friends. Then we would load up and head back to the company area where Dusty and I would take the newbies to the bunker to blow them away again. In many cases, the rest of the time they were in the company they were in the bunker with us. We always sent them off to their duty assignments with a good buzz, friendship and all the low down on the places they were going to.

After my arrival at 35th Group I got a birthday package in the mail from my younger brother.

It was filled with munchies, reading material, and hidden in one bag of candy was a little plastic box with an assortment of LSD and mescaline tablets. This was a welcome addition and I shared it with friends. It took the edge off things and with the cosmic cookies, kept us wired. For many of us dope was the common ground upon which we stood. We were from a variety of backgrounds, ethnicities, cultures and represented a cross section of American youth. The Army, the draft and Vietnam were common denominators for us. We fought the insanity, with insanity. Dope brought many of us together and it was a matter of strangers becoming brothers and every so often it brought old friends together.

One evening we were having a party down in the S-4 storage yard below the hill and behind the USO stage near South Beach. One of the boys in the group, SP5 Harry Arnold, worked in the S-4 yard where he drove a huge forklift. He was on his second tour in the Nam and often remarked about the differences between his two tours. His first tour found people possessed with a "gung-ho" attitude and there were many juicers and virtually no heads or drug use. By his second tour he'd turned on to smoking pot and the whole scene in Vietnam had changed; he said it was like two different tours. He would repack White Owl cigars with pot, leaving the outer wrap of tobacco leaves. We often saw him during the day driving that huge forklift through the S-4 yard or the company area with that White Owl cigar in his mouth and a big shit-eatin' grin on his face.

Arnold's forklift was an immense machine and on this night we were having a party up on the forklift. That's how big it was! There were about ten or fifteen of us and the forklift was parked in the center of the S-4 yard. Being in the dark, no one could approach unobserved, so we relaxed all over the machine. A short distance away, the asphalt road passed by the yard and across from that was a PX snack bar trailer, assorted hooches and buildings of a number of transportation companies along South Beach. The lights from the snack bar trailer illuminated the area enough for us to see soldiers lounging around and lining up to buy snacks and drinks.

It was not long before we were felt the dryness in our throats from smoking, so a few of us climbed down off the forklift and hiked across to the snack bar to procure some drinks. As we approached out of the darkness and into the light around the snack bar, I became aware of four GIs sitting on a small picnic table beside the trailer. They were horsing around and being loud and we ignored them at first, concentrating on getting our orders straight. The guys at the table struck up a conversation with us and one fellow came over and asked if we knew where they could get some smoke. I was noncommittal but said they were welcome to come to the party and then disengaged myself from the conversation.

There was something familiar about that fellow, something about his face, the way he talked. I tried to place the face with a name and then it came to me. He looked like Dan Reeder from my college days at Platteville. Dan was from Platteville and been one of the campus radicals when I was in school there. We'd spent a lot of time together back then but somewhere along the way, after I'd left school, we'd lost track of one another. But here I was looking at a fellow who reminded me of old Dan Reeder. As I looked at him, I decided that it must be a coincidence.

We gathered our drinks and started back to the S-4 yard when this fellow came rushing up and again asked if we knew where they could get some smoke. We talked amongst ourselves for a moment and I suggested again that they come over to the S-4 yard with us. A convoy was in and there was a lot of smoke among the drivers so we told them to come along.

The fellow motioned to his three buddies and they all followed us to the S-4 yard.

When we arrived, we tossed the canned drinks to the boys on the forklift and explained the new additions to our group. Everyone climbed up on the forklift until it was packed and there was no more room. I found myself on the ground with one other fellow and strangely enough, it was the dude who looked like Dan Reeder. We started talking and realized that we'd been thinking the same thing about each other from the moment our eyes met. It was Dan Reeder! A long-lost friend had been found. What an amazing coincidence, to have parted ways in Wisconsin in 1968 only to find ourselves in the Nam three years later and residing only a short distance apart.

We talked and laughed sitting on the immense tires of the forklift. We had a lot of catching up to do, not to mention figuring out how our individual paths had led us to this moment. Dan had been down at Phan Rang and had been transferred to a transportation company on South Beach, just below Engineer Hill. He'd been living there for a while and we'd been so close to finding one another but hadn't until that night. After that Dan and I saw each other frequently and he became a part of our group and we a part of his. He would come up to visit our bunker and we would hike down off the Hill and return the visit to South Beach.

Running into Dan Reeder from my college days was one example of how small the world could be. Another example turned up in the S-3 office one day when a tanned GI in faded fatigues came looking for me. At first I didn't recognize him but when I looked at the nametape on his fatigues, I recognized the name "Valentine." It was John Valentine, who I had crossed paths with in college and who had visited Billy Casick and me in Dong Ba Thin after John came through there as a newbie. That time he had some Purple Haze LSD he'd brought from the States and the three of us tripped one wild evening. John was on his way home and had tracked me down at 35th Group HQ. He was on his way to the 22nd Replacement and went out of his way to come by and express his appreciation for the hospitality we had shown him when he was an apprehensive newbie. We chatted and I took him to the bunker to celebrate his departure in proper style. I explained to him why I was still in-country but also pointed out that I was fast approaching my own date of departure. We parted with a handshake and a hug and I never saw him again.

Sunday was a day of rest for us. S-3 had no Sunday duty for staff such as we had at Dong Ba Thin so we had the day off. Trips to the beaches were always popular on Sundays and we' procure a truck and head out. Since our old Vinnell Beach hangouts had been closed down by this time we sought other places. One destination was the beach at a Navy installation at Market Time, just down the road from Vinnell Beach. It was a small post with well-kept buildings, paved streets and situated on a beautiful cove backed by high, rocky ridges. The beach was beautiful white sand and the water crystal blue. The cove was large enough that you could hike down to the far end where it disappeared against sheer, rocky heights and be relatively safe from intrusion. Plus, no one could approach unseen and the people that far down the beach were doing the same thing we were.

When Ralph, Chris Wilson and I first arrived at 35th Group, we were already familiar with Market Time Beach. In fact, it was the site of the last Sunday outing we'd had with Ski, Hud and Schives before they departed. One Sunday after we'd joined 35th Group the guys were looking for some new place to go. Ralph and I suggested Market Time Beach. They were unaware of the place so we took them there. They liked it and we made frequent Sunday trips there to smoke, toke, and soak. However, with the close proximity of the Navy installation, we could never really be as relaxed as we had been at Vinnell Beach and we all wanted to find a place where we could get laid back without having to keep an eye over our shoulders.

Pete Simpson mentioned the existence of a park near Market Time.

Graffiti up in the rocks at Market Time. Left to right: Mike Stigg, Harry Peterson, Tommy Tomason, Dave Friday and Mark "Frizzle" Fritzo. "We are the people our parents warned against."

This was questioned because in all the times we'd been out there we'd never seen anything that looked like a park. He insisted it was there and even had directions. It was small and little used which was evidenced by our having overlooked it. One afternoon, Pete took a drive out that way to check it out; he reported back that it was there and was satisfactory.

Preparations were made for a mission to the park near Market Time for Sunday. We had Chris Wilson's cosmic cookies and after lunch we headed down the Hill to Market Time with Pete driving the lead truck since he knew where we were going. As we approached the end of Market Time Road, we could see the gates to the Navy installation down the road, but Pete slowed and turned off onto a dirt road that led across a grassy field to a clump of large trees. On two sides there were rocky ridges, escarpments and mountains that rose up providing a breath-taking backdrop. To the south, across an open expanse of fields, was the Market Time installation and to the east lay a large rocky mountain that blocked the view of the South China Sea.

The trucks pulled under the shade of several huge mango trees and then we saw a barbecue pit and two picnic tables. We swarmed over the area and claimed a spot. The place was deserted so we fanned out to explore and found a long rope ladder that went up into one of the large mango trees and a long rope hung down from a high branch. It didn't take us long to make use of this. Some fellows scrambled up into the far reaches of the tree by climbing up the rope ladder while others took turns giving us the old Tarzan routine on the hanging rope Others branched out into the surrounding brush and up into the rocks of the ridge directly behind us. We were totally whacked out about the trees since they were the only real trees we'd stood under in a long time.

We were wired up on the cosmic cookies and pipes were kindled and passed around. The day was beautiful and the rocks up in the ridge behind us sparkled in the sunshine like there were diamonds up there. I'd noticed this on the drive into the place but decided it was the mescaline rather than reality. As we climbed up into the rocks, I saw it wasn't the mescaline at all. The rocks were full of quartz crystals of various sizes. They were everywhere and of every shape and size. We went nuts looking at them as if the ground was covered in diamonds. Some of the boys filled their pockets and hauled down some good-sized chunks. We made many trips to the park on subsequent Sundays and it became our private Sunday party spot.

15

The Incorrigibles

Dave Friday was one of the old-timers at 35th Group when I arrived. He lived in Stigg's Room so when his departure approached, we had to send him off in style. Whenever any of the guys left the Nam it was cause for celebration. Dave was going to E.T.S. (Expiration Term of Service) thus the end of his tour in the Nam and subsequent E.T.S. was a big affair. He was one of ours going home and it was milestone in all our journeys through the Nam. As befitting such a milestone, his ETS party was to be a big affair and much planning went into it. We anticipated a full throttle party, so we needed a place where we could have it with some degree of security.

After casting about for a suitable place, we found a spot that seemed ideal up at the apex of Engineer Hill. The Hill was a long, high sand ridge that connected at the North end to a high, rocky mountain, like a large "V" with the sand dune forming one arm and the mountain forming the other. Where these two ridges met was a large, rocky bluff that overlooked a rock quarry, and motor pool, directly below, and spread out beyond was Times Square, Cam Ranh Main Army HQ, most of main Cam Ranh Army and the docks down on the bay. A narrow, brush-shielded path led up to the bluff and it appeared to be the ideal place because it was isolated and away from the inhabited areas on Engineer Hill. There were convoys coming in so their drivers were alerted to the pending festivities and funds were put together for a run to Su Chin to score some smoke. We looked forward with much anticipation to the event although we hated to see Dave leave. However, everyone knew that his departure meant their own was that much closer.

As the day approached, preparations progressed, and Stigg's Room was a bee hive of activity all day with joint rolling machines turning out one after another until a shoe box full had been accumulated. The day arrived but we still had to work. After supper there was a mass gathering around the picnic table and in Stigg's Room. There were a number of convoy drivers and gun truck crews present, as well as Freddie Warren and the well drillers. Even C.W Stinson was in the area for a few days and able to participate.

15. The Incorrigibles

About dusk there was an air of anticipation as we began the trek up to the party site. There must have been fifty people straggling out across the sand like an arrow pointing to where we were going. Others joined the procession along the way. We had coolers, cassette players and enough smoke to choke a horse. I guess we were so fired up that our "common sense" was buried under all the anticipation. Ralph, Frizzle, C.W., Chris and I had all consumed some cosmic cookies and we were a pretty zonked bunch of troopers by the time we walked up the rocky pathway to the promontory on the bluff. In the gathering darkness we sat in a huge circle with cassette players putting out tunes in the center. The box of joints was opened, and assorted pipes started passing around. Joints were lit at various points in the circle and passed down the line never to be seen again, although others were fired up to take their places. It was an unbelievable sight, a mass meeting of smokers from all over 35th Group set upon one of the highest points overlooking Cam Ranh Bay.

Darkness descended upon us and the party roared on as we lost all sense of time. At one point someone said something about a jeep driving around in the rock quarry below us. We walked to the edge where we could see the lights of a jeep far below, apparently trying to shine a spotlight up to where we were. I plainly saw that it was an MP jeep and even though a red light flashed in my brain, my mind was too perforated to be alarmed.

I don't know how long we sat there in that blasted state of ignorant bliss, but things continued as before until we saw several people on the far side of the circle get up and look down the access pathway behind them. I felt a flash of concern just in observing the way they got up. Then more people began to get up and everyone seemed to be peering through the darkness at something behind and below us. One man was pointing at something down the pathway.

I didn't like the look of things; there was a growing sense of panic in the group like there was something wrong. We looked at each other, then got up and walked over where the group stood. "What's down there?" I asked. Someone replied "A jeep drove up but we can't see it now." The convoy drivers were pretty hard core individuals and a couple of them were not intimidated by the situation. Several started walking down the path to investigate when suddenly there was the unmistakable clatter of an M-16 bolt slamming a round into its chamber. The boys down the path dropped all pretense at bravery and fled back to where we stood, hardly pausing there as some continued on in the dark, clamoring up the rock and boulder-strewn face of the slope behind us.

Panic exploded everywhere, many not caring what was being fled from but merely accepting the fact that whatever it was, they too, should be elsewhere. For a moment all we could hear were the sounds of falling rocks and pebbles as they scrambled up the rocky slope in an attempt to escape this unknown threat that had yet to materialize. A small portion of the group stood their ground, some wanting to know exactly what was happening.

We stood there trying to figure out that out. I knew I was not going to do much climbing in those rocks with my flimsy flip flops, plus the mescaline was doing a job on me. I said to Ralph "Let's just hang loose here. I've got nothing on me. What can they do to us?"

Ralph agreed but then he looked around and a surge of panic hit him. He grabbed me and said "Yes, we haven't got any dope on us but look around you! We gotta get outta here!" I looked around me and could see his point. Scattered around us all I could see were burning joints, smoking pipes, soda cans and bags of pot all over the ground. It looked like a disaster area and panic gripped me when I realized I had to get away from there, regardless of my flip flops.

We made our way out of the open area and into the rocks and boulders along the slope where Ralph, CW, Frizzle and I hid behind a large rock where we could still see what was happening. We sat quietly among others and the party site remained empty and quiet. We waited. Nothing happened. Then a shadowy figure emerged from the thicket below and approached the head of the pathway. Another shadow joined him. We sat there behind our boulder hoping we were well hidden but getting impatient with the uncertainty. Frizzle kept asking "Are we busted? Hey, are we busted?" and Ralph and I kept telling him to "Shut up!" because we weren't busted—yet. Frizzle was having his first experience with Mescaline and he was zapped pretty good.

It couldn't have been very long, but to those of us hiding in the rocks, it felt like hours. Gradually others joined the guys standing at the head of the pathway until a small group had gathered there. We felt rather ridiculous sitting there behind that rock and as far as we could tell, nothing had happened so we decided to join the group. There were about twenty people clustered around the head of the pathway. No one seemed to know what was happening so Ralph, CW, Frizzle and I clustered together to one side of the group. A little ways down the path I could see a figure standing there dressed in a multi-colored Hawaiian shirt and everyone seemed to be watching him. He walked up the path towards us and then stopped and walked back down again. I couldn't determine whether he was one of our group or not. Finally, he turned and came up the path and in the darkness behind him we saw another shadow move into the brush.

The fellow walked up to us and stopped. He didn't seem such a threat as to warrant the kind of panic that had resulted. The group gathered in a semi-circle around the head of the path and this fellow stood on the path below us, looking up at us. I realized that this guy must be part of what the problem was all about but I did not envy him his position facing all of us, considering the hard character of some of those present. He then broke the silence by saying in a rather disgusted tone of voice "Is there a spokesman among you guys?" No one replied and no one moved. I realized that every one of those guys were so fucked up they just wanted out. No one was even capable of talking much less serve as a group spokesman.

Once again the man in the Hawaiian shirt asked if someone could explain why we were up there. No one replied. Then he said "You guys are really stupid. Everyone in Cam Ranh can see what you're doing up here!" We listened in stunned silence. I didn't understand who this guy was, scolding us like we were a bunch of errant children. He didn't look much older than us and was dressed in civilian clothes. He continued saying "If there weren't so many of you, I'd march you all down to your respective companies. Are you all from the Hill?" No one replied. "I want you guys to get outta here and fast! I should report you all, but you be dammed thankful there are too many of you for me to do that. Now, if I were you, I'd get the fuck outta here!"

We didn't need to be told twice. All we wanted at that moment was to get "outta" there too. He stepped aside and we surged past him and down the path in a ragged, single file, walking silently except for the sound of Frizzle asking Ralph "Are we busted? Hey, are we busted?" We told him to "shut up and keep walking."

Parked at the bottom of the path was a jeep with a starched fatigue, spit-shined MP NCO standing there with a shotgun and another soldier with an M-16 behind the jeep. They didn't say a word to us and we kept walking, heading for the anonymity of our company area. Frizzle kept asking "Are we busted, are we busted?" and we kept telling him to "Shut up and keep walking." We straggled out of the shadows, past the shitters headed for our company. Others stood by and watched this procession that wound out of the darkness and wondered what was going on. It appeared my guardian angel had been doing her job.

The sight of the company drew us onward and we headed for the cooling comfort of Stigg's Room. Dave Friday joined us and hardly believed what had just transpired. What a way to end your tour by narrowly avoiding being busted by the MP's! It was not long before the group in Stigg's Room began to swell in numbers as others gradually made their way back. We sat up for hours consuming sodas, toking on the occasional joint and re-hashing the evening's experience. We took a head count to see just who was accounted for and who was still out there. Others continued to make their way off the rocky mountain all night long and we waited to see who would be the last to come out. Finally, about midnight, Chris Wilson came in. He had been stumbling around the mountain in the dark for several hours. We found out later that a number of the convoy drivers spent the night up on the mountain and did not come down until daylight.

The next morning, we were pretty strung out and expected to hear about it from the 1SGT at morning formation. However, much to our surprise, nothing was ever said about the party and it having been raided. That morning we sent Dave Friday off to the World but there was much talk about all the smoke and stuff that had been left up there. We didn't know if they had picked up all of it after we left or was it still up there? Indeed, was it safe to go up there in the daylight so soon after the event? Could we return to the scene of the "crime?" That question was kicked around and it was felt the investment in the smoke alone was worth the risk. That following afternoon, Stigg, Tommy Tomason, Andy Davidson and a few others hiked up to the bluff and amazingly, found everything undisturbed. They cleaned it up and managed to salvage almost everything.

As we later learned, it seemed that our choice of the promontory, because of its scenic attraction and inaccessibility had almost been our undoing. We didn't stop to think that the view from the top of the bluff worked both ways. We could see the beautiful lights of Cam Ranh very well, but by the same regard, everyone in Cam Ranh could see us up there. We heard later from friends and from Dusty who had been on guard duty down at Cam Ranh village, that all they could see up there was a multitude of little glowing dots that were all the joints being smoked and the flashes of every match and cigarette lighter as well.

Apparently since everyone could see what was taking place up on that bluff, there was a big fuss about finding out what was going on up there. This is what led to the jeep running around the rock quarry and eventually the visit we received from the MP's. Our shit was in the wind but we managed to get through by the grace of God and guardian angels. This response to our party had been unanticipated but we'd been saved by the large numbers in our group. I'm sure we presented a formidable sight but what saved the situation was the fact we were so messed up and had no stomach for fighting our way out although these MP's had no knowledge of that fact. They were smart enough to let us all go.

Dave Friday's ETS party was a grand time and in no time became the stuff of legend with stories told and re-told about who had fled into the hills and only came out at daylight, or who had faced the problem and gotten away. Ralph, CW, Frizzle and I survived. Poor Mark "Frizzle" Frizzo never did quite know what to make of it. Even after we were safe in Stigg's Room, he was not sure if he had been busted or not.

In June, I marked my twelfth month in-country, one full year, a complete tour of duty and then started serving my extension. It had been a long trip from being a green newbie to being an old timer and now being a short

15. The Incorrigibles

timer. I'd changed through those many months. Somehow, I had become one of those people I had once looked upon with awe and disbelief when I was first in-country, those who looked like they'd never set foot on a sidewalk in the World. They looked like they'd always been in Vietnam. Their fatigues were faded and spoke of long service in-country. Their faces and arms were deeply tanned, and their expression appeared as if they were looking at something in the distance.

I was thin, tan and my fatigues well-worn and faded. I wore beads, brass Montagnard bracelets and other unauthorized individual expressions of personal adornment. My hair was too long for the Stateside Army and my moustache was untrimmed. My speech had become exceedingly profane, liberally sprinkled with Vietnamese phrases and military slang and I came to look upon the Vietnamese themselves with a sort of disdain. I had become hardened through all those months and in some ways couldn't see myself assimilating into civilized society again.

I had become one of the "Incorrigibles," the short-timers who had become uncivilized, foul-mouthed, intolerant of bull shit and authority and obnoxious. Being that short gave one a terrible attitude. I mean, what were they going to do to you, extend your tour? Hell, some of those guys would have welcomed that punishment. Some guys didn't want to go home. Some went AWOL until they were ready or they were caught and sent home. The Incorrigibles were counting weeks and days now, not months. They were not ready for the World and the World wasn't ready for them. It seemed nothing short of a crime to turn some of these guys loose into civilized society straight out of months in Vietnam. But they did it anyway.

By mid–July 1971 I began to realize how short I was. I'd been running the Construction Projects Section for about two months when a new typist arrived. I was relieved to have someone take that burden, so I trained him until he had a grasp of what the section did and finally, we got a new NCO to run the section. He was SFC Reno, a healthy fellow in his late thirties, a career Army man who tried very hard to be likeable. I had to train him so he would know how our section operated. He seemed to resent the fact that he had to be trained by me and I didn't much care for his attitude. It seemed like he was always trying to make things more difficult than they had to be. I'm sure Reno saw me as a stubborn, hippy short timer. Our relations deteriorated by the day.

It finally got to the point where I began training the typist to be the file clerk so he could help keep up with the work. SFC Reno and I butted heads over how things were done in the section. To me, the system worked fine, and I knew how to make it work. For some reason, Reno was determined to change everything from top to bottom. To me it seemed a case of fixing something that wasn't broken. He was my superior in rank, but I outranked him in experience in the section, and time in country. I continued to work since our section was at full strength again, but the day came when my replacement arrived. Then I knew how short I was.

SFC Reno continued to aggravate me by questioning procedures. We came to verbal conflict on a number of occasions and there was a growing resentment. By late July of '71, he'd had enough. I came to work one morning and he told me to get out of the office and not come back except to get my mail. I thought he was joking but he was serious. I was instructed to stay in the company area so they could get me if I was needed. Besides, I was too short anyway. My replacement was there and I was no longer needed to run the section.

I was shocked at first. The very idea of being thrown out of the office was one thing, but over a month before I was due to quit work? Who wouldn't make use of extra help? I knew it was partly because SFC Reno was tired of arguing with me and didn't want to put up with my short timer attitude.

Thus, for over a month, I spent my time lying in the sun, keeping my head and taking several showers a day. I enjoyed the time to myself, as there was much to ponder. Being as short as I was, I decided since I wasn't working anymore, I didn't need to make company formations either. So I quit getting up for them. No one said anything about it. Even so, I rarely slept in. By force of habit, I was up at 6:00 a.m. in order to be at the bunker for the morning activities. However, when everyone went to morning formation and then to work, I changed clothes and laid in the sun.

During the many hours I spent in the sun beside that old bunker, I had much to think about. Just letting it sink in that all those months had passed was enough to stagger my mind. It seemed so long ago that I had arrived "in-country" and yet it felt like only yesterday. Surprisingly, the thought of going home, back to the States, back to the World, was more than a little disconcerting. It was a strange fact, but true. By this time I was accustomed to life in Vietnam and the thought of facing unknown changes was unsettling. The media was filled with news about antiwar, anti-draft, anti-anything demonstrations. Places were being bombed and burned. There was unrest and discontent. People were being killed. What kind of peace would I return to? How would I be received? It was ironic to think that I'd been afraid to go to Vietnam because it was a dangerous place and people got killed. Now I was afraid to go back to the World because it was a dangerous place and people got killed. But, Life is dangerous. No one gets out alive.

Ultimately, I would be going back to the World and getting out of the Army. Then I would have to find a job to support myself and become "responsible." I'd saved money but not nearly enough considering the

15. The Incorrigibles

After I was thrown out of the office, when my services were no longer needed, I spent every day at the beach, lying in the sand across the street from my hooch at the big bunker.

expenses I would have to bear. I would have to buy a car, insurance, probably new clothes, keeping a roof over my head, food in my mouth, and money in my pocket. I wanted to finish college but that would take money, even with the GI Bill.

Indeed, many aspects of going home were frightening when I considered that in Vietnam my clothing, food and housing were provided. Plus, the money was good, I paid no income taxes, was with good companions, drugs were plentiful and cheap as were many other vices. The PX provided deals on anything from cameras to appliances and we were in a setting of tropical beauty. It was no wonder some guys went home, turned around and came back for another tour. It was what kept Freddie Warren in Vietnam for twenty-four months, and I finally understood those guys at Hunter Army Airfield, who came into the company from Vietnam, but wanted to go back after only a few weeks. I'd seen guys who had to be carried to the plane when it came time for them to leave. Some people did not want to leave when it was time for them to go home. I felt some of those same emotions as the time approached for my return to the World and I felt guilty for feeling that way. Of course, I probably would have felt differently had I been serving all that time in a line company somewhere rather than what my reality had been. But my reality had been determined by circumstances beyond my control more than through anything I did. Ultimately it was my skill with a typewriter that determined my fate.

After fourteen months Vietnam was home. That ragged hooch on top of that pile of sand in Cam Ranh was my home. Friends were there and so many memories, that the World with all of its family and related associations seemed far away, almost as if my life before the Nam had never happened. I felt in some ways like I'd always been in Vietnam. In some ways, I resented the thought of going home, of leaving my friends behind. But the "going home" like the "going over," was not in my power to influence. I realized I could not continue to live the Nam insanity forever. I wanted out of the Army and that was the goal I had striven to reach all those months. But in getting out, I would be complicating my life.

Vietnam kept life to its basics. You lived each day as it came and didn't worry about yesterday or tomorrow because you only had today. But by getting out, I was letting myself in for a lot more to deal with. In civilian life, I could not live the day by day, devil-may-care lifestyle I'd been living in Vietnam.

By August 1971, I was so short I barely gave a shit about anything. At this time we received word that we were going to a state of "Yellow Alert" because national elections were to take place and there were expectations of increased enemy activity. Rockets had been a nuisance and sappers had penetrated Cam Ranh before, so we knew that anything was possible. As a result the order came down to post guards around the perimeter of Engineer Hill. We'd never pulled guard duty on the Hill before, only a guard post or two every so often down by the village or at the officers club. None of us could really understand what was up on that pile of sand that was worth anything to some VC sapper.

The perimeter bunkers were manned at night and machine guns posted at key bunkers. The career soldiers took the whole thing quite seriously, as if they expected an assault at any moment. However, to combat it we were given M-16s and a few M-60 machine guns with 200 rounds for each. It seemed ridiculous since 200 rounds of ammo would have been consumed in seconds in an attack. I caught the duty once and as you might have guessed, Ralph was also called for duty, so we were out there that evening for guard mount, Gung Ho to get the information and passwords.

There were two to three men to a bunker, depending on circumstances and the bunker's location. It was not like standing guard in those towers at Dong Ba Thin, but we passed the night without incident other than an

15. The Incorrigibles

Guard Mount. 1SGT briefing the guards, August 1971. I'm not happy at having to do this shit because I'm about two weeks from getting out of Vietnam and the Army. I'm too short for this.

inebriated GI with a .45 automatic pistol who shot up the barracks behind us. Although there were no hostilities while I was on guard, it didn't mean the V.C. would leave us alone. A few days after my stint on guard duty, the shit did hit the fan in the early morning darkness of 25 August 1971. It was a hot night and I lay in my bed trying to sleep, serenaded by the hum of a small electric fan mounted on the wall over the head of my bunk. Freddie Warren was rooming with me and he slept with his desk light on which cast a dim glow on my side of the room. About 2:00 a.m., I heard stray rockets whiz by overhead and detonate against the mountain behind us. This had happened before. I didn't give it much thought.

On the other side of that mountain behind us were large storage yards as well as petroleum and ammo dumps. They were tempting targets for the VC and if their rocket trajectories were too low, they struck the mountain behind us. I'd heard them before, usually late at night and never in great quantity. However, on this night there were many more than usual. There were no sirens or alert notice taken with the exception of one newbie in the hooch who went berserk and ran up and down the hall banging on everyone's door, yelling for them to get up. I ignored him because I was far too short to be fucking around if we had incoming.

Shortly after, the lights went out in the hooch and my fan quit running. I knew the power had gone out and that meant something had happened to the generator. Heavy explosions reverberated farther away but still healthy enough to shake my bed. There were sudden rippling explosions, again far away, but these were serious detonations, not from rockets or mortars. I knew something beyond the ordinary was happening, and with all the noise and no fan, lights or electricity there was no sense trying to sleep.

I sat on the edge of the bed. There was a continuous, distant rumbling like thunder, and I could feel shock waves moving through the ground. Freddie had not budged from his bed. He was still asleep, oblivious to it all. I put on my flip flops and shuffled into the darkened hallway. I could barely see the open doorway at the end of the hall, but I could make out a faint, glimmering red hue illuminating shadows that passed by the open door.

When I stepped outside it was like walking into another world. To the north, a mile or so away from us, the whole night sky was a mass of rolling, black clouds, laced with a deep, red light that glowed and glimmered, casting a lurid glare over everything. There were flashes and rumbling and flames over the rocky ridge behind us. One of Cam Ranh's main ammo dumps was going up in a blaze of smoke and fire like an erupting volcano. Ammunition went up in horrendous, exploding balls of fire. Small arms ammo, artillery shells, all exploded with tremendous displays that shook the ground where we stood. The lights all over Cam Ranh were still out and everything was illuminated by the eerie red glow from the ammo dump. The revetments and walkway were filled with people lounging about, watching the fireworks.

I walked out and sat down on the revetment between some people there. Across the street I could see the small guard station between the two big bunkers was manned and there was a group of shadows clustered around it. As I watched, one shadow detached itself from the group and slowly shuffled across the sand. I would have recognized that shuffle anywhere. It was Dusty. It seemed to me as if he knew I was there because he walked across the street and up to where I sat on the revetments, turned around and boosted himself up next to me. He turned and asked if I had a light. I had my lighter and with no further word he handed me a joint and said "light this." I fired it up and we each took a few hits. In a moment, a couple more joints appeared from somewhere and the aroma of "peace" drifted through the group as we sat there dumbfounded by the spectacle.

He was on bunker guard that night and after sharing a few joints we went back across the street to the bunker where he was on duty. I did not

15. The Incorrigibles

know his fellow guards, nor did Dusty but I joined the group around the bunker. About 4:30 a.m., I returned to my darkened room and tried to sleep. Freddie was still out cold, oblivious to it all. I realized that tomorrow, 26 August, was my father's birthday and exactly one year from my near-death experience at Dong Ba Thin.

The next morning it was still dark when I awoke and the sky seemed eerily overcast, like a fog was hanging over us and there was the smell of cordite in the air. When I walked outside the scene was as bizarre as the one of the night before. A huge, black pall of smoke hung over us for miles, blotting out all sunlight, yet out across the bay, on the mainland, I could clearly see the sun shining. But all over Cam Ranh peninsula, this pall of thick, black smoke hung over us and the ammo dump continued rumbling and spewing smoke and spouting fire. To top it off, old Freddie slept through the entire thing! It wasn't until he woke up that he realized something had occurred.

It continued to blow off all morning and wasn't until afternoon when it finally began to burn out. Although the explosions ceased, the fires burned for hours and the ominous pall hung over us the rest of the day. I later learned this operation resulted in the destruction of over 6,000 tons of munitions valued in excess of $10.3 million dollars and six U.S. personnel were wounded.*

Ralph and I sat in the bunker that afternoon talking things over. It was an impressive event, but illustrated no matter how secure we felt atop our little pile of sand in Cam Ranh, there actually *was* a war out there. It was always there in the background and this occasion reminded us of that.

Another milestone you passed in getting short was the day you got your DEROS orders.

This was your "Date of Estimated Return from Over Seas" and these were the orders that started the wheels turning to get you sent home. On one of those late August afternoons while I was laying in the sun by the bunker, my DEROS orders came through. When I went to my room to get cleaned up, they were laying on my bunk. They'd been cut in the personnel office that day and the boys there sped them along with a hand-delivery to the S-3 office where they were picked up and brought to my hooch. There in my hands were my DEROS orders sending me home to ETS from the Army. Now it was official. I was an Incorrigible Short-Timer on the downhill slide.

In a year I'd accumulated a lot. There was no way I could carry it all home so excess was shipped home in "hold baggage." My most massive accumulation was books. I'd consumed paperback books like candy. Ralph and I were always the first ones in the day room when a shipment of free paperbacks came in each month and we always came away with pockets and arms bulging with books to read. I began sorting through my accumulation

---

*Schrader, Person Papers Collection; Fox, p. 199 #407.

and decided to sell the guitar I'd carried over rather than carry it back since I had other guitars at home so I sold it to C.W. Stinson. I kept the old battered Vietnamese guitar that John Robards had given me on that fateful day in Dong Ba Thin when he'd been shipped out during the Bust.

After receiving my orders, Ralph, Stigg and I drove down to the hold baggage building near the docks where I made an appointment for them to pick up my excess. On the appointed afternoon, I was on the revetment at the end of my hooch waiting for the arrival of the hold baggage van. I had my stuff sorted and the excess ready for packing. I saw the truck coming up the road. When they pulled over beside the hooch and stopped, five Vietnamese men jumped off and an NCO with clipboard in hand and cigar in mouth climbed out of the cab and approached me. "You Durham?" he asked. I replied in the affirmative and he says "Let's get on with it."

He whistled and motioned to the Vietnamese men who were in the process of pulling a huge, empty crate off the back of the truck. I led him down the dim hallway of the hooch to my room and indicated the material that was to go. He sat down on my bed with his clipboard and whistled at the Vietnamese who were struggling down the hall with the bulky crate. They brought it in the room, set it down and stood back. The NCO chewed his cigar and sorted through my books and paraphernalia before giving them to two of the Vietnamese who stood by. They packed everything away. The pile of stuff I was shipping home seemed like a lot as it sat on the floor but once tucked in that crate it hardly filled it.

Once packed away the lid was nailed down, the crate hauled out to the truck, weighed, my name stenciled on the side and then hoisted onto the back of the truck. I was given paperwork copies and the NCO climbed back into the cab of the truck and they were off.

Indeed, I was getting short. All I had to do was clear the post at the proper time and leave. But I'd decided a long time before that when I got short I was going out in a blaze of glory. I'd taken two R&R's to Sydney already and I had one more to take and decided to take that one right before rotating home; I was headed to Sydney for a third time. Most of the gang at 35th Group hadn't taken their R&R's yet and they were interested in Ralph and my experiences in Australia.

When Ralph extended his tour of duty for two months, he also got another R&R so we started talking about going on R&R together. When word of this got out, Dusty decided to take his R&R and go with us. Then Mike Stigg decided to do likewise. In conjunction with these developments, Pete Simpson, Harry Arnold, Frizzle, Tommy Tomason and a few others from the company all decided to go on R&R as well, but they were going to Bangkok. Still, we were all going to leave from Da Nang together. I was told we had the limit of men authorized to be absent from the company on R&R at one time.

I wrote letters to Renny and Neil and Pat Morrison and Gypsy to tell them I was coming again and bringing reinforcements. We put our requests in and when our orders came back, Ralph was booked on a flight that left the day before the rest of us. There was nothing to be done about it so Dusty, Stigg and I sent Ralph off a day early to scout things out for us. I gave Ralph instructions on where to go to find the house on Bourke Street and we were all set. My last R&R, September 1971, arrived at last. I was set to ETS on 17 September. With two weeks left in the Army, I was going to spend one of them in Sydney, Australia. Ralph left the company on 2 September, heading for Da Nang. The rest of us would be a day behind him and anticipated an outrageous reunion in Sydney.

16

Bourke Street Again: R&R #3

We sent Ralph off on 2 September then had ourselves a send-off party that night in Stigg's Room. Almost everyone in our group was going on R&R. Ten were headed out the next day and Ralph, who was already gone, made eleven of us absent for a week. We were booked on an early flight to Da Nang so we had to get an early start. As a result, Dusty was at my door before the sun peeked over the horizon. There were so many of us that we had to get a deuce-and-a-half to take us to the airport. Others came along for the ride including my old, roommate, Freddie Warren. We fired up a pipe at the revetments before throwing our luggage aboard the truck, climbing in the back and off to the airport. It was 3 September 1971 and I had two weeks left in the Army.

We arrived at the 14th Aerial Port as dawn was breaking, collected our bags, and headed for the terminal to book flights and booked the first flight to Da Nang. About 11:00 a.m. we touched down at Da Nang and rumbled to a halt near the terminal. We entered and scattered to find our bags while others looked into how we were supposed to get to the Freedom Hill R&R Center. We found a bus stop outside where we could catch a bus to Freedom Hill, however it had just departed and another run would not be made for an hour. We went about collecting our bags and congregating at the bus stop to await the next bus.

Across the street there was a line of parked vehicles and as we sat with our luggage a ragged GI walked up to us. "You guys going to Freedom Hill?" We replied that we were and he said "I'll give you a ride but you'll have to give my truck a push so I can get it started." We agreed although I decided I was far too short to be working up a sweat in that manner. There were enough of us to get the job done without my efforts, so I sat back.

The assembled group followed the fellow to a ¾-ton truck. After the driver got in, the boys applied their shoulders to the front and pushed the truck out into the street. Once in the street everyone went to the rear end and began pushing the truck. It jerked down the street a little but would not start. By this time traffic was backing up behind us and right up on our bumper came a battered Vietnamese garbage truck. The Vietnamese on the truck jumped off and shuffled up to our group. They jabbered at us with smiles on their face.

After a bit of talking and hand gestures, we understood they wanted to push us with the truck so Harry Peterson directed the truck against our bumper, we loaded our bags, and everyone climbed in. They gave us a push, the driver let out the clutch and the truck coughed to life. We thanked the garbage men, sped off down the street and passed through a gate in a chain link fence, and were in downtown Da Nang. We soon left the town behind and the road stretched out toward an installation we could see in the distance. The driver pulled off the road at the gate and said "Freedom Hill. Thanks for your trouble, fellas." We wished him "peace" and climbed out.

After checking in at the gate we trudged down an asphalt road that ran along row after row of unoccupied barracks to the left and a chain link fence on the right with open fields and paddies beyond. We worked up a sweat and grumbled about the damn R&R center being so far from the gate

Waiting for them to announce the R&R flights going out. Freedom Hill R&R Center, Da Nang, RVN.

but we finally rounded a corner and the activity ahead indicated we were there. To our left was a large A-frame shelter under which was a small snack bar and picnic tables. Ahead of us was a street bordered by two-story barracks on the left side and a one-story building on the right that held the processing facilities.

There wasn't much activity and we only saw a few GIs in fatigues and others in civilian clothes here and there. At an information window we learned the Bangkok flight would process that night and the next Sydney flight was not until the following evening. Since the barracks had not been opened we who were bound for Sydney, were obliged to wait before we could get a bunk. The others, who were off for Thailand, were not worried about bunks as they would be in Thailand before the sun rose again.

We ate lunch from the snack bar at the A-frame shelter, then located a room in an empty barracks to secure our bags. We'd passed a USO coming in so we went to see what was there. It was on the bottom floor of an air-conditioned two-story barracks and upon entering, it seemed we had found where everyone in Freedom Hill was hiding as it was filled with GIs.

There was a snack bar to one side, pool tables that were doing a brisk business and other diversions, so we gathered at a group of couches while some investigated a pool table. Those of us with less energy kicked back relaxed and managed to pass the hours until the barracks opened.

We found the barracks uninhabited with only a few bunks occupied as the scattered bags gave evidence. Stigg, Dusty and I picked out bunks while the guys heading to Thailand changed into civilian clothes as their flight would process soon. As the time approached for the Bangkok flight, we moved outside where we sat in the shade.

The loudspeaker announced processing for the Bangkok flight, which brought life to our boys headed there so last minute goodbyes and good lucks were exchanged as well as various admonishments on what to look out for. The boys bound for Thailand hustled off for processing leaving Dusty, Stigg and me in the silence of their departure.

The Bangkok flight took practically everyone out of the R&R center thus only a few of us heading out on the next day's flights were still around. Dusty, Stigg and I returned to the USO which we found deserted and passed the time until supper. Between us we had a deck of joints and had been looking for a safe place to sneak off to and get a buzz. However, we were not familiar with the complexities of the compound and had not been able to find a place. With nightfall our chances would be better.

The sun disappeared behind the hills after supper and we went out for a walk as darkness fell. We followed the street around the far side of the processing building and arrived at a corner in the chain link fencing that seemed to suit our needs. Outside the fence, spotlights illuminated the fields beyond and this light provided just enough illumination but there was a shadow in the corner where we stood with a perfectly unobstructed view down the only routes of approach anyone would use. There we fired up some numbers and discussed all manner of things from my getting short to what we would find in Sydney.

By this time the processing center was deserted, and we walked back toward our barracks The flash of a cigarette lighter in the distance near the darkened USO attracted our attention. Through the half light we could see another little group huddling together in the darkness passing numbers around. We finally headed to the barracks to hit the sack.

During the night a returning R&R flight arrived, and our sleep was disturbed by the influx of rowdy GIs coming in to bed down. There was much horse play going on and showers taken, and we tried to ignore them and sleep but without much luck.

We were rousted early the next morning as they cleared the barracks, so we followed the procession of grumbling GIs out to the street. We had an entire day to kill before our flight, so we stashed our bags in one of the empty barracks again. The USO was filling up fast as new arrivals poured into the center as R&R flights began to arrive. We made our way to a large PX just up the road and spent the morning there before returning to the USO. After lunch we found a secure place to smoke a joint.

That afternoon we changed into civilian clothes and stored our fatigues in a room opened for that purpose. As the sun slipped behind the mountain, the loudspeaker blared that processing for the Sydney flight was to begin so we grabbed our bags and joined others at the entrance, then elbowed our way into a large room with chairs with desk tops. An NCO stepped to the podium and processing began. It was the usual, forms, currency conversion, and all that until we were dismissed to go to customs and convert our MPC to greenbacks. As before, we were dismissed according to rank and when the call for officers came I motioned to Stigg and Dusty to follow me and we walked out with the officers to board the buses.

Soon we were headed into Da Nang and toward the airfield where we rolled out onto the runway toward a big, blue and white Pan Am jet. When the call for officers came, we scrambled off the bus and up the boarding ramp where round-eyed girls greeted us at the entrance. They directed us into the interior where we claimed three seats. Soon the doors were latched and in no time we were hurtling off into the night sky bound for Australia with a stop in Darwin.

We dozed and when I opened my eyes the sun was rising which meant we were approaching Sydney. The pilot soon informed us we were on our descent into Sydney Airport. "Sydney, here we come!" Dusty said as we buckled our seat belts. The runway rose up, the plane thumped to a landing, and we taxied to the terminal.

The door opened and we followed the call for officers and hurried into the terminal, down the long hallway towards the customs area and recovered our luggage. Once through there we followed the flow outside to the line of waiting buses. As we boarded, it occurred to me that Renny might come to meet us at the airport as it would be just like her to do that, but we were hustled through so quickly I hardly had a chance to look for her. Then Dusty nudged me and pointed out the window. At first glance, it was just two girls walking along the parking lot across the street, but on closer inspection I saw that it was RENNY and a girl named Patty from the Bourke Street Commune. I laughed and told Dusty he would meet those two ladies very soon.

Apparently Renny had arrived too late to meet us since we were already boarding the buses.

I hurried off the bus and called to her. She waved and I ran over to where she was. She gave me a hug and we had a brief reunion. This really startled Dusty and Stigg since to them it appeared as if I had just approached an unknown stranger on street and started hugging her. The buses were ready to depart so I told Renny I would see them shortly and hurried back to the bus.

The buses soon headed for downtown Sydney. It was hard to believe I was in Sydney for the third time in six months. Stigg and Dusty were watching all that was passing, and everyone was taking in the sight of Hot Pants, mini-skirts and the like which evoked an outburst of enthusiasm and appreciation from the occupants of the bus. We turned down a lane and pulled up to the front of the processing building.

The bus doors opened, and we filed into the processing building. When I entered the lobby, I was surprised to see Gypsy sitting among those waiting in the lobby. She looked radiant and smiled at me when our eyes met. We were hustled through the lobby so quickly that I hardly had a chance to exchange a word with her and followed the group through a door and down an all too familiar hall to an all too familiar processing room where we took our seats.

It was the same old procedure with forms to fill out, currency to convert, then briefings. During the break, messages were given out and I was surprised to hear my name called out. I was handed a sheet of paper that had been folded several times. Dusty and Stigg looked on with much curiosity as I unfolded it. There were only three words written in pencil on the center of the page.

"Gypsy is here." Dusty and Stigg began to razz me a little after I showed them the paper but I told them I'd already seen her in the lobby so I knew she was there.

16. Bourke Street Again: R&R #3

The briefing concluded and we were released, officers first, so we snuck out with them. When we got into the hallway to get our luggage we ran into Renny and Patty. I gave Renny a big hug while she went on about missing our flight's arrival at the airport and having to rush downtown to catch the buses. I introduced Dusty and Stigg and asked about Ralph who was conspicuous by his absence. Renny related that Ralph was in rare form, had latched onto some hot young red head, hadn't been seen since early the night before, and had not come home all night.

Renny had a car outside to give us a ride to the house but I told her I had to see Gypsy and Renny said they would wait while I went to get her. I made my way down the hallway which was rapidly filling as the processing let out and others were flooding into the lobby. When I entered, there was Gypsy with her little girl smile and her sparkling eyes. We embraced and kissed. I told her what the situation was as Renny and the others arrived. Dusty and Stigg had procured my bag and they were ready to get moving. I introduced them to Gypsy and in no time we were all crammed into Renny's little car and heading for Bourke Street.

Renny related the story of going to the airport to meet Ralph. She blew him away as he expected to meet a "guy" named Renny, not some good-looking, long-legged, red-headed Aussie chick in Hot Pants. Renny said they all liked Ralph immediately and he had kept them in stitches. She inquired about Ski and I told her that he had gone home and I'd not heard from him since.

We arrived at the Bourke Street house, parked and hurried inside. Many of the same people were living there and I renewed old acquaintances while introducing Dusty and Stigg whose reputations had preceded them due to Ralph's stories. The smoking room in the basement of the house next door was still the smoking room and we retired there to get our heads, courtesy of some GIs already there. Gypsy had to work as she had a new job as a waitress at a restaurant in Kings Cross and was living with Pat Morrison and Elaine in an apartment at Bondi Beach.

Gypsy had brought Pat and Elaine together and they'd set up housekeeping. Pat provided something of a "father" figure for Elaine's little girl, Tara. Shortly after I'd left in May, Pat got a part time job in a music store downtown which gave him some income. The cost of living in Australia was such that Pat's part time job was enough to support them. Gypsy and Elaine were close friends and, since the apartment at Bondi Beach was large enough, Gypsy moved in to help with the expenses and take care of Tara. Gypsy wanted me to come to Bondi Beach and stay with them, which I promised to do but I told her I was obligated to stay at the Bourke Street house for a while to help Dusty and Stigg get acclimated, which I knew would not take long.

Dusty and Stigg were in good hands so I left them at the house while Gypsy and I went out to walk downtown to see Pat at work. Everywhere there were images of the recent past. I could see Janet Carr and Ski and Sue in the park all wired up on Acid. We walked the same streets I'd pounded before as we followed the sidewalks into downtown Sydney. We passed shops and stores until we entered a large music store where I saw Pat standing behind the counter. He smiled warmly when he saw me and we shook hands and embraced like long lost brothers. Pat and I had been corresponding through the intervening months since my May R&R, so I was aware of his situation and that life in Australia agreed with him.

As business picked up we let Pat get back to work with promises of getting together soon, then Gypsy and I walked back up the street towards Kings Cross. It was about time for her to go to work so I escorted her there and made plans to meet later.

When I returned to Bourke Street, I found Dusty and Stigg at the kitchen table visiting with Renny and Neil. Since the day was still young we hit the streets and wandered all over Kings Cross and took taxi rides here and there. We sat at the same fountain where Ski and I had been beckoned by the two girls hanging out of a window eight stories up. I told them the story and marveled at the fact that I was sitting there on the same fountain six months later with two guys I hadn't even known then. It seemed like a dream. With the constant Déjà vu, my pending ETS, being back in a real city, I was losing my grip on reality. My mind was so drawn to the past and the impending future that I had little time to deal with the present.

We spent the day getting used to the feel of a city again and when we returned to Bourke Street there was still no sign of Ralph. I began to worry a little as no one had seen him since the evening before. However, I knew how events could run away with you, and all you could do was go with the flow and I knew he would surface sooner or later. Ralph finally called in to say that he and his young lady were at some place owned by her friends at Bondi Beach. They would be back at the house the next day. Needless to say, Ralph was having a good time.

By this time we'd been assigned rooms and I'd made arrangements with Renny to stay a few days before I went out to Bondi Beach. We got acquainted with the other GIs who were there and, as always there was a feeling of brotherhood and good vibes amongst us all. It was a wild, good time, ending up back at the house where we gathered around the kitchen table for coffee, smoke and late-night conversation.

That last R&R blurred into a surreal haze as there were a number of things that blew my mind. I was in Sydney with good buddies and around good people. I was shortly to leave the Nam and get out of the Army. My life would soon be mine to live as I pleased for the very first time. My life would

16. Bourke Street Again: R&R #3

be my own, bought and paid for. It wasn't cheap, only about five of the best years of my life. It wasn't exactly a bargain price, but it was soon to be paid in full.

We didn't meet up with Ralph until late the next afternoon when we returned to Bourke Street from a trip downtown. We walked in the front room to find Ralph sitting there with this totally smashed, shit-eatin' grin on his face and a long, slinky, red head attached to his arm. Dusty, Stigg and I jumped on him as we hadn't seen him since the night before we left Engineer Hill. "Dog pile on Ralph!" It was funny to see him in civilian clothes but it was Ralph.

In the intervening time we met a fellow GI at the house who turned out to be a good friend of Pete Simpson. He was on our R&R flight and his name was Mike. He had spent his first night in Sydney in a hotel until he met one of the girls from the house. She brought him in and he never went back to the hotel. It was one of those "small world" things I'd experienced several times since being in the Nam. In Sydney, of all places, we met a fellow who had grown up with Pete Simpson. We told him Pete was on R&R in Thailand right then. Mike joined us in our wanderings.

One evening I took a cab to Bondi Beach to visit Gypsy, Pat and Elaine. We had a pleasant reunion. Pat was doing well and quite happy. He worked at the music store and in his spare time walked to the beach and fished. Fish he caught were brought home, cleaned and frozen to supplement their food stocks. They seemed quite content. It was inevitable the conversation turned to my future as it was soon to be in my hands to be determined.

We talked about me coming back to Australia or perhaps staying there and not going back since I was so close to getting out of the Army and I had plenty of leave time accrued. Who would worry about one lousy week? I had to admit the idea crossed my mind and I had considered the possibility but at that point in time I had reached no decision.

I spent an enjoyable evening with them. Gypsy and I walked to the beach and sat in the sand, talking of many things there in the darkness. I returned to Bourke Street that night but not before promising to come and stay a few nights with them. Once arrangements had been made, I went to see Ralph, who was now on the downhill side of his R&R.

About the time we were in mid–R&R, Ralph was finishing his. On one of his last nights we had a big blow-out at the Bourke Street house. The kitchen table crowd was already collecting and others were already tripping when we arrived and we joined them. It was a riotous night that became one of those all night mass trips and at first light we were still laughing, joking, toking, and drinking coffee. It was a wild night that kept us going into the next day. No time to sleep. As the sun came up we headed out to take an early morning walk then it was time to send Ralph back to the Nam. We told him to make sure the company was prepared because the whole troop of us would all be returning about the same time so it was bound to be another wild time.

As the day dawned, I got a cab and moved out to Bondi Beach to stay with Pat, Elaine and Gypsy. She took time off from her job and we spent several days together, riding the double-decker buses all over town, visiting the botanical gardens downtown and having lunch on the terrace of a tea room. We sat in the yard behind their Bondi Beach apartment and enjoyed the sun and the moon and walked through the little shops and stores and markets in their neighborhood.

The end approached all too quickly. I began to freak out when I realized R&R was almost over and I was seven days SHORT! When I got back to Vietnam all I had to do was clear post and report for processing at the appointed time. I was in a daze those last days in Sydney.

Pat and Gypsy wanted me to come back to Australia when I got out of the Army but I couldn't decide. I needed to finish my college degree as I only lacked one year before graduating. Without that degree I didn't think I could do much in Australia and felt it would be a problem to try and finish it there. And in the back of my mind was my Stateside Janet whom I hadn't seen in two years. There were many implications and unfinished business between us and I was curious to see her again, so that was an attraction to return to the States.

When the day arrived, I rode the bus back to the Bourke Street house and found Dusty and Stigg in fine spirits. Stigg had latched onto a foxy-looking Aussie lass who was petite, well proportioned and nicely assembled. He was in love and talking about coming back to Australia to be with her and she was talking about going to the States to be with him. That conversation sounded familiar. Dusty was holding his own. We had one day and that night to get it together. There was one last blow-out and we ended up around the kitchen table until all hours and never made it to bed that night. As the sun crept through the windows, the house was buzzing. Everybody was running all over, upstairs and down, until 7:00 a.m. when we gathered on the sidewalk out front. Renny pulled up in her car and we packed ourselves in. Besides Stigg, Dusty, Mike and I, there was also Renny, Sandy, Patty and Stigg's girl, all crammed in Renny's little car. She fired up the engine and we were off.

We pulled up near the processing center and piled out. There was already a gathering of GIs and their ladies involved in saying their farewells. Stigg immediately got involved with his lady while we collected in an alley near the entrance to the R & R center, goofed off, took pictures, and said our goodbyes to the people from Bourke Street. Renny asked me to keep in touch and reassured me I always had a place to stay if I ever

Tara (child), Elaine, and Pat, Bondi Beach, 1971.

came back again. The fellows from our flight made their return to the processing center. It wasn't that they wanted to go back, but rather that they had to. I was the shortest man there and not bashful in letting them all know it. The call for processing was issued so our last goodbyes were said and we joined the crush as everyone shuffled into the briefing room. It was the usual forms and currency conversion before we were herded off to the buses. We piled in and in no time were off, waving to Renny and the gang as they stood by the car yelling something at us as we sped off.

We zoomed down the city streets. Stigg and Dusty and everyone on our bus were quiet and subdued. I knew the feeling only too well. It was my third trip there but for most it was their first and probably only trip to Sydney. We were lost in thought as our late-night hours and early morning rushing around began to catch up with us. We arrived at the airport, were hustled to the waiting plane where we boarded, collapsed in our seats and in no time were off into the skies heading toward Vietnam via the Philippines. We were so worn out it was almost a relief to be heading for Da Nang. It was dark by the time we arrived and got off the plane, "officers first."

The buses rolled up, we unloaded, went to the processing building, converted our currency to MPC, collected our bedding, and found empty bunks in a barracks. A few people were trying to sleep but the influx turned on the lights and the business of making beds, and taking showers began. I remembered when we had been so disturbed a week earlier by returning R&R GIs.

We noticed fellows returning with their fatigues that had been stored at the far end of the processing building so we hurried down to get our fatigues out of storage.

Once settled in the barracks we found we were too wide awake to think of sleep. However, we had nothing to smoke which was a sad situation, but

Renny Vorsa sees me off after my last R&R. Heading back to Vietnam one more time.

16. Bourke Street Again: R&R #3

we decided there must be something burning somewhere and went out for a walk. I remembered seeing others out toking in the shadows when we were there a week before and figured the odds were good we would stumble upon someone we might bum a joint from. The odds were in our favor. On the backside of the processing building, near where we had smoked before, we saw a little cluster of people standing in the shadows between two spotlights on the wall.

We walked down the street toward them and as we approached, we could see the glowing coals of the joints, smell the pungent aroma and hear their muffled conversation. When they noticed our approach their conversation hushed. As we walked up to them, Stigg stepped forward and asked if we might bum a joint. He explained our position and in no time we were welcomed into their group. These fellows were on their way to Sydney the next day. We laughed and told them to check out the house on Bourke Street and to tell the folks there we'd sent them.

We were mellowed out when we finally retired to our bunks. I tried to sleep but my mind was so full of thoughts about what lay ahead that sleep was hard to find. On the next morning my final roller coaster ride to ETS would begin.

As soon as they rousted us out of our beds that morning, I hit the floor running. Dusty and Stigg understood perfectly that my getting back to the company as quickly as possible was a priority. I grabbed my bag and headed out to hike to the front gate where I hoped to hitch a ride to the airport. Dusty and Stigg would follow shortly. It was early but the heat of the day was already gaining in intensity and I worked up a sweat as I hurried down that long street past all those empty barracks with my mind swimming with ideas of "if" and "when" and "how."

I exited Freedom Hill and saw that I was the only person trying to catch a ride so I parked myself opposite the gate on the other side of the highway. It was early morning and the traffic had not started yet. Only an occasional Army vehicle came by and just zoomed past me. I was a little miffed since we always picked up hitchhikers back in Cam Ranh and Dong Ba Thin. It was not long before I was joined by others trying to catch rides. Dusty and Stigg then joined me.

It seemed to me we stood there on that roadside with an increasing crowd for at least an hour. At last, a jeep pulled over beside us but there were three people in it. The lieutenant in front said "We can take one." Dusty and Stigg told me to get in which I did with no further encouragement. The jeep took off, heading for the airport. When I explained my rush to them I was roundly congratulated by the other three in the jeep and they drove me right to the front of the terminal where they left me amid shouts of "Good luck!"

I hurried to the counter and found the morning flight to Cam Ranh was open so I booked it and checked my bag. Dusty and Stigg arrived a short time later and booked the same flight. When our flight was called, we trekked across the runway to a C-130 where the two huge cargo doors were opened, and the loading ramp was down. Inside there were NO seats, only the floor.

We climbed in, sitting in rows with one large cargo strap across our collective laps, one for each row like one large seat belt for fifteen people in each row. Once situated with our luggage strapped to a huge pallet secured behind us, the doors shut and the engines started. As the plane began moving it was easy to see that this deal of one seat belt was not all it was cracked up to be.

We hung on for dear life as the plane roared down the runway and took off. The centrifugal force tumbled us into one another as one by one, each row collapsed into the one behind it. Once the plane leveled off we unscrambled ourselves amid grumbling and laughter. It was about this time we learned our flight was not the express flight since we were going to Cam Ranh by way of Pleiku with an hour hold over somewhere along the way.

It was late afternoon when we touched down at Cam Ranh. We hurried off the plane, gathered our bags, headed out the door and down the street, stretching our thumbs at everything going our way. We had not hiked down the road too far when an OD green special services van pulled off the road ahead of us. We hurried down and climbed in. The fellow in the van took us to South Beach but declined to take his van up that pile of sand where we lived, because he could not believe that what was the road was in fact a road. He let us out instead and we trudged up the road.

When we reached the top of the Hill, Dusty and Stigg headed for their hooch and I walked down the duckboards to mine. It was about 3:00 p.m. when I walked into my room. It was just as I'd left it, devoid of any belongings since I'd sold them off or shipped them home, but I noticed that Freddie and his stuff were gone. We learned later that one morning while we were gone the 1SGT walked through the hooch and found Fred just waking up. In the ensuing conversation it came out that Fred was freeloading off our company and was sent packing back up the Hill to the 497th PCC where the oversight was pointed out to them. This meant the loss of my roommate, but Fred still held up his part and was with us to the bitter end.

I dropped my suitcase, saw the accumulated mail on my bed, turned around and headed back down the hall. There was something on my mind at that moment and it was more important than mail. I walked to the orderly room and told the clerk I was back from R&R and I wanted my Clearance Papers. He shuffled through his IN box, finally pulling out some papers that he handed to me. Clearance papers were a form that you had to take to all the little places indicated and get someone to initial it. Once you had checked in at all those places and gotten your records and all the necessary initials, you were considered "cleared" to leave. I returned to my hooch and looked at those coveted pieces of paper before sorting through my mail. Then I hiked down to the motor pool to get that checked off. I had three days to clear post and what days they would be.

When we returned, the gang was once again reunited after about ten days. The fellows who had flown out to Thailand had gotten back the day before and Ralph had returned shortly before they did. Ralph said the company was pretty dull when he got back and if it hadn't been for Chris Wilson, he would have gone bonkers smoking by himself. That night we gathered in Stigg's Room It was a riotous night filled with stories and jokes and laughs that would have rivaled anything ever seen around the kitchen table at Bourke Street. Everyone had something to relate and we all enjoyed hearing about everyone's adventures. All in all, it was still good to be back on top of that pile of sand, laid back in familiar surroundings with the guys. The party soon deteriorated, and we got back into our old grooves. My time was growing shorter by the minute. I had to finish clearing and already plans were being made to throw an ETS party for me that might rival Dave Friday's and would take place in a few days.

17

Straight On Till Morning

I was out of bed early on the morning of 13 September 1971 and joined the boys in the bunker for our regular post-breakfast break. One by one they came out to sit and share a moment of reflection. It was like any typical morning I'd lived the past few months except now I had my clearance papers and, with luck, would clear as many places as I could on this day. We were still recovering from our R&R, plus the wild welcome-back smoke-down of the night before and I'd let everyone know I had my clearance papers. They pooh-poohed me and said they'd be glad to get rid of me which I knew was true since my departure brought them closer to their own.

When they went to work, I grabbed a ride to finance. I remembered processing there when I arrived and felt certain it could not possibly take as long to process out as it had to process in. The finance building looked the same. Newbies milled about outside the entrance as I walked in and it was the same dark interior with newbies filling the bleachers set against the wall. They were processing in and I was processing out. I went to the counter to one side where the sign read "OUT PROCESSING" and was sent from one desk clerk to another, filled out forms, and was told it would be a half-hour before my records would be ready to pick up.

When my name was called, I hustled to the desk, signed for my records, got my clearance papers initialed, and received my "good luck" from the clerk. I turned and smiled at the newbies and let them know that I was four days short, then was out the door in a flash. Next stop was to get my medical records from the dispensary and my dental records from the dental clinic.

In that first full day of clearing post I got everything checked off except the company supply room and orderly room which I would clear on my last day. So I was finished until I signed out to go home. I stashed my records and papers in my wall locker, changed my clothes and headed for the bunker to take up my spot in the sun. I had two more days of laying in the sun reading, thinking, smoking and joking with the guys who came out to the bunker.

17. Straight On Till Morning

It was inevitable that my ETS party would come about. It was to be another of those all out smokestack, mind-blowing affairs and the boys got ready well in advance. It was intended to be memorable, but with not quite the intensity of Dave Friday's party, so it was time to get in a stock of smoke. With a big party in the offing a resupply run was necessary. However, smoke was getting harder to find in large quantities. In answer to the call, the hat was passed, about $100 raised, and Dusty, Stigg and Pete got the paperwork to drive off the Cam Ranh peninsula so they could get out into the countryside. On 14 September, the day before the party, the trio took off. They were gone most of the afternoon and it was nearly 4:30 p.m. when they pulled in but they were all smiles which attested to the success of their mission.

That night we gathered in Stigg's Room and rolled joints in assembly line fashion as we had for Dave Friday's party. We had wash pans filled with loose pot, rolling papers and cigarette rolling machines and we got busy. This routine went on almost all night.

On 15 September, I laid in the sun all morning and part of the afternoon and made occasional trips Stigg's Room where the boys were still rolling numbers. That afternoon, I showered early and went to Stigg's Room to relax and listen to some tunes. Everyone else was at work so I had the room to myself. I was resigned to my fate and realized it was very much the same attitude that had come over me when I was facing orders sending me to Vietnam.

As closing time approached in the offices about 5:30 p.m., we headed for the bunker. After supper we regrouped around the picnic table by the revetments and waited until everyone arrived. As the evening sky darkened, we went to the bunker to sit in the sand and fire up a few numbers. Once the evening was launched, we returned to Stigg's Room where the stereo was cranked up and the grocery bag of joints opened up.

The room filled in no time and everyone was there, Dusty, Ralph, Stigg, Andy Davidson, Arnold, Frizzle, Freddie, Pete Mendez, Pete Simpson, Chris Wilson, Bo Long, Denny Roberts and many others The air-conditioner kept us cool and it was a riotous evening on the order of Dave Friday's party but without all the added excitement. Denny Roberts passed around a notebook and returned it to me with everyone's home address in it. There were photographs taken to mark the occasion and provide a visual record of the moment. As the hours passed the company settled in after the movie was over but we came out of the room to take in some fresh air at the picnic table.

We freaked around the picnic table until the wee hours of the morning when gradually, one by one, everyone came to shake hands, pat me on the back, wish me luck and say goodbye. Some goodbyes were harder to say than others but the hardest goodbyes were yet to come. It came down to a bare handful of the hard-core and finally, in self-defense, I had to call it quits.

I stumbled back to my room one last time. When I got there I looked at its barren interior with my bags packed and ready, my extra fatigues stacked and ready to turn in. There was nothing in my wall locker. I marked off the last days on my short timer calendar, packed it away, crawled in bed and turned out the light.

The sun rose as it had on countless days I'd spent in-country. When I awoke, there was such an air of routine that I felt like I could get up, lay in the sun and it would keep going. But this was the day I had lived through almost sixteen months for. I could report to process for shipment back to the States. Look out World, here I come! I dressed in my fatigues and met most of the boys out in the bunker one last time for the morning smoke. Many were absent, victims of the night before. Dusty, Ralph, Stigg and I went to eat breakfast and while they went for morning formation, I returned to the hooch, gathered my bedding and remaining sets of fatigues and took them to the supply room to turn in. I got my clearance papers initialed and now all that remained was for me to sign out of the company at the orderly room.

Feeling the regular after-breakfast call of nature, I walked to the pisser and relieved myself.

As I returned across the street to my hooch, a jeep pulled up and Dusty and Stigg hopped out. We walked to my room and met Ralph coming down the hallway from the opposite direction.

Everyone seemed as if it were just another day. We entered my barren room where only my bags sat in the middle of the floor. My bed was merely the metal frame, bare mattress and pillow.

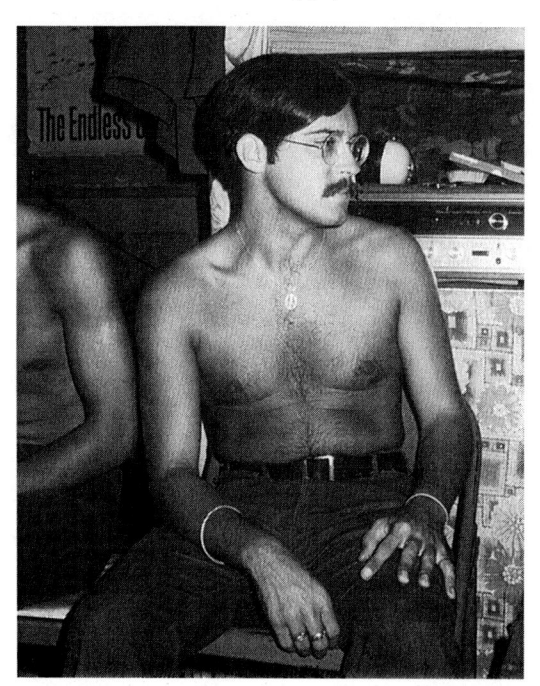

My last night in the company and my ETS party. I'm totally freaking out in spite of the calm façade.

17. Straight On Till Morning

I tucked away a few joints in a plastic bag and stashed them in my pocket. Dusty, Stigg and Ralph stood by silently while I reviewed everything to see that nothing was forgotten or remained to be done. "That's it!" I said. Stigg and Ralph grabbed my bags and we headed to the jeep outside. While they put my bags in, I walked down the duckboards one last time and entered the orderly room. "All set to go!" I announced to the 1SGT and clerks as I walked in. They extended their "good lucks" to me and I walked over to the company register. With that I picked up the pen and signed myself out of Headquarters and Headquarters Company, 35th Engineer Group.

I walked to where the boys sat waiting in the jeep and climbed in the front seat beside Stigg with Dusty and Ralph in the back. Stigg fired up the engine, made a "U" turn and headed down the sandy street leaving Engineer Hill behind me forever. At the bottom of the hill, we turned onto the asphalt heading north toward Times Square and the 22nd Replacement. Dusty and Ralph fired up some joints and we smoked a silent tribute. There was very little conversation as we drove.

We turned off at the sign for the 22nd Replacement. It had been a while since I'd been there but as we rounded the curve it spread out before us looking the same as the first time I'd seen it. It was a depressing sight when I first saw it, but at this point in time it was a beautiful sight. The only difference was a small building with a chain-link fence around the back side, built next to the entrance to the compound. We pulled up at the gate where a big sign instructed personnel reporting for out-processing to report to the new building.

We parked on the shoulder of the road across from the building while I went to see what the deal was. I entered and found myself in a small room with several men sitting behind tables and a rack with suitcases in it. Through a door in the back, I could see a large room with urinals along one wall. It was the "piss test." Every out-processing GI had to take a piss test. If they found traces of heroin, you went to a hospital for detoxification, then back to the States for more detox. If you were going to ETS, a positive result would delay your separation by up to two months.

I talked to one of the clerks as to what the procedure was, then hustled back outside to where Dusty, Stigg and Ralph stood waiting with my bags by the jeep. "I guess this is it" I said as I approached. There was nothing more to do. We shook hands and hugged and said our goodbyes. It was hard to leave these good people who had become my brothers over the months. Old Ralph smiled because he knew we would be reuniting in about a month since he was already pressing thirty days short himself and his home was a mere thirty-minute drive from my own.

I picked up my bags, turned my back and walked toward the building. I heard the jeep engine and I stopped to look back as they turned and sped out the gate, heading back to Engineer Hill. A large part of me wanted to climb back in that jeep and go back to the Hill but I watched the jeep disappear, then I went inside. I checked my bags, filled out a card, and was handed a paper cup and directed to "fill it up" in the adjoining room.

I walked into the other room, which I found to be four walls of wall-to-wall urinals with a fellow sitting in an elevated chair that resembled a lifeguard's chair at the beach. He was to see that no funny business occurred, and he personally examined each cup to make certain it was "up to snuff" before allowing the individuals to proceed. There were others doing their duty, so I picked a random urinal and prepared to do my stuff. As I stood staring at the wall, a sinking feeling swept over me as I realized that I had done my regular morning business before I left the company a short time back. Now there was barely enough urine to fill the bottom of the cup, far from sufficient, I knew.

I walked over to the dude on duty in the big chair. "What happens now?" I inquired as I showed him my deficient cup. He instructed me to leave my cup and card on the table in front of him and to go to the adjoining room where I would find coffee and water to help my system, but I could not leave until my cup was filled. As I set my cup and card on the table I saw that I was not the only one in that predicament as there were other cups already on the table being held hostage to the demand for a cup of warm pee. I silently cursed myself for being so absent-minded as to forget about the piss test that morning.

I gave the old cup a few more tries and managed to squeeze out a few more drops, gradually adding to the contents. The dude on duty still said "NO" so I waited, frustrated at having missed the morning out-process briefing. I finally managed to dispense the required amount of yellow gold into the cup and the dude on duty said "OK." I turned in my sample with a degree of certainty that it was not tainted in the least by any opiate traces. My bags were returned to me and I shuffled out into the mid-morning sun to hike over to the processing center.

It was not a long walk but the heat of the sun and the weight of my bags made it seem like an uphill climb. I passed the same central issue facility building where EJ and I had spent our first night in-country sleeping on luggage racks. I passed the in-processing building where we had come in and I went by the same PSP matting hardstand where we stood in the sun on that first day. There were newbies standing around the in-processing area looking rather lost.

I reached the out-processing building and set my bags in the shade under a covered walkway leading up to the entrance of the building. The briefing I had missed due to my difficulties at the pee test was still in progress so I settled by my bags and opened up my book. I was not more than

17. Straight On Till Morning

The out-processing building. Waiting to go home.

ten feet from the front door of the processing hall so figured there was no way I could miss the call for the next briefing. I became engrossed in my book but kept an eye on the entrance. The briefing let out and the hall emptied. There would be about a half hour between briefings so I continued to read and listen for the call.

When I looked up again I could not believe my eyes. The processing hall was filled and the briefing was in progress. I looked at my watch. It was five minutes past one! The 1:00 p.m. briefing started and I heard no call nor noticed any activity at the door even though I was but ten feet away. I grabbed my records and hurried over to a fellow standing in the doorway. He barred me from entering and was unsympathetic to my pleas. I had to wait until the 2:30 p.m. briefing due to this.

Doing a "slow burn" I turned away just as a soul brother came rushing up, obviously in the same plight as me. I watched a replay of the same scene I'd just played. The fellow in the doorway disposed of the soul brother, and walked away, leaving us to stand there gritting our teeth. "Same shit for you, too?" I said to the brother.

He turned and looked at me, then spewed forth a string of profanity that ended up stating that the Army keeps fucking with you right up to the end. Amen! I told him how I'd waited right there and still managed to miss the briefing, which made him laugh. We decided we would not miss the 2:30 p.m. briefing, shook hands on it, and introduced ourselves to each other. His name was Archie and he was about my height and build, with a friendly manner and pleasant personality. Some of the soul brothers were very clannish and you could not get close to them easily but usually it was dope that provided a common link between many whites and blacks. We talked as Archie brought his duffle bag over to where my bags sat in the shade of the covered walkway. As it turned out he was looking to ETS the same day as me. We laughed at how we'd each been looking for this day to come for so long and suddenly it was here. To top it off, we'd both missed the same briefing by minutes. We talked about a multitude of things and in a short time developed a sort of bond.

The out-processing center consisted of a cluster of two-story barracks, a large, single-story building, sand, boardwalks and a multitude of GIs milling about. Archie was the only one I knew and I felt it was probably likewise for him. When I began to figure out that he was probably a fellow head, he showed me he was when he said "You look like a man who knows where his head is at. Do you think there's a place we could get off to and smoke a bone?"

I felt a reassured. Call it human nature or intuition but I laughed when he asked me. It was as if he had taken down the last barrier between us. "I'm sure something can be done" I replied. We decided to get away from there and find a bunker. Archie had some joints and I had a small stash so we agreed to get our heads together for the next briefing. We made our way past the cluster of barracks to the far end of the line where there was not much activity and slipped into a bunker, relaxed in the sand, and fired up a couple of numbers.

Suddenly, another fellow entered the bunker and walked in on us. He was friendly enough and quickly explained that he was looking for a toke or two to get his head. He'd seen us go in the bunker and assumed we had gone in for that purpose so we invited him to join us. He was also looking to ETS but had not made arrangements to bring anything to smoke with him. We had a good visit until the joint was burned and then he thanked us and left.

By this time Archie and I were better friends than when we had gone in the bunker. Time was of the essence so we headed to the processing building. In the distance, a mile or so across the bay, I could see Dong Ba Thin stretching along the far shore. I pointed it out to Archie and told him about EJ and I watching it get hit our second night in-country and my time there.

We arrived at the processing building as the briefing was letting out. The room was empty and it would be a half hour until the next briefing. We walked in. There were long rows of tables with a counter and podium set up along one side. Soon we were joined by others and gradually the room came to life. Clerks distributed forms on the tables while the hall filled to capacity. I could see there was no call being given. They just started on time and if you were there, that was fine.

At the appropriate time, an NCO stepped to the podium, turned on the microphone and brought things to order. We were given a manifest number and instructed to assemble in that building when that number was called. We were told to tattoo it to our eyelids as it was the key to our way out. If we missed the call, we had to start processing all over again. We filled out forms, signed papers, turned in our records, received instructions, and were told to be at every formation since that was where we would get our information. With that we were released.

We returned outside to our place under the covered walkway. Since it was late we figured we would not get out of there until the next day or that night. There were of rumors about leaving fast or being held up by delays. Some guys said they'd been waiting for two days to get out and word was that things were backed up so we hauled our bags down the board walk in hopes of finding a bunk, located an empty barracks and staked a claim on some empty bunks.

We then hiked to the USO which hadn't changed a bit from the day I'd first set foot in it nearly sixteen months ago. We then took a leisurely walk down the street to the out-processing area, where we saw a crowd gathering around the podium set up in front of the barracks so we joined them. The 1SGT ascended the podium. His fatigues were starched, pressed and creased to a razor's edge. His hair close cut and his baseball cap worn just right. He surveyed us quietly for a moment, almost disapprovingly, before he brought us to order. His attitude towards us was almost belligerent. It was as if he held complete control of everything and no one would be allowed to go home until he had given his personal approval. His attitude put us all off and we did not like him. Many others quietly voiced their opinions about him, but we had to do what we were told to get out of there. He passed along information regarding manifest processing, made announcements, and impressed upon us the necessity to get ourselves clean and "regulation."

We were finally released and as we milled about we ran into the fellow who we'd turned on in the bunker that afternoon. He came over to us and slapped us on the back and stated once again how much he appreciated us turning him on. He had just gotten a bunch of smack from a buddy and was going to have a big party that night out behind the movie screen after the evening movie was over and we were invited. We said "Sure, sure" but didn't think messing with smack just now was the best thing to be doing. After all,

I'd seen how Dave Friday's big party had become a disaster and this felt as if it had the same potential.

He'd been clean for his piss test and would pass with no problems. Having already taken the test, he felt no qualms about indulging in some smack. As he walked away, he said for us to be sure and come out after the movie. Archie and I both felt that it might be best to forego this party since it seemed like a potential for problems. We headed off to find supper. I would have to spend one more day in the Nam and I considered hitching a ride back to Engineer Hill to spend the night. Archie considered the same but we decided there was no sense in going back and prolonging things. As the sun slipped behind the distant mountains, we headed to the out-processing area to take in the evening movie. It didn't matter what it was; it was a way to pass the time.

The movie had not started when we arrived in the area but a crowd was gathered around the makeshift screen constructed in a large open area behind the barracks. We found a spot on the revetments and settled back to watch. The movie didn't last long enough and when it ended, everyone went off in different directions. We saw a group making their way toward the movie screen and the darkened brush beyond. That looked like our party. Archie and I decided to let the party go and started back towards the barracks. We had no sooner turned around when we ran into the dude who had invited us to the party. Once again he told us of the incredible supply of smack he had and how they were all going to get loose for one last night in-country and we should come along. I made some excuse for us to go to the barracks first and told him we'd meet him out there.

That suited him and we parted company. Archie and I walked through the barracks and exited from the other end of the building and headed out for a walk along the deserted streets.

Once safely out of the milling mass at the company area, we fired up a couple of numbers and walked on. It was a cool evening and the sky was clear and a portion of the moon overhead gave off enough light to illuminate the dark. We walked along the road that ran parallel to the bay and turned up the street toward the darkened USO building. On several occasions we passed individuals coming from the opposite direction who were obviously out for the same purpose and pleasantries were exchanged in the darkness as we passed. We knew they were short-timers like us for no newbies would be out there taking an evening walk. We continued until we cut across a large, open, sandy field and when we were in the center of the field we sat down in the sand and shared war stories until the hands of the watch told us that the 17th of September 1971 had arrived. We would leave the Nam today. It would be my re-birthday. We shared a joint and

17. Straight On Till Morning

shook hands to congratulate each other, then got up and wandered back to the barracks.

We awoke to the noise in the barracks as everyone was getting dressed for morning formation where the same 1SGT was reading off a list of names and the named individuals were gathering at the podium. Once finished they were marched off by another NCO. I nudged the fellow standing next to me. "What was all that about?" I asked.

"Flunked their piss tests" he replied.

I hoped that was one list my name wouldn't show up on. We listened to information about the backlog of manifests and flights that were responsible for the delays and continued processing problems. Before dismissing the formation, the 1SGT gave us a lecture about looking sharp when we reported for boarding. He said moustaches that were not regulation, hair too long, dirty khakis, etc., etc., would get us bumped from the manifest and as a final word of warning, he would be inspecting us as we came through. This brought a chorus of catcalls and jeers from the assembled group but the 1SGT stood there glaring as the catcalls continued. It was that old short-timer attitude and I suppose the 1SGT had seen enough of it to know he wouldn't win the confrontation, so he turned and descended the platform. A rousing cheer went up as the crowd dispersed.

I knew my hair was not regulation enough for the 1SGT and my moustache certainly wasn't so we decided to treat ourselves to a PX haircut and shave, so we'd look good for our boarding call. Once we were cleaned up and paid our bills, we walked out into the early morning sun.

The in-processing center had received a shipment of newbies and the area was once again swamped with "fresh fish" in brand new green fatigues, baseball caps and unscuffed boots. We maintained our superior air of the "veteran" and walked through their groups like a hot knife through butter as if they weren't there. The newbies looked at us with envy on their faces as they abandoned the sidewalks to let us pass through their groups.

At lunch we went to the out-processing area for the noon formation where we hoped to get a surprise and have our manifest number called. Everyone was gathering around the podium when we arrived, so we made our way into the crowd and awaited the 1SGT. On the outside stairs of the barracks behind us I saw our party friend from the night before standing among the group gathered there. He was joking with the fellows and didn't seem to have a care in the world.

The 1SGT ascended the podium and called us to order. The first order of business was another list of names for the failed piss tests. I didn't expect to hear my name but was prepared for anything as the unexpected was frequently the most common occurrence in Vietnam. The 1SGT called off names, none of which were familiar. The named individuals filtered through the crowd to gather in the open area beside the podium. Then there was one name that Archie and I both recognized. It was the fellow we had turned on the day before and who had invited us to his big smack party the night before. I looked over my shoulder and saw him descending the stairs. As he made his way through the crowd, I could see the dejected look of surprise on his face that contrasted greatly with the smiling, confident face I had seen on those stairs a moment before.

It didn't matter whether it was a mistake or not. He would be taken for another piss test and if his party had been anything like he said it would, he would fail that piss test and continue to fail them for two weeks or so. Now he was in for hospitalization and detoxification. He anticipated being back in the World in a week but now he wouldn't see it for at least another month. The list was completed, and we watched the dude march away with the others.

The formation continued and a new manifest was called, however it was not ours. Some GIs among us whooped with joy and made their way out of the crowd to gather their bags. Things were backlogged but we were promised everything was being done to speed it up.

After the 1SGT's lectures, he dismissed the formation. I was getting tired of going to formation and not having our manifest called but we figured our time was about due. We'd been there a day already and watched several other manifests ship out. Our time was surely at hand and we would soon be changing into our khakis. We spent the afternoon walking the streets of the replacement center, haunting the PX and the USO and taking the occasional toke. Our supply of joints was dwindling but we had calculated finishing them before our last briefing.

We found a bunker and relaxed in the shade until about 4:00 p.m. when it was time to change into our khakis since we both had a feeling our manifest would be called at the evening formation. We hiked to the barracks and retrieved our khakis from our bags. We'd been told that we could take one set of jungle fatigues and boots back to the States with us and as I changed into my khakis I surveyed my worn fatigues. The jacket and pants were faded and frayed. I realized in looking at them that they would serve no useful purpose in the World and likewise, my boots had little useful wear left in them. However, they would be keepsakes, silent witnesses to the reality I had lived, the history I had been a part of so I carefully packed them away with my boonie hats.

After putting on my khakis I felt like a new man. The clean fit of the khaki shirt and pants felt somewhat uncomfortable after my loose-fitting, baggy fatigues. When it was time for evening formation, we walked to the area which was filling with GIs anticipating the call.

The 1SGT ascended the podium and called the formation to order.

17. Straight On Till Morning

The first order of business was another roster of failed piss tests. Another unfortunate group gathered at the podium and was taken away. Then manifest numbers were called and *ours was called*. Archie and I looked at each other for a moment before bursting out in laughter. Those of us on this manifest were instructed to report for processing in one hour, at 6:00 p.m.

We took off, elbowing our way through the crowd to get our bags. We were too fired up to worry about eating supper and hauled our bags to the entrance of the processing building. Since we had time on our hands, we casually walked around back to the far corner of the processing building and ducked behind the revetments at an opening left for two large doors in the corner. We sat on the sandbags and fired up. I finished off my joint and as 6:00 p.m. approached stashed them under a sandbag atop the revetment near the doors in the corner.

We walked to the front of the processing building where our manifest was gathering. The doors of the building were opened when we arrived, so we grabbed our bags and joined the rush inside to find a seat. The NCO in charge called us to order. There were more lectures, forms to fill out and paperwork to sign. We were each given a number that corresponded to a number on our manifest. Once again, we surrendered our names for a number just as we had at the reception station at basic training. Our records were returned to us and then it was time to start moving. We were dismissed a table at a time and instructed to take our bags through a door near the entrance of the hall. Beyond that door was customs.

We joined the line when our table was dismissed and once through the door found ourselves in a long, narrow room with a counter down the center. A line of husky MP's were situated behind the counter rummaging through the bags presented to them. Other MP's walked among us picking people for a body search. Several unfortunate individuals were leaning against a wall while an MP frisked them and went through their pockets. I didn't have anything on me and felt certain that I didn't have anything in my suitcases that would be objectionable, but one never knew. I picked up my bags and joined a line in front of the counter.

When it was my turn, I laid my bags on the counter as I faced a big, burly MP. He spoke not a word but proceeded to open my bags and finger everything within. He found a little cardboard box where I had pipes packed away. He looked at me a moment, then opened it. There were several pipes inside, two carved ivory ones, my Australian "smokestack" pipe and an ornate German one I'd gotten in Sydney and two small ivory "roach" pipes that had never been used. All of the used pipes I'd left with the guys on the Hill. He picked up an ivory pipe, cast a wary glance at me and dumped all the pipes in a box behind the counter. I could have taken issue with this since they were brand new but I bit my tongue and figured it was a lost cause to protest.

The MP searched the remainder of my luggage thoroughly before closing it up, attaching a baggage claim tag to it and stacking it on a rack behind him. I was given the claim stubs and told to go through the door at the far end of the room. I shouldered my multi-colored haversack with my camera and book in it and walked down the room past others who were being searched or having their luggage checked. There was no sign of Archie in the crowd.

In the other room were booths where I exchanged my MPC for U.S. greenback currency and turned in my MACV card. From there I was instructed to go through another door where I found myself in a large enclosed hard-stand with plywood walls and ceiling. There were others sitting about in little groups on folding chairs, so I entered and found a chair near the doorway. Archie sat down with me and gradually our flight collected.

The flight was processed and all that remained was to get on the buses, go to our Freedom Bird and fly out of there. One of the NCOs walked in with a clipboard in hand and called for our attention. Everyone began cheering, however our excitement was premature because he informed us our flight had been delayed for two hours and since we had already cleared customs and changed our MPC, we had to stay cooped up in that room! This news was greeted with a good deal of grumbling. We waited while Archie got acquainted with other soul brothers sitting nearby.

About 10:00 p.m. we heard the buses pull up outside which brought a stir to the crowd and a ragged cheer went up. The arrival of the buses meant one thing—it was almost time to go to the airport. Then the NCO appeared to tell us we would be boarding while we clustered around the two big doors at the end of the long room. The rumble of idling bus engines seemed like the song of sirens beckoning us.

Finally, the NCO with the clipboard returned. The two big doors were opened, and the NCO began calling off numbers. Individuals answered the numbers and hustled out the open doors into the night. The flow of people continued, then my number was called, and I hurried to the NCO at the doorway. He checked my number off and I went out the door where I found a line of OD buses waiting. Some were almost filled so I walked down the line and found one that was almost empty, entered and found a seat. Archie was right behind me.

We waited while the bus filled. We'd lost all sense of time at this point. Once every seat was filled the driver boarded our bus, shut the door and we began to move. A lusty cheer filled the bus and windows were lowered as we yelled our pleasure to those who stood around outside to watch us move off into the darkness.

17. Straight On Till Morning

I watched the processing center disappear behind us. We passed the USO, the CIF buildings, the piss test building and headed out the gate, leaving the 22nd Replacement behind forever. We were yelling, screaming and cheering something terrible at this point. Our bus followed the line of buses down that familiar road, heading for the airport. It was a pitch-black night but we were going home and that was all that mattered. We raised HELL in that bus.

The buses bearing their exuberant cargo of ecstatic GIs proceeded to the 14th Aerial Port where a rousing cheer went up as the lights of the airport came into view. The buses continued straight on, taking the same route as the day we had arrived. We approached a gate in a high wall and drove through the gate, past darkened buildings, blast walls, parked planes and out onto the runway. The bus cleared the cluster of buildings and proceeded down the runway. Then we all saw our Freedom Bird sitting in the distance, bathed in floodlights and the loudest cheer yet broke through that bus as we approached. The line of buses proceeded while everyone was eyeing the big, beautiful jet illuminated before us. The buses pulled to the loading ramp and unloaded one bus at a time. When our bus pulled up to the bottom of the loading ramp, the doors flew open and we crammed into the aisle in our rush to get on that plane.

I stepped off the bus, headed up the ramp and looked at my watch. It was a little past 11:00 p.m. At the top of the ramp I was greeted by two young round-eyed stewardesses. I entered and joined the crush of GIs in the aisles. Archie was behind me and we staked a claim on two seats while his new soul brother friends sat across the aisle from us. The pilot welcomed us, indicating we would be taking off shortly. This news brought another rousing cheer. The engines picked up and we taxied down the runway then halted. It was time. The engines revved up and the plane vibrated and shuddered. Then we were free, rolling down the runway, picking up speed.

We all felt that moment when the nose of the plane rose and we left the runway. The noise of the landing gear being retracted hit our ears, and a tremendous cheer filled the interior of the plane, continuing for several minutes. It was an explosion of emotion and people were shaking hands, smiling, laughing and slapping each other on the back. The plane gained altitude and we could see the lights of Cam Ranh spread out below and dropping away behind us. We could see the parachute flares drifting in the distance as the war continued, but it was no longer our war.

The seat belt light went off and some got up in the aisle while getting things from the overhead compartments. Suddenly, there was a terrific BANG and the plane lurched wildly, throwing people down in the aisle and pillows, blankets and bags fell from the overhead compartments. It was like the plane had hit a big bump and all our hearts skipped a beat. I was sure we'd been hit by something as it was such a tremendous and violent blast that I didn't see how the plane could survive. Somehow, it seemed fitting I would die in a plane crash full of short-timer Incorrigibles leaving the Nam. But nothing happened. Those strewn in the aisles got up and surveyed themselves. There were no injuries other than a few bruises.

The pilot came over the intercom to say we'd hit some turbulence but everything was under control. The stewardesses served sandwiches and drinks and we relaxed. It was late. I breathed a sigh of relief. Sleep came easily.

When I awoke it was daylight and the stewardesses were rousing those who still slept and breakfast was being served. By now we were in our descent into Yokota Air Base, Japan and through the clouds below we could make out patches of a green landscape that was Japan. In no time the landing gear hummed into place and we settled back as the plane thumped onto the runway, then taxied to the terminal. After it halted, we filed off, heading for the same terminal where EJ and I had waited on our flight the other way so many months ago.

As we walked across the tarmac I saw an approaching group of newbies all dressed in their new green fatigues. They were halted so we could pass. It was history repeating itself for as newbies, EJ and I had stood with a group of FNGs when we'd been halted to let a flight of short-timer Incorrigibles pass. They had heckled us unmercifully, just as we heckled the subdued newbies when we passed them, and I almost expected to see EJ and myself among the cluster.

The interior of the terminal looked the same as that day so many months before when EJ and I waited there on our way to Vietnam. I marveled at the *sameness* of everything and how time seemed to stand still, despite my knowledge that many months had passed. I felt as if it could still be that June day in 1970, rather than this September day in 1971 that I had looked forward to.

After making the rounds of the shops, I joined the crowd milling about the terminal where I ran into Archie. He was with his new soul brother pals and I began to see that he probably felt no further need of our friendship. He was back with a group of brothers and I was the only white, or tanned, face among them. I had a good tan, but not good enough to blend in with Archie and his buddies. It was awkward and I realized the comradeship that sustained us during out-processing served no useful purpose once we were out of Vietnam and we were most definitely OUT.

Perhaps it was because we were going back to different concepts of the WORLD.

The call came to re-board for the final leg of the flight. We boarded and got re-situated.

17. Straight On Till Morning

Archie was there with me and we joked a little as the plane taxied down the runway and took off. Soon we were heading out, high over the Pacific Ocean, the nose of our Freedom Bird pointed toward Seattle, Washington. I thought about the boys back on the Hill who were living the 18th of September while I was still living the 17th of September all over again. By crossing the International Date Line, I gained a day while my buddies on the Hill were living tomorrow.

While I was streaking across the Pacific at that moment, waiting over in Bremerton, Washington, was John Criner, a good buddy from my grade school and high school days. We had grown up together and shared many of the same friends and experiences. John now worked for General Electric and had been transferred to Bremerton about a week earlier after living near Newport News, Virginia. We had kept up correspondence while I was in-country and when John wrote of his impending move, I saw that he would be within an easy drive of Fort Lewis. I pointed this out to him in a letter and plans were made for him to meet me at Fort Lewis when I got out. Then we would have some time to catch up on things before I headed for home. I had his phone number and instructions to call him as soon as I could after I got to Fort Lewis.

As the jet sailed across the ocean, I wondered about John. The last time I'd seen him was that July of 1969 when we gathered to send the Phantom off to the Army. This was the same gathering where I had reunited with Stateside Janet that led to our emotional entanglements.

While I was looking forward to seeing John, Janet was also high on my list of people I needed to see. She was in Atlanta and expecting me to visit her so I planned on going to Atlanta before going home. I owed her that since I had reneged on our plans for a Hawaiian R&R and there was much we needed to discuss. We corresponded through the last part of my Vietnam tour and many things had been expressed to one another in those letters. Now the time was at hand where we would need to face one another to determine if the emotions were behind the words.

Gradually the sky darkened, and excitement filled the plane as we got close to the States. The pilot came over the intercom to tell us that Seattle was visible ahead of us and we would be landing at McChord in a short time. We strained to catch that first glimpse of the WORLD. There ahead and below us lay an expanse of glittering lights shining against the darkness.

18

Wandering and Wondering

The jet eased onto the runway at McChord Air Base and came to a halt amid a rousing cheer from those aboard. I stared out the window at the terminal bathed in light. It looked exactly the same as that night over a year earlier when EJ and I had taken off for Anchorage, Alaska, on our way to Vietnam. The plane taxied to the hardstand where the Flying Tiger Airlines jet had been when I'd gotten on almost sixteen months before, so I'd come full circle. When engines shut down we watched them wheel ramps to the doors of the plane. Then the doors opened and we disembarked. Everyone was quiet, lost in their own thoughts at this moment. I eased down the aisle as the crowd made its way to the door. Then I was standing on the ramp with the cool September night air brushing my face. I walked down the stairs watching those ahead of me file across the tarmac toward the terminal. Some stopped to kiss the ground.

I stepped off the bottom step and my foot touched the ground of the good old U.S.A. I was back! I followed the file across the hardstand, pausing momentarily to bend down and touch the ground as if to reassure myself that it was indeed real, and then went on into the terminal. Once inside the brightly lit room I could see the familiar counters of customs looking something like a supermarket checkout. Pallets with our bags had been brought into the room and I joined the crush of people who were retrieving them.

Feeling certain that I had nothing to fear from these customs people who looked as though they were just going through the motions, I joined the line. The customs man opened my bags, rummaged around and then motioned me on through. I shut my bags and headed for the door where everyone was disappearing. Security guards directed me to where I found typical OD Army buses waiting with engines idling at the front of the terminal. I climbed aboard, found an empty seat and collapsed, luggage and all. Others filed on behind me and it seemed as though we proceeded through the terminal in record time. It was about 10:00 p.m. on 17 September 1971.

The driver finally boarded, and we took off following the other buses down the street, out the main gate, and onto the highway toward Fort Lewis. The multitude of glittering neon lights was a sight to see. There were motels, liquor stores, fast food places, gas stations, etc., and we all began to remember things we'd forgotten we'd even missed. The question "Has it really been all that time?" kept ringing in my mind. It seemed as though nothing outside the bus had changed. I knew I had changed and in a way, I'd given up almost three years of my life to a multitude of changes, that didn't matter to anyone outside the bus. I realized that it didn't matter. None of it mattered to anyone but me. The bus approached Fort Lewis and butterflies stirred in my stomach when I saw the exit sign. The bus turned off toward the installation. Ahead was the main gate.

We arrived at the replacement center and the buses stopped at one of the supply buildings. An NCO came on board and instructed us to get our razors, soap, toothbrushes, etc., out of our luggage and then to check our bags in the building beside the buses. With that we were released. We filed off the bus, collected our gear and checked our bags as instructed, then joined the milling crowd where NCOs were dividing up the group and leading them off to barracks at the corner of the area where EJ and I had stood formations back in June of 1970.

I joined a group and we were marched to a barracks where we stormed inside, turned on the lights and laid claim to beds, but no one was in any mood to sleep although it was close to 11:00 p.m. Having been cooped up on an airplane for eighteen hours could have had something to do with it, plus there was the traditional steak dinner that all returning Nam vets were promised. We settled into the barracks and were called together by our NCO who told us we would be going to the mess hall for that steak dinner. This brought a rousing cheer from everyone and we headed outside to form up for the trip to the mess hall.

Since it was so late the replacement center was quiet, and seemed deserted. Only the bare street lights and an occasional light in a window could be seen. It was easy to see what barracks had been assigned to those in our flight since they glowed with light from every window and door. We headed for the NCO club where our dinner was to be served.

We entered the NCO club, the same one EJ and I had been in back in June of '70. It was clean, well-decorated and looked most inviting. The only problem was—no food. We stormed in and the quiet calm of the empty room suddenly burst into a cacophony of chairs and tables being shuffled around and the noise of loud conversation. We were back and we didn't give a damn who knew it so we were being as loud as hell. It was almost as if we were drunk on the headiness of the moment. The group settled noisily around the cluster of tables and groused loudly for food. However, we were informed that due to a typical Army SNAFU and our late arrival, the cooks had not been ready, so our steak dinner would be a little late but it would be forthcoming. Of course this did not sit well with us and we loudly voiced our displeasure. When the cooks arrived we gave them a loud razzing of verbal abuse. They knew what they had on their hands and they tried very hard to please a bunch of men who would not be easily pleased. The cooks immediately got to work, bringing out toast, rolls, coffee and juice while they got steaks cooking.

Food in our stomachs definitely brought a change of attitude. The cooks soon rolled out pans of scrambled eggs, potatoes, vegetables and steaks cooked to order. It was set up buffet style and we spent the next hour and a half gorging ourselves. I ate three steaks, but others seemed to have the proverbial bottomless pits for stomachs. By 1:30 a.m. we were all laid back in our chairs and stuffed to the gills. One by one or in small groups, we made our way back to our respective barracks. Even though we were told we would be rising early, no one was ready to hit the sack.

I went to my bunk at the far end of the top floor. Others were taking showers, laughing, poking fun, etc. There were no cell phones in 1971 so there was also a rush to phone booths as people sought to re-establish contact with loved ones and family. I'd lost Archie by this time as he was now a full-fledged member of that group of soul brothers and had no further use for me.

The hooting and hollering seemed to go on forever. I went to bed.

The following morning, we were awakened early and instructed to get dressed, eat breakfast and fall out in front of the barracks at 7:00 a.m. It seemed as though I had just shut my eyes but I dragged myself out of bed hoping it would be the last night I would spend in an Army bunk. Everyone was subdued and there was not nearly as much enthusiasm as the night before due more to the early hour than any change in attitude.

We fell in at 7:00 a.m. as our enthusiasm returned. The flight had been broken down into platoon-sized groups; each group assigned a barracks and an NCO. We were told we followed the same backlog we had run up against in the Nam and that it was still ahead of us but we would begin processing by taking a thorough physical exam. After that we could be called to other briefings at any moment and since we would process as a group, it was important for us to stay together, close to the barracks in our off time. If one person was missing when our briefings were called, the entire group would be held back until missing individuals were located. Since no one wanted to screw things up and we all wanted out, these instructions were taken to heart. We were also warned about rough-housing and noise which was frowned upon, but how does one contain such exuberance? What were they going to do with us if we didn't comply, send us to Vietnam?

In a short time buses halted in the street behind the barracks. We were

18. Wandering and Wondering

instructed to get our medical records and board the buses so we, hooting and hollering, stampeded to the barracks and back. Our processing had begun and it would be the last morning we would spend in the U.S. Army. We were taken to a three-story building where we disembarked and spent the morning being weighed, measured, poked, prodded, inspected, gave urine samples, had our blood taken and on and on. When finished we assembled outside until buses arrived to carry us to the barracks.

At the barracks there was more waiting to do. I began to think about trying to call John Criner since I needed to make arrangements with him. John knew when I'd be arriving but not exactly when I'd get out but I was reluctant to wander off in search of a vacant phone. I also considered phoning my parents to let them know I was back in the States. They knew I was coming home but did not know exactly when. However, I purposely kept them in the dark because I did not want any kind of big surprise welcome home party when I got there. I just wanted to come home and kind of surprise them. I was planning to see Janet in Atlanta before going home and I didn't know how to explain that to them. It was better they did not know so I decided not to try and call them. They knew I was on my way home and that was enough for the time being.

Lunch time arrived and we availed ourselves of chow. There were all kinds of rumors about the backlog of out-processing people and it seemed as bad as waiting in Vietnam for the manifest to fly out, but at least we were Stateside and no longer in a combat zone. After lunch we went to the central issue facility to be outfitted in winter Class "A" dress greens. Since it was a bit nippy and khakis were not authorized for wear after 1 September, so we had to get "regulation."

The buses arrived, we piled aboard with our supply records and were driven to the very same CIF where we had received our brand-new jungle fatigues and boots. The buses halted and we filed into a large room where we were briefed, filled out supply forms and went through the motions of getting fitted for our winter greens. Pants were altered and we were issued new underwear, shirts and all. With production line efficiency, we were shortly in our winter greens looking nice, cleaned up and regulation.

By mid-afternoon we were back at the barracks and I managed to find an empty phone booth within sight of the barracks and dialed John's number. No answer. No John. About 4:00 p.m. we were called to formation again and marched to a building where we received information from representatives of the Veteran's Administration concerning our benefits. This lasted about an hour and then we found ourselves back at the barracks—waiting. I hurried over to the same phone booth to try and call John. Still no answer. I began to worry that I might miss my connection with him and have to fly out without seeing him. I returned to the barracks to wait. The latest word was that we would be out by 8:30 that night.

Supper time arrived and while our group went off to eat I tried to call John again. At last, it was John! He was happy to hear I was back, and he was ready to come get me whenever I said. I told him the word was we'd be out by 8:30 that night and gave him detailed directions on how to get to the replacement center. We agreed to meet at the bus terminal there since that was probably the most prominent feature in front of the replacement center. With that, I went off to eat, relieved I'd been able to make my connection.

Our group returned to the barracks where we got word that our physicals had been processed and everyone in our group had passed. The best news was that the group immediately preceding ours was soon to go to their final briefing. That meant our time was surely close at hand. About 7:30 p.m. our call finally came. We eagerly scrambled out of the barracks to form up. Once heads were counted, (no pun intended) we marched to the same processing building where I had in-processed during May 1969 and again in June 1970. We entered and hurried up the steps to the same processing room where the rest of our flight sat waiting. An NCO and assistants arrived, and our briefing began. We were informed about accrued leave payments, reserve obligations and given more forms to fill out and sign. It seemed that the darned thing was going to go on forever and we began to get impatient as the time dragged on. At last, our final pay vouchers were brought in and those all-important DD-214s, our proof that we had indeed been in the Army and they'd let us go honorably when our time was done.

As our pay vouchers and 214s were distributed we were released. With vouchers in hand, we hustled across the street to a window where they were presented for our final pay. I got to the window, presented my voucher and got a fist full of brand-new U.S. greenback twenty-dollar bills. This was it! I was out! A free man at last! I had my DD-214 in hand, my last pay, and I was out.

My life belonged to me for the first time in twenty-four years.

I looked at my watch; it was close to 8:30 p.m., the time I had told John to come so I hoped he was at the bus terminal waiting. I decided to go there first rather than get my bags because I assumed John and I could drive over and pick them up later. No sense hauling them all the way to the depot. I rushed down the street toward the terminal feeling like a new person, which in a sense, I was. I was happy and excited and totally freaked out.

The bus terminal was brightly illuminated and there were a number of fellows there having tearful reunions with wives, mothers, fathers, brothers, sisters, and sweethearts. I walked around the building but no John

18. Wandering and Wondering

Criner was to be seen. I went into the waiting room where there were soldiers lounging in the chairs but still no John Criner. I thought it was odd that he wasn't there as I was almost a half-hour late but I decided he could have been held up by some delay. After all, he had just moved to the area so perhaps he was unfamiliar with the roads.

I was too excited to sit and wait so I decided to go fetch my bags and haul them to the terminal. That would give John some time to get there. There was a lot of hooting and hollering going on and I realized I was witnessing and participating in a scene that was played out in the replacement center every day and night. It was the rejoicing of soldiers who had paid their dues, had met their obligations to their country, paid the ransom and had been freed. There seemed to be jubilation everywhere around me.

At the baggage building I got my bags and shuffled toward the bus terminal, anticipating John's arrival but when I got there, still no John. I went into the waiting room, sat down in a chair, pulled out my trusty book and began to read.

I read, anxiously looking up when anyone came in, but still no sign of John. I had about resigned myself to a long wait when I noticed someone enter and begin walking toward me. I looked up from my book. It was John. "Hey, Shadow!" he said, using an old high school nickname. "You're looking good." A wave of relief swept over me as I stood to shake his hand and exchange a brotherly hug.

We hauled my bags to the parking lot, talking as we went. The last time we had been together was in July 1969 when we sent our buddy the Phantom, off to the Army and Janet and I reconnected. It had been a long time and there was so much to get caught up on. We climbed into his car and John said "Where to?"

"Anywhere" I replied. "Let's just get out of here."

He started the engine and drove out of the parking lot. "Really good to see you again, Shadowie" John said. We drove toward the gate which I could see in the distance. In the quiet of that moment, my mind drifted and I wondered about Stigg and Ralph and Dusty and the boys on the Hill. It would be morning there about now, probably break time and I had a feeling they were gathering in the bunker for a smoke break, maybe even wondering about me at that moment, and maybe that was why I was thinking about them. We drove through the gate and onto the street. "Any place special you want to go or you just want to go back to my place?" John asked I thought for a moment but I could see just what I wanted a short ways down the road. "I want a fucking hamburger and a real fucking milk shake!" I replied.

When the golden arches of a McDonalds appeared, John turned in and parked. This was the days before "drive through service" and John asked "You want to go in?" I looked around the parking lot. There were young people gathered in small groups here and there. It was Friday night and they were laughing and having a good time and they weren't worried about Vietnam and it didn't matter to them who I was or where I'd just come from. I felt very old and very conspicuous and out of place in my dress greens and GI haircut. I couldn't face it and decided to stay in the car while John fetched my food. I could not bring myself to get out of the car. I was overwhelmed by everything that had happened to me, and here I was, back where it started. I felt like a ghost sitting in John's car in a McDonald's parking lot.

John walked up to the building while I sat lost in thought, watching the groups of youngsters. Life went on. I realized all that knowledge crammed in my brain no longer had any value. I had knowledge of the organization of engineer units in Vietnam, where certain industrial sites were, what they did, what their output of material was. I knew cost figures for projects, filing systems, procedures, regulations, etc. The knowledge one gains, not just of job-related items, but also of living and surviving in Vietnam was tremendous. It defined your existence. Yet, as I sat there in the parking lot of that McDonalds, I realized that all that information was now worthless. I would never draw on that body of knowledge again. It was only to be forgotten.

John returned with my burger and shake and we sat quietly eating in the car. When I took the first bite of that Big Mac, I knew I was "back on the block." I fairly inhaled the burger and fries and savored that first real American milk shake for as long as it would last. When John finished, we headed to his apartment. I wished so much for a joint as it seemed like months since I'd gotten a good buzz but I had none and John had none so there was no use worrying about it. As we drove toward John's apartment, he said "Well, tell me about it, Shadowie. What was it like? You're home and a free man. How's it feel?"

How could I condense all those months of insanity into a few sentences and provide a concise, focused response? It was not possible. All I could say was: "It was like Boy Scouts with guns." Having been Boy Scouts together, I knew John would understand. I also knew this wasn't the first time these questions would be asked and I would have to deal with it whenever I met any friends or family. I told John I felt great but there was an incredible sense of unreality. Even the thirty minute ride to his apartment wouldn't be enough time to answer his questions.

When we arrived at John's we were too wound up to sleep and there was much catching up to do as our lives had taken many twists and turns since we'd last seen each other in July 1969. We sat up and talked until 3:30 a.m. when we both went to bed. I crashed on the sofa but my sleep was one of physical exhaustion and not restful since my mind would not shut down.

18. Wandering and Wondering

It may have been the excitement of the moment or the jet lag from traveling through so many time zones.

I only slept a few hours as I was too attuned to early rising to break old habits even with the jet lag. As soon as the first light of day filtered through the living room curtains, I was awake.

While John slept I occupied myself poking about the apartment, marveling at modern toilet facilities and peering out the windows at the green landscape and typical American houses and apartment buildings. No more sand, no more duckboard walks, no more blast walls, revetments, weathered, tin-roofed hooches, shitters, pissers, bunkers, guard towers, perimeter wire, helicopters and all that. There was an unreality about the experience, as if it had been a dream.

A siren began wailing nearby, a police car perhaps, but my reaction was one ingrained in me at Dong Ba Thin. I momentarily scrambled around the room looking for something to get under before I realized there were no Red Alerts here. There were no falling mortar rounds here nor incoming rockets, no perimeters to man, no bunkers to get into, no guard towers.

When John rolled out of bed, we had breakfast before we went for a drive around Bremerton, a community situated on Puget Sound. I was amazed at everything I saw, as though I was seeing it for the first time. We drove to the navy yard where John worked and toured the battleship U.S.S. *Missouri* upon whose decks the Japanese surrendered in September 1945, twenty-six years earlier. It seemed fitting to visit the *Missouri* since my war had ended as well.

We returned to John's apartment where I telephoned the airport to make reservations for a flight to Atlanta. Then I called Janet in Atlanta to inform her of my imminent arrival. We visited briefly since it was the first time we had actually spoken to one another in over two years. Many letters and thoughts had passed between us in that time but this conversation was different. I could sense the tension in her voice about what lay ahead.

That night I accompanied John to a party some of his co-workers were hosting. John was a newcomer to their group and I only knew John. I had a hard time relating and we left the party after a short time and headed for the airport so I could catch my flight. Since the airport was across Puget Sound we took a ferry across rather than drive around it. When we reached the other side John drove while I changed from my civilian clothes to my dress greens so I could get the military discount for the flight. In a short time we were there. I didn't see any sense in having John see me off since it was late so he drove me to the front of the terminal where we shook hands and said our farewells. We both knew we would see each other again.

I grabbed my bags and hurried into the terminal as John drove off. I checked in for my flight and found I would fly to Chicago O'Hare and change planes there, heading on for Atlanta. In a short time I was once again on a big jet streaking eastward. I wondered how traveling would be since we'd all heard stories about how returning Vietnam vets had been treated by the American public. I felt certain that my status as a returning Nam vet was something that could not be disguised as my dress greens bore Vietnam unit insignia, Nam service ribbons, and my deep tan and Montagnard bracelets certainly indicated service in Southeast Asia. People were not overtly hostile to me but I noticed their stares and the manner in which I was shunned, almost as if I was not there. I felt like a ghost. I ignored them. Returning vets were met with anger, ridicule and hatred as a welcome home gift from those we served. Those wounds cut deeper than any we received in Vietnam.

I arrived at Chicago's O'Hare Airport early on 20 September. It was pouring rain and as I waited for my connecting flight to Atlanta, I couldn't help thinking about my parents and brothers only a few miles away in Naperville. I felt guilty for not going home first but there were things I needed to see to first and I was soon on my way South. I was uncertain about what I was walking into in Atlanta. Janet and I had a moment of mutual realization back in July 1969 but it had not been consummated. There were many questions but few answers until we began corresponding while I was in the Nam. A great many feelings and emotions had been expressed on paper, however much time had passed since we had been together. Would those emotions be valid once we were together and not separated by 10,000 miles? That was part of the reason I was on my way to Atlanta but I had no idea what to expect or what I wanted to come away with from there.

I arrived at the Atlanta airport on a bright, sunny day. Janet was there waiting with Tony Phillips and Tom Nelson, two old high school friends whose presence was a pleasant surprise to me. They were on their way to Miami, Florida, and had stopped to visit Janet. She was radiant, tall, long dark hair, brown eyes, and looked much more of a woman than I remembered. The insecure little girl from high school was now a woman of the world, confident, self-assured, and beautiful. We embraced for a long moment. There were tears, there were questions but there was not much that could be said as we stood there amid the disembarking passengers.

We went to her apartment where I finally got a buzz thanks to Tony and Tom. As for Janet and me and my two friends who were also there, it had been so long since our paths had crossed that we were almost strangers to each other. They had not changed, but I had. I felt out of place and continued to suffer from Vietnam jet lag. Tony and Tom had some decent smoke that helped me ease into the reality of being back in the World. They asked those questions about the Nam and my experiences there. What

18. Wandering and Wondering

could I tell them? Where should I start? I thought about Ralph, Dusty, Stigg, Pete and the Engineer Hill gang as they were all constantly in my mind and my thoughts were always with them. I felt an incredible sense of guilt for having left them; I felt as if I should be there and not in Atlanta.

Janet and I talked when we could but with our two friends and her roommate around, it was difficult for us to find some quiet time together. I didn't know what the sleeping arrangements were to be in the apartment, but I didn't care. I'd slept in guard towers, bunkers, a roadside ditch, luggage racks, and vermin infested hooches, so the floor was fine with me and with evening upon us after that first day in Atlanta, the floor looked pretty good to me. By this time, I was descending into a state of physical and mental exhaustion due to the excitement, the adrenalin rush and the jet lag of the past few days. It was not long before I sought only to sleep, right there on the floor of the living room and in no time I passed out.

I don't know how long I slept but I was oblivious to everything until Janet woke me and despite my protests to be left alone, insisted I come with her. I wearily followed her into her bedroom where she closed the door and answered many of my questions.

We spent the next day out and about Atlanta visiting the Atlanta Zoo, Grant Park and other sights and I felt like I was on R&R again, like in Sydney, since the sights and sounds of a large metropolitan city were so foreign to me.

Atlanta was merely a stop on my road home and it came time to get on to Chicago to relieve my parents' apprehensions about my fate. I'd kept them in the dark long enough. From Atlanta I called my older brother and made arrangements for him and my younger brother to meet me at the airport. I wanted them to meet me and take me home since I was afraid if my parents had too much time to prepare for my return, I would walk into some kind of "welcome home" party I didn't want to have anything to do with. I just wanted to come home and be done with it.

I flew back to Chicago on 22 September and my brothers were there to greet me. It was good to be together and we drove home where I proceeded to surprise my poor, worried mother. She was surprised to see me and I imagine I was quite a sight to both my parents. I was thin, darkly tanned from all those days laying in the sun out by the bunker, wearing Montagnard bracelets, and not looking at all like the young man they had seen depart for Vietnam. She was happy to see me but upset I hadn't called first to give them a warning of my arrival. I winked at my brothers and explained that I didn't have firm dates and times until almost time to fly home. My father hugged me and shook my hand. The pride he felt was clearly seen in his face. I was home, out of the Army and from that point a whole new chapter of my life was opening.

My parents were glad to have me home after so many months of worrying about my welfare and safety. My mother said "It's all over now. You can put it all behind you." I didn't know how to tell her that it was not over, that it was still going on and I knew the boys on Engineer Hill were still carrying on at that moment. I eventually would put it all behind me but it was always there, right behind me, just over my shoulder, not like a monkey on my back but rather like a shadow. They asked numerous questions about my experiences and I tried to find the words to convey what I had seen and felt and done. I showed them photographs but it was hard for them to grasp their significance and what they represented.

My parents had seen the TV news and read all the articles so were well aware of the drug problem in Vietnam. I had dreaded the inevitable questions they would ask about the drugs, but they only asked me one question about them. My father asked, "Was the drug problem over there as bad as we've heard?" My response was "No, there was no problem. You could get all the drugs you wanted, any time, any place." They never brought the subject up again.

I came home expecting to pick up a reality I'd left behind almost three years before, but I found that reality had changed in my absence and I was unprepared for what I found because I had changed as well. My first few months at home were the strangest since flush toilets were still a novelty as well as unlimited hot water, not to mention television, wall to wall carpeting, and almost everything around me. In a way, I was still an Incorrigible and not fit to be in civilized society after living in that male-dominated society for sixteen months. I had to clean up my language, my attitudes and reactions were thoroughly in-grained and it was hard to break old habits. My response to sirens and my urge to listen for the rounds to fall did not go away for a while. My thoughts were often with the boys still over there on the Hill. As I lay in bed at night I knew they were facing another day. Even though I was back in the States, my heart was still over there with the boys on top of that sand pile. In a sense, I still felt guilty for having left them.

Living with my parents was a nice change to a certain extent. After all, there was mom's home cooking and relaxing in front of the TV was a nice way to pass the time but it wasn't the same as laying in the sun beside the bunker. My parents treated me differently than they had before because I was not the immature person they had seen go off to military service. But they did not want me to vegetate and seemed to think that after all those months in Vietnam I should be able to put it behind me and move on. They didn't understand that it wasn't that simple.

Being back in the States trying to pick up the pieces of my life was disconcerting. The reality I left behind was no longer there. My parents wanted me to go back to college and finish my degree. I did not want to do that

18. Wandering and Wondering

because I was not ready. I'd spent three years in college struggling to maintain my deferment and I did not want to go directly back into that academic environment. The Army and Vietnam had been an education and my DD-214 was my diploma.

At that point I didn't know exactly what I wanted to do with my life. Should I go to Atlanta to see Janet, or get a job, travel, pursue my music with my old friend Captain Marvel? I wasn't sure, most of all I just wanted to take a year off and decompress before returning to school. I had many adjustments to make before I could re-assimilate. The grub stake I'd saved during my service quickly disappeared. I needed a car and it needed tires and insurance. I needed clothes since my old ones no longer fit or were out of style. I was soon broke and needed a job.

I collected unemployment, perused the classified ads and applied for jobs but none of them paid any money. I finally got a job working for the DuPage County, Sewer and Water Division where I worked as a laborer, mowing grass, painting, shoveling out sludge beds, hauling it to disposal areas, cleaning lift stations, etc. It was dirty, shitty work but it paid me more money than any of the other jobs I'd sought and I didn't mind it since I worked pretty much on my own. The job was dirty but it put money in my pocket and my bank account so I could build my grub stake and look toward college. Since I had my own car I traveled on weekends to see family and friends.

After I'd been home about a month, Ralph returned. He called me from his parents' home in Western Springs where we soon reunited. It was good to see an old comrade, someone with whom I had shared those experiences, who I could identify with on a unique basis and who understood and felt the same. We freaked out on the reality of driving around suburban Chicago while getting a buzz on.

We sat in his bedroom at his parents' home, toking up and marveling that Vietnam, Dong Ba Thin, Cam Ranh Bay, 18th ENGR BDE, 35th ENGR GRP, Engineer Hill, all that had really happened, while his mother stood

You can take the boy out of Vietnam but you can't take Vietnam out of the boy.

outside his door asking what that funny smell was. Chicago brought to mind Freddie Warren of well-driller fame and a vet of double Nam tours. We tracked Fred down to his homestead on the south side of Chicago and went to spend a day with him. He'd put on some weight, but it was still Fred and he was back on the block. However, Ralph soon departed since he had stateside duty to serve as he had not ETS'd when he left Vietnam.

Later that winter I had a call from Dusty, who was passing through Chicago on his way home to Ohio and was at O'Hare airport. I drove out to get him and bring him home for a short visit. He was still Dusty but now with a well-trimmed moustache rather than the ornately waxed handlebar he used to sport. He was dressed in crisp Class "A" winter dress greens and I hardly recognized him at first glance. He was free of the Army at last and the first place he wanted to go was to a store to buy some civilian clothes, so we headed to a K-Mart where he bought some blue jeans and a shirt. He paid for them and wore them out of the store, changing clothes right there at the checkout cash register and stuffing his greens into the sack. I entertained him at home briefly, drove him around the suburbs for a short time and then took him back to O'Hare so he could continue on to Ohio.

19

To the Wicky Wick Woods

I found myself among family and friends and in familiar surroundings but felt very disconnected like I shouldn't be there. I also had a sense of guilt that I didn't understand. I had no sense of pride in what I'd been a part of; the prevailing attitude around me was very negative where the topic of Vietnam was concerned. I did not talk about my service with people I didn't know and didn't admit that I was a Nam vet. I had trouble dealing with people, was not comfortable in crowds, sought isolation and wanted to crawl under a rock to keep the world out.

But I was in a hurry to get on with my life. Many of my contemporaries from high school and college were out of school now and in the working world while my college years were interrupted by military service; I felt very much behind the curve. I needed to return to school; I only had a year remaining to finish my degree so planned on working until the fall 1972 and then finish my degree.

But my future lay wide open. I could go anywhere, do anything, and I had a lot of options. Going to Atlanta was one of those options but I wasn't sure it was the right thing to do. Was Janet anticipating my return to Atlanta? After I got over the excitement of being home, I called her to check in as we'd not spoken since I'd left Atlanta. I mulled over what to say and really did not know what to expect when she answered. We had a pleasant conversation but when it turned to plans for the future, she informed me that she was moving to Peoria, Illinois, and would be rooming with several high school girl friends there. This took me by surprise. Peoria was a short drive from Naperville, and I had family there and my old pickin' buddy, Captain Marvel, as well. I expected to spend a lot of time in Peoria and now Janet would be there. Was she coming back because I was there?

Working at the county sewer and water department gave me an income while I was sorting out my life, living at home, and going to Peoria on the weekends where I saw a lot of my extended family there and my buddy Captain Marvel. But I could hardly go see them and not see Janet. When I went to see her in Peoria we picked up where we left off and gradually her attraction meant I spent more time with her and less with family and Captain Marvel. But there was tension. It was a rocky courtship aggravated by the fact she had been my buddy's girlfriend all through high school and here we were carrying on in a most familiar way while he was still in the Army. However, they had not been going together for several years, and the sense of betrayal I felt was not justified.

My relationship with Janet grew out of a long friendship and in a way seemed logical it would progress to something more as we matured. It almost seemed "storybook" destined, like it was meant to be. But we both had a stake in our relationships with the Phantom and if it all went wrong it could destroy the friendship we all shared with each other all those years growing up together. Phantom was a counterculture warrior serving in Germany and was due to ETS soon. He would be coming home, and we didn't know what he expected to find. He had no inkling of the relationship that had grown between us and I was concerned about what he expected to come home to. I finally wrote him and laid it out for him. He responded with a very positive letter, happy for both of us, and wanted to get together when he got home.

We were married in August 1972 and the Phantom was my Best Man. The next month we moved to Platteville, Wisconsin, where Janet worked while I went back to school at the University of Wisconsin there. For me, the campus was haunted with people and events from my years there in the late 1960s. Although the stage was the same, the players had changed, ghosts were everywhere. My wife and our new life together anchored me. But Vietnam followed me. One day as I walked through the student center I heard someone call my name. I stopped and looked around then I saw him. Dan Reeder, my old college buddy from before the Army, who I'd run into at Cam Ranh when I was on

Non-regulation at last.

Engineer Hill. Now we'd come full circle and he was back in school same as me. We saw each other that year, often shaking our heads in disbelief at how ironic the road of life could be.

While finishing school, we lived for a period of time in an old log cabin down at the end of a long gravel road. We had electricity and a "two-hole shitter" out back, water provided from a free flowing spring, but no satellite TV, no cable, no phone, no internet, no computer, no hot water. It was rather like Vietnam without the sand.

As my time at school drew to a close I had to come to grips with something I'd forgotten—there was life after college. Janet and I wanted to flee the northern winters and Georgia beckoned, Savannah for me, Atlanta for her. She contacted an old boss from her Atlanta days who promised her a job if she came back. So, one of us had employment once I graduated; based on that, when I finished my last class we packed and headed for Georgia that night.

My degree was in history and I put it to work for the State of Georgia as a historic site superintendent operating several state historic sites on the Georgia coast near Savannah at Sunbury and Midway in Liberty County. I was fortunate in finding employment that allowed me to live and work at isolated sites. I had become uncomfortable in the urban environment and crowds bothered me. Finding a job that allowed me to live where I worked, located in a beautiful, isolated, coastal setting, became that rock I'd been looking to crawl under.

During this time, I lost my Australian friends. I had been corresponding with Gypsy, Renny and Pat Murphy and the ties were still strong. They pressed me to return. However, Janet objected to my corresponding with "women" in Australia, and in a move to placate her, I let go of the threads that bound me to Australia. It was a move I would come to regret.

I watched the Vietnam War come to an end on TV in the spring of 1975 and wondered what it would be like without Vietnam in the news and in our lives. I'd lived with it since 1965. But the end of the Vietnam War was not the only thing coming to an end. My marriage to Janet didn't last. There was no storybook ending for that saga. It survived four years and collapsed in 1976. We went our separate ways. I retreated to Liberty County, Georgia, to a friend's summer cabin at Sunbury while I tried to put my life back together.

But Janet didn't leave me without connecting me to the lady who would become my spouse for the long term. I married a second time to JoAnn, a wonderful lady whom I'd met through Janet. Circumstances brought us together and after a period of time pursuing different paths our roads came back together and we found love.

I continued my career in museums and historic sites. History was an interest I put to work for me and it took me many different places to live and work all over the country. Then, in the irony to end all ironies, my career led me back to the U.S. Army. When I'd left the Nam I swore I'd never have anything to do with the Army again. I was wrong. In 1985, I went to work for the Army as a civilian employee at Fort Bliss, Texas, operating the Fort Bliss Museum.

I'd not been in that Army environment since leaving Fort Lewis in 1971. Fort Bliss; how odd it was to be back on an Army base again. Old memories and attitudes long repressed rose to the surface of my consciousness. But it didn't take long to realize this was not the same Army. There was no FTA attitude, no draftees with bad attitudes, or resisters in the ranks. This was an all-volunteer Army and everyone was there because they'd chosen to be. I worked for the Army running their museums for twenty years. It was the first place where I met young soldiers who expressed appreciation for my service. It was awkward. I didn't appreciate my service. How could they?

While at Ft. Bliss, our first child arrived, a daughter we named Star, since she had been born in the Lone Star State. Shortly after her birth we relocated back to Georgia where I went to work at Fort Stewart operating the Fort Stewart Museum.*

Over the years I maintained contact with C.W. Stinson in Atlanta, and Ralph Dexter was a member of the family by this time, but everyone else had scattered. After about twenty-five years I started looking for the guys because I was curious about how they were doing. I didn't find them all but did find some. A few didn't want to be found so I left them alone. Others were surprised or overjoyed to reconnect. I was amazed at how so many had gone off to parts unknown but eventually came back to their home ground. I managed to find Ronnie "Hard Dick" Hardwick, Greg "Ski" Kowalski, Jay "Antman" Barton, Tom "Dusty" Dustman, Mike Stigg, Tommy Tomason, Mark "Frizzle" Fritzo, Andy Davidson, Garry "Hud" Huddleman, John "JC" Arthur, McGregor, Ralph "Hardcore" Dexter and Everett "EJ" Nance.

As the years pass, I often wonder about going back to Vietnam, to see what's there some years later. It's gone today, the graffiti-filled bunkers over by finance, the shitters, the pissers, the guard towers. I've wondered if anybody found any of those plastic practice golf balls that were lost in the

---

*In 1988, while employed by the US Army as Director of the 24th Infantry Division and Fort Stewart Museum in Georgia, LTG McCaffrey's son, Barry R. McCaffrey, was in command of the 24th Division and took them to Saudi Arabia for the Desert Shield and Desert Storm operations. While he was in command of the post of Fort Stewart, his father, the MG McCaffrey who gave us a lift to Long Binh in his chopper that May evening so long ago, visited the post and was honored by one of the units on post. Part of those activities included visit to the post museum where I had the opportunity to cross paths with him again. I gave him a tour of the museum and talk turned to the topic of Vietnam. I mentioned that we had once crossed paths in Vietnam and he wanted to know when. I related the details to which he smiled and said: "I'm glad I gave you a ride."

course of the great Dong Ba Thin Golf Tournaments.

The memory of that time remains sharp and clear. It's all gone today but I know it's still there, just below the surface of my conscious mind and it doesn't take much to pull it up, to go back. I can go back, in my mind's eye, back to the shitters and the sand, pissers and prostitutes, guard duty and bunker duty. I can walk the streets of Dong Ba Thin or Engineer Hill and see it exactly as it was. I can see it, hear it and smell it and if I look I can see the people, Ski and Hud and JC and Ralph.

Ralph shows the benefits of Army chow.

I know Ralph is still there. He was stricken with cancer in 1990 and in spite of all treatment efforts lost his battle. The doctors sent him home from the hospital because they'd done everything they could. He went home to await the end. When his wife told me, I hurried to Chicago to see him one last time. I found him in his room, in a hospital bed. He was the same old Ralph. He was always so thin he looked like a concentration camp survivor so I couldn't tell if he'd lost weight. We greeted each other as brothers and Ralph laid it all out for me. We knew our roads would separate and this would be the last time we'd be together in this life.

We squeezed as much as we could out of our meager time together reminiscing, laughing, crying and reliving our adventures until it came time for us to part. We hugged and after a brief exchange of farewells I slowly made my way to the door and paused in the doorway to look back and take my last look at Ralph. He was lying in bed with that "Cheshire Cat" smile on his face, like he knew something I didn't, and as our eyes met he said: "I'll be in-country before you are this time." I threw him a peace sign and walked out. The symbolism of equating Vietnam to heaven was not lost on me. It blew me away. When Ralph got to Dong Ba Thin as a newbie, I had been in-country four months already and was considered an old timer. Now here was Ralph telling me that he would be the old-timer when I got "there" this time.

We lost Ralph in October 1990. He answered the draft once more and had to leave the party early. As time has gone by, he's been joined by others such as Mark "Frizzle" Fritzo who was claimed by cancer, and EJ who also fell to cancer, and the Antman who was claimed by a questionable suicide. But Ralph was the first of my Vietnam brothers to go.

About four months after his passing, I was doing some work around the house when I had to take something to the hall closet by the front door. As I placed the item on a shelf in the closet, I noticed my Class A Greens hanging there, the ones that I'd worn home from Fort Lewis after returning from Vietnam. I'd not paid any attention to them since the day I took them off and hung them up and wondered what might be in the pockets. Did I clean them out when I took the jacket off? Curiosity got the better of me and I started checking the pockets.

Not much to be found other than a deck of USO playing cards in one pocket. Then I checked the inside breast pocket and there was something there. I couldn't tell what it was at first, but as I pulled it out I recognized a "garrison" cap folded in half. In the Army the cap is known by another name based on the cap's resemblance to an item of the female anatomy. It looks like a large letter envelope, rectangular in shape and with one long edge open. Inside there was a leather sweatband and we were required to put our names and service numbers inside the sweatband. I was known to place a few suitable epithets inside the sweatband in addition to my name and service number, so I wondered what I'd written in this one.

I folded back the sweatband and was astounded to find it was not my name inside the sweatband. It was "Ralph H. Dexter SN: 247830261" It was Ralph's cap! How did I get that? We never served anywhere together where we would have been required to wear that cap. I knew him in Vietnam, not before, and we did not wear those garrison caps

Uncle George in 1945.

19. To the Wicky Wick Woods

in Vietnam. I have absolutely no idea how I ended up with Ralph's garrison cap but I began to think perhaps it was a sign from him that he's back on the hill, everything is OK, and he'll see me when I get there. Dog pile on Ralph!

In December 1994 the 50th anniversary of the Battle of the Bulge was observed. I called my Uncle George and asked him what he was doing fifty years ago. He said: "Hmmmm, let me think. Oh shit! Was in the Battle of the Bulge, got shot, froze my ass off. Wouldn't want to do it again." We chuckled and I thanked him for his service as one veteran to another and not just as a nephew to his uncle. We visited and he talked about where he was in Luxembourg in December 1944 when the battle started. He described a small town with a large church in the center of the town. I didn't keep him long, but I felt that my uncle was pleased I'd made the connection and remembered him.

In 1995, I travelled to Germany on Army museum business and while there we visited Battle of the Bulge battlefields which made me think of Uncle George. We visited Luxembourg during this time and stayed in Diekirch a small town with a large church in the center reminding me very much of the town he had described in our phone conversation. As we toured the area I noticed monuments and markers bearing the Keystone insignia of the 28th Infantry Division, my uncle's unit. I knew nothing of his service but determined to talk to him about it when I returned home.

After coaxing, he agreed to talk about his experiences and over a period of time we exchanged letters, phone calls and books about the Battle of the Bulge. It finally came to the point where I knew I had to sit down with him and a tape recorder. He agreed and on 12 August 1997 we sat on his back porch with the recorder running. I asked questions and he would answer, one thing leading to another.

He'd gone in the Army in June '41 and reported for induction at Camp Grant, near Chicago.

While there his typing abilities were discovered because he noted on a form that he had two years of high school typing experience. He was given a typing test and soon detailed to administrative duties until sent to basic training. George recalled that once he arrived at the basic training center:

> They put me in headquarters because they found out I could type. They didn't care how smart you were, if you could type, they could use you at headquarters…. They just saw in my records that I had typed at Camp Grant when I came in and they transferred me up there with no problem. Word came down I'm to report to battalion headquarters. That was a good deal for me. A 40-hour week, and before that I'd been working, oh, I don't know how many hours, and on the marches I was in a jeep. It was great.

As he spoke these words a light went off in my head as my mind said: "Whoa! I've heard this story before!" It was as if he was reciting my own experience. At basic training he was put to work in the HQ unit and when the officer he worked for was transferred to Camp Blanding, Florida, he had George transferred to Blanding to work for him. So George spent almost four years there on the cadre at an infantry training center in Florida, just because he could type.

As the war entered 1944, he began to get nervous because he was a prime candidate for an overseas assignment. He didn't want to go to the Pacific theater. Letters from his younger brother serving there with the Marines convinced him of that. This left the European Theater. D-Day had passed, Paris had fallen and it looked like the war in Europe would be over by Christmas so he put in a request for transfer to Europe. He never foresaw the Battle of the Bulge in his future.

That experience led to our meeting on that August afternoon in 1997. His revelation about how his typing skills served him well in the Army was like a light turned on. Suddenly, it all fell into place. My father's insistence on my learning how to type now made sense. It was 1963 and Vietnam was a growing conflict about to consume thousands of Americans. He had a son who would be draft age and would be facing military service unless he could obtain a deferment, which seemed unlikely in 1963 considering my grades. He was a father and he wanted to do something to prepare his son with a skill the military would find useful. His brother's experience in the military and his own military experiences had shown what a little knowledge of typing could do in that environment.

I realized how this little fact had affected my whole life. Although I didn't understand his

Uncle George and my father, July 1945. George is home after serving in the ETO. My father is home on leave after basic training.

insistence at the time, as I got older, I gained a deeper understanding of his motive. Learning how to type was responsible for the direction my life took from the time I entered the Army. Perhaps the most critical moment was July 1969 when I reported to Fort Lewis processing for Vietnam, only to have them change my orders and divert me to Hunter Army Airfield in Savannah. My subsequent life hinged on that moment. What would my life have been like if I'd gone to Vietnam in July of 1969? What a narrow edge my fate teetered on and I didn't even know it. That decision by some person at Fort Lewis sent me to Hunter Army Air Field in Savannah rather than Vietnam.

I guess my guardian angel was looking out for me. If I'd gone to Vietnam in July '69, I would not have had the clerical experience I got at HHC#2 orderly room, so my duty assignment in Vietnam might have been much different from what I received in 1970, all due to that clerical experience, not to mention that MAJ Wells put a letter of recommendation in my records, another thing that would not have happened if I had not gone to Savannah. What would my fate have been had I gone in 1969? There's no way to know but one thing is certain—the life I would have lived from that point forward would not have been the life I did live when I came home in 1971.

I never had the chance to properly thank my father, in part because I didn't really comprehend what he had done for me. I took much of it for granted then but now I understand better than when it was happening. He set me upon the road of life with all the advantages he could give me, including typing. While I understood what he did regarding my military service, I never fully appreciated the significance and impact of it until after he passed.

Typing. It doesn't sound like much today because far more people are familiar with a keyboard given the now ubiquitous use of computers and smart phones. But back in 1968 there were no desktop computers, tablets, or cell phones, and the only people who dealt with keyboards were typically secretaries, clerical people and academics. The keyboards were on typewriters. It was a significant, but uncommon skill outside those occupations, but not so much today where a person at a keyboard can sit in an office and launch smart bombs toward targets located on the other side of the planet. Now I understand the role it played in determining the road I traveled.

When I looked at the future that lay before me at the end of my time in Vietnam, it was an unwritten book, a road not yet traveled. Now, as I stand some fifty years down that road since Vietnam, I look back across a past that was once my future and now understand what was going on then and how I've gotten to where I am today. I realized how much it affected my life and put me on roads I would never have traveled otherwise.

I learned many things from my time in Vietnam, but it wasn't until twenty years had passed before I learned the most stunning lesson of all. We were living in Hinesville, Georgia, and I was working at Fort Stewart.

In March of 1990 our second child was born, another daughter we named Lacy. Daughter Star was 3½ and pleased to be a big sister. Living in an Army town and exposed to the base activity, it was to be expected that she would absorb some of her surroundings as she grew up.

We frequently went on walks around the neighborhood and being in the vicinity of the base, helicopter traffic overhead was normal. On our walks Star always wanted to see them as they flew overhead. She eventually became so attuned to the sound of helicopter rotors, that she could distinguish the sound of a Huey from the sound of a Cobra or Chinook and could identify the helicopter before we saw it pass by overhead.

Not long after our newborn daughter was brought home from the hospital, Star and I went on one of our walks in the neighborhood. We talked about whatever she wanted to talk about and on this day we were chatting about her new baby sister. This led to discussing the fact that her mommy and daddy had been together before she was born. Then she asked a rather startling question.

"Where was I before I was with you and Mommy?"

This caught me off-guard but, pointing to the sky, I responded: "You were a bright light in the heavens, waiting to come and be with us when the time was right."

She pondered this a moment and then asked: "Where was Lacy before she came here?"

I responded: "She was up in Heaven with you, waiting until it was time for her to come and be with us. You girls were out there until it was time for you to come and bless your mommy and daddy. You came first, and now it's Lacy's time to be with us"

She became excited, like she just remembered something. I was not prepared to hear what she had to say: "Yes, yes! I remember, I remember!" she exclaimed. "I watched over you when you were a soldier!"

I hardly knew what to say. I clearly remembered the times I felt

My guardian angel.

like I had a guardian angel watching over me. I realized she could be reaching pre-birth memories and I knew this was a briefly opened window to find validation. She said she "watched" over me.

"What did you see?" I asked.

Without hesitation she said one word—twice. "Sand ... Sand"

"What did you do?"

Sounding little irritated that I'd asked her that, she replied: "I had to bring you home." Before I could ask her "why" she changed the subject as if to indicate she was finished with that conversation. "Let's go to the Wicky Wick Woods" she said.

The Wicky Wick Woods were just a few blocks away where a residential street ended at a large patch of thick woods with old trees and Spanish moss draped over their limbs. To her it looked just like the dark woods in "The Wizard of Oz" where Dorothy and her companions passed on their way to the Wicked Witch's castle. Since she couldn't pronounce "Wicked Witch" they became the Wicky Wick Woods to her. So we went to the Wicky Wick Woods.

Roger S. Durham
Service History

U.S. Army

Basic Training, Fort Bragg, NC, February–April 1969
Advanced Training, Fort Lee, VA—78Y30, Armorer and Supply, April–June 1969
HHC #2, Hunter Army Airfield, GA , July 1969–April 1970
HHC, 18th Engineer Brigade, Dong Ba Thin, RVN, June 1970–April 1971
HHC, 35th Engineer Group, Cam Ranh Army, RVN, April–September 1971

U.S. Army—Civilian Employment

Fort Bliss, TX, Director, Fort Bliss Museum, July 1985–October 1986
Fort Stewart, GA, Director, Fort Stewart and 24th Infantry Division Museum, October 1986–April 1994
Fort Stewart, GA, Director, Fort Stewart and 3rd Infantry Division Museum, April 1994–August 1998.
Carlisle Barracks, PA, U.S. Army Heritage and Education Center. Director, U.S. Army Heritage Museum, October 2003–July 2009.

Index

Anderson, Willie 33–35, 37, 57, 63 72, 74, 113
Anthony, Philip 130, 274
Antman see Barton, Jay
Archie 256, 258, 261–265
Arecon, Gary 57, 64
Arnold, John C. 87, 88, 93, 97, 98, 101, 120–122, 124, 125, 135, 136, 143, 145, 147, 166, 168, 170, 171, 182
Australia Janet see Carr, Janet

Baldwin, MAJ 128
Barton, Jay 11, 282, 284
B-Chuck see Beshak
Berdman, Stewart 34, 35, 110–113
Beshak, Chris 33–35, 45, 57, 74, 94, 106, 108, 110–114, 125
Binder, John 130, 265, 269, 270–273
Boone, Robert 34, 36, 41, 57, 77–80, 82, 83, 89
Boy Scouts 40, 68
Brown, Bruce 130, 277, 279, 280
Brown, CPT 121, 133–135
Brozic, Dan 94, 104, 174, 175
Burns, 1LT 45, 54, 80–83, 117, 118, 133, 135

Calaber, CPT 94, 95, 111, 113, 120–122, 133, 134, 174
Cam Ranh Air Force Base 8, 14, 68
Cam Ranh Army HQ 222
Cam Ranh Bay 7, 11–14, 20, 24, 26, 42, 51, 52, 63, 66, 67, 74, 91, 95–97, 99, 100, 109, 117, 121, 123, 125–128, 143, 164, 170, 171, 177, 180, 195, 196, 204–206, 211, 215, 222, 223, 225, 226, 230, 232, 233, 248, 251, 263, 277, 280
Cam Ranh Village 183, 211, 226
Camp Alpha 144, 145, 164, 187, 193, 195
Carr, Janet 148–151, 153–164, 166, 167, 186–191, 196
Casick, William 44, 45, 82–84, 86, 87, 89, 116, 219

Danang 27, 116, 169, 170, 176, 234–237, 239, 246
Davidson, Andy 209, 226, 282
Democratic Convention 8
Dexter, Ralph 87–89, 93, 95, 101, 103, 124, 125, 133–136, 139, 143, 145, 147, 166, 168–171, 174,
175, 179, 181, 182, 184, 185, 206, 208–214, 220, 223–225, 230, 233–236, 241–243, 249, 251–253, 271, 275, 277, 278, 282–285
Don Dzom 197, 198
Dong Ba Thin 21, 24, 29, 43, 44, 59–61, 63, 66, 68, 71, 72, 74, 83, 85–87, 90–93, 95, 108, 115, 117, 120–122, 125, 134, 140, 162, 165–167, 170, 172, 174, 176, 177, 179, 181, 183, 200, 202, 206, 208, 209, 211, 219, 230, 233, 273, 277, 283
Dong Ba Thin Anti-Doobie Band 127–129, 136, 164, 167–169, 174, 256, 283
Dow Chemical Demonstrations 7
Durham, John 1
Dustman, Thomas (Dusty) 184, 209, 216, 217, 226, 232–234, 236, 238–244, 246–248, 251–253, 271, 275, 278, 282

864th Engineer Battalion 199
EJ see Nance, Everett

Ferrill, James 31, 32, 34, 42–44, 48, 50–52, 62, 63, 72, 90
Fields, Glenn 38, 39, 45, 59, 82, 133
553rd Float Bridge Company 25, 58
Fix, Chaplain 128
Florence, MSG 27, 30–34, 37, 41–44, 50, 52, 53, 56, 62–64, 72, 74, 83, 89, 115, 118–120, 127, 128
Forrest, SFC 183, 196
Fort Bliss 282
Fort Bragg, NC 8
Fort Lee, VA 9, 11
Fort Lewis, WA 9, 12, 13, 265, 267, 282, 284, 287
45th Engineer Group 27, 116, 169, 170, 174, 176
497th Port Construction 214, 215, 248
Franklin, Thomas 34, 36, 94, 104, 108, 110, 112, 113
Fritzo, Mark 178, 181, 220, 222, 225, 226, 234, 251, 282, 284

Gomez, "Big" 40
Gomez, Steve "Little" 39, 40, 47, 59
Gregson, Robert 34, 36
Groucho see Berdman, Stewart

293

Index

Guardian Angel 11, 78, 123, 226
Gun Trucks 83, 85, 208, 211–213

Hagberg, SFC 30, 31, 53, 89, 115
Hardwick, Ronald 32, 34, 37, 39–41, 49, 61–66, 70, 72, 78, 92–94, 101, 103–105, 110–115, 118, 119, 122–125, 127, 128, 135, 139–141, 143, 166, 168, 170, 171, 282
Harris, lSGT 49, 54, 56, 60, 69, 92, 132, 133
HHC #2 10, 26
HHC 18th Engineer Brigade 42, 91
Howell Beach 100
HQ, 18th Engineer Brigade 128, 167
Huddleman, Gary "Hud" 90, 91, 93, 97, 98, 109, 122, 124, 139–141, 170, 174, 175, 220, 282–283
Hunter Army Airfield 10–12, 14, 26, 170, 228, 287

Janet, "Australia" *see* Carr, Janet
Janet, "Stateside" 130, 132, 150, 152, 166, 167, 186, 196, 244, 265, 269, 273–275, 277, 279, 280, 281

Kent, Gypsy 190–192, 196, 235, 240–243, 281
Kowalski, Greg 87, 90–93, 109, 110, 121–125, 143–145, 147, 149, 152–159, 161–163, 166, 170, 171, 174, 175, 187, 189, 190, 193, 208, 220, 241, 242, 282–283

Long, Bo 126–128, 167–169, 175, 251

Market Time Beach and Naval Facility 100, 170, 219–221
Marks, MAJ 31, 65, 113, 128
Mathison, Robert 90, 91, 122, 123, 166, 170
Mayaguez, Dennis 212–214
McCaffrey, LTG 194–201
McChord Air Force Base 12, 13, 265, 266
McGregor, Robert 43, 44, 60, 61, 67–69, 90–92, 122, 123, 170
Mendez, Peter 214, 251
Myca Bridge 63, 99, 100, 165
Myca Checkpoint 42, 63
Myca Crossroads 60, 177

Nance, Everett (EJ) 11, 12, 18–23, 25, 86, 254, 256, 264, 266, 267, 282, 284
Nha Trang 20, 38, 127
937th Engineer Group 27, 83–85, 128

Peterson, Harry 220, 237
Phan Rang 82, 197, 198, 205, 219
Preston, George 11, 12

Qhin Nhon 27

Reeder, Dan 218, 219, 280
Reno, SFC 227, 228
Robards, John 34, 36, 37, 40, 45, 58, 61, 77, 81, 82, 90, 118, 133, 234

Roberts, Dennis 251
Rosberg, Dan 38, 39, 45

S-3 Office 183, 197, 205, 219, 233
S-4 Office 38, 44, 55, 56, 63–65, 72, 75, 81, 83, 89, 94, 120, 121, 171, 173, 202
Sanger, Mike 34, 36, 37, 39, 40, 44, 45, 47, 58, 70, 71, 77–82, 90, 118, 133, 135
Schrader, BG Henry 80, 94, 113, 116, 137, 168, 173–174, 194
Schives, Warren 90, 122, 170, 220
Simpson, Pete 184, 209, 220, 221, 243, 251, 275
610th Engineer Battalion 208
Smith, Mike 47, 132, 133
Sparks, SFC 64, 202
Stance, Major 126–129, 167–169
Stigg, Mike 184, 209, 211, 220, 222, 225, 226, 234, 236, 238–245, 247–249, 251–253, 275, 282
Stiner, Major 128
Su Chin 60, 123, 165, 211, 222

Tan Son Hhut 143–145, 164, 165, 187, 193, 194, 196
Tanh Tonh 45, 92, 123, 175
Taske, Frank 39, 40, 45, 48, 82
35th Engineer Group 86, 126, 127, 168–170, 174–179, 181, 183, 185, 186, 202, 210, 213, 214, 217, 219, 220, 222, 223, 234, 253, 277
Thomas, John 274
Torres, Willie 101
Tower 15 46, 47, 78, 96, 97, 134, 13
Tower 16 96, 97
Tower 17 69, 73, 78, 87, 88, 95–97, 99, 119, 136–138
Tower 18 46
Tower 19 45, 46, 96, 97, 136–140
Tower 20 46, 98, 99, 138, 139
22nd Replacement Company 15, 44, 84, 86, 97, 174, 219, 253, 263
299th Engineer Battalion 82, 83, 85, 126, 198
Typhoon Kate 109, 116, 120

Valdez, Tony 214
Valentine, John 84, 219
Vinnell Beach 63, 100, 101, 120, 121, 141, 142, 219, 220
Vorsa, Renny 150, 151, 158, 187–189, 192, 235, 240–242, 244–246, 281

Walters, James 31–37, 41, 44, 62, 63, 79, 90
Warren, Fred 214, 215, 222, 229, 231–233, 236, 248, 251, 277
Wells, MAJ Larry 4, 287
Whiskey Mountain Industrial Site 199, 200
White, CPT 32
Wilks, Robert 38–40, 45–47, 59, 82, 87, 107, 135
Wilson, Chris 125, 168, 169, 175, 178, 179, 181, 186, 220, 221, 223–225, 249, 251
Witner, Andy 34, 36, 72

Yakota, Japan 13, 264